JURISPRUDENCE FOR AN INTERCONNECTED GLOBE

Jurisprudence for an Interconnected Globe

Edited by

CATHERINE DAUVERGNE

ASHGATE

Published by
Ashgate Publishing Limited
Gower House
Croft Road
Aldershot
Hampshire GU11 3HR
England

Ashgate Publishing Company
Suite 420
101 Cherry Street
Burlington, VT 05401-4405 USA

Ashgate website: http://www.ashgate.com

British Library Cataloguing in Publication Data
Jurisprudence for an interconnected globe. - (Applied legal philosophy)
1. Jurisprudence 2. Globalization
I. Dauvergne, Catherine
340

Library of Congress Cataloging-in-Publication Data
Jurisprudence for an interconnected globe / edited by Catherine Dauvergne.
p.cm. -- (Applied legal philosophy)
Includes bibliographical references.
ISBN 0-7546-2282-7 (alk.paper)
1. Jurisprudence. 2. Globalization. I. Dauvergne, Catherine. II. Series.

K235 .J865 2002
340--dc21

2002027921

ISBN 0 7546 2282 7

Printed and bound in Great Britain by MPG Books Ltd, Bodmin, Cornwall

Contents

List of Contributors *vii*
Series Preface *ix*
Acknowledgments *xi*

1 New Directions for Jurisprudence 1
Catherine Dauvergne

PART 1: KEY THEMES IN JURISPRUDENCE FOR AN INTERCONNECTED GLOBE

2 The Province of Jurisprudence Re-examined 13
William Twining
3 Historical Aspects of Globalization and Law 43
David B. Goldman

PART II: GLOBALIZATION AND THE LAWS OF MONEY

4 Globalization and International Economic Law 71
Sundhya Pahuja
5 Networks, Norms and the Nation State: Thoughts on Pluralism and Globalized Securities Regulation 93
Dimity Kingsford Smith

PART III: GLOBALIZATION AND THE LAWS OF PEOPLE

6 Relabelling the International Labour Problem: Globalization and Ideology 129
Jill Murray
7 Globalization and Citizenship and Nationality 159
Kim Rubenstein
8 Illegal Migration and Sovereignty 187
Catherine Dauvergne

PART IV: GLOBALIZATION, CULTURES AND COMPARISONS

9 Globalization, Legal Transplants and Unhappiness: Post-Communist Experiences 213
Adam Czarnota
10 Crime, Terror and Transitional Cultures in a Contracting Globe 231
Mark Findlay

Index *249*

List of Contributors

Adam Czarnota is Senior Lecturer in the Faculty of Law, University of New South Wales. He has published widely on Eastern European transformations and is co-editor of two recent collections on political, legal and sociological interpretations of transformations in former communist countries. He is currently engaged in a project on quasi-judicial institutions, time and collective memories.

Catherine Dauvergne is Associate Professor and Canada Research Chair in Migration Law, University of British Columbia. She works primarily in the areas of refugee and immigration law and is presently coordinating a research project canvassing how migration laws in the Asia Pacific region are responding to globalization. Her work appears in *Res Publica*, the *International Journal of Refugee Law* and the *Osgoode Hall Law Journal* among others.

Mark Findlay has recently published *The Globalization of Crime* in which he explores the recent manifestation of globalization and the way in which crime is one of its essential features. This work arose out of earlier considerations of crime and development and the relationship between crime, control and transitional cultures. Mark is now researching the dimensions of international criminal justice procedures. He holds chairs in the Faculty of Law, University of Sydney, and Nottingham Law School.

David B. Goldman is writing a PhD on globalization and the Western legal tradition, under an Australian Postgraduate Award at the Faculty of Law, University of Sydney. He has taught History and Philosophy of Law at Macquarie University and practises part-time as a solicitor at Deacons Lawyers, Sydney.

Dimity Kingsford Smith holds a Chair in the Faculty of Law, Monash University. She researches in the area of financial regulation, with a particular interest in the insights that various theoretical perspectives lend to the operation of law in the context of financial markets. Her writing addresses the nature and effect of financial regulation and the contribution of various theories of regulation across a range of markets – from corporate securities to collective investments, including managed investments and superannuation. Professor Kingsford Smith is a Director of the Centre for Law in the Digital Economy in the Monash University Faculty of Law.

Jill Murray is Research Fellow at the Centre for Employment and Labour Relations Law at the University of Melbourne. After many years as a trade union advocate, she completed a doctorate in law at Oxford University, and recently published *Transnational Labour Regulation: the ILO and EU Compared*. Her research interests centre on the international regulation of labour. Her other published work appears in the *Industrial Law Journal*, the *International Journal of Comparative Labour Law and Industrial Relations* and the *Australian Journal of Labour Law*.

Sundhya Pahuja is a Lecturer in the Law School at the University of Melbourne and a Barrister and Solicitor of the Supreme Court of Victoria, Australia. Her current research interests include processes of globalization and law and theory, with a particular emphasis on International Economic Organizations and South/North relationships. Her work appears in the *Leiden Journal of International Law*, the *Hague Yearbook of International Law*, and the *Australian Feminist Law Journal* among others.

Kim Rubenstein is Senior Lecturer in Law at the University of Melbourne. She teaches Constitutional law, Administrative law and Migration law. Her primary research is in the area of citizenship and she has recently completed a book entitled *Australian Citizenship Law in Context*.

William Twining was Quain Professor of Jurisprudence from 1983-96 at University College London, where he is now Research Professor of Law. His books include *Karl Llewellyn and the Realist Movement*, *Rethinking Evidence*, *Law in Context: Enlarging a Discipline*, *Globalization and Legal Theory* and most recently *The Great Juristic Bazaar: Jurists' Texts and Lawyers' Stories*.

Series Preface

The objective of this series in Applied Legal Philosophy is to publish work which adopts a theoretical approach to the study of particular areas or aspects of law or deals with general theories of law in a way which focuses on issues of practical moral and political concern in specific legal contexts.

In recent years there has been an encouraging tendency for legal philosophers to utilize detailed knowledge of the substance and practicalities of law and a noteworthy development in the theoretical sophistication of much legal research. The series seeks to encourage these trends and to make available studies in law which are both genuinely philosophical in approach and at the same time based on appropriate legal knowledge and directed towards issues in the criticism and reform of actual laws and legal systems.

The series will include studies in all the main areas of law, presented in a manner which relates to the concerns of specialist legal academics and practitioners. Each book makes an original contribution to an area of legal study while being comprehensible to those engaged in a wide variety of disciplines. Their legal content is principally Anglo-American, but a wide-ranging comparative approach is encouraged and authors are drawn from a variety of jurisdictions.

Tom D. Campbell
Series Editor
Centre for Applied Philosophy and Public Ethics,
Charles Sturt University, Australia

Acknowledgments

This collection arose out of the Symposium on Globalization and the Universalization of Legal Norms hosted by the Julius Stone Institute of Jurisprudence at the Faculty of Law, University of Sydney. The Symposium was convened to coincide with Professor William Twining's delivery of the Inaugural Julius Stone Address in August 2000. Professor Twining's visit was supported by the Julius Stone Institute and especially by a gift to that Institute from the Jewish Heritage Foundation that supports the annual address. The Symposium was supported by Ebsworth and Ebsworth Sydney.

We are grateful also to the diverse audience whose participation enriched our discussions. Jennifer Braid and Michelle Burgis provided vital support in the editing process.

Chapter 1

New Directions for Jurisprudence

Catherine Dauvergne

This collection grew out of the events of the Inaugural Julius Stone Lecture at the University of Sydney Faculty of Law in August 2000. Professor William Twining, Research Professor of Law at University College London, delivered the Inaugural Address. In order to provide a forum for discussing with Professor Twining some of the themes of his most recent writings, the Julius Stone Institute at Sydney University organized a day-long Symposium gathering together Australian-based scholars interested in the way globalization and jurisprudence are, or ought to be, interrelated. The forum provided, in that sense, for an interaction of the global and the local.

The scholars who attended the Symposium, and those whose work is collected here, approach the question of the interrelationship between jurisprudence and globalization from diverse angles. Looking at the traditional division of the discipline of law into sub-disciplinary teaching or subject areas, we work in different areas of law. Both the fictions of disciplinary cleavages and the role of legal theory within the discipline are, however, underscored by the work of the Symposium. The work gathered here presents a body of common themes, interests and insights that would not necessarily be expected from a gathering of criminal, corporate, immigration, international and property law scholars. The role of legal theory in mapping movements in the law and exploring how the law responds to the changing world around it was demonstrated at the Symposium through the convergence of ideas and the conversations which followed from them. Professor Twining delivered his Inaugural Address following the close of the Symposium proceedings. His re-examination of the province of jurisprudence provided a serendipitous finale to the proceedings by staking a broad terrain within which the work of the Symposium can be located, analyzed and evaluated.

William Twining's central concern in reviving the idea of general jurisprudence as a response to the challenges which globalization poses to legal theory is to situate the question of generalizability high on the agenda of jurisprudential inquiry. The framework and inspiration of his analysis pay tribute to the work of Julius Stone. However, both Twining and Stone acknowledge the vital role that historical location plays in defining the appropriate place of jurisprudence. Since Julius Stone completed his final version of the redetermination of the province of jurisprudence in 1968,[1] the most significant challenges for jurisprudential inquiry that have emerged can be grouped together under the rubric of 'globalization'. These challenges provide the basis for William Twining's inquiry, and are the reason that generalizability is at its centre. It is no longer appropriate for legal theorists in the Western, or indeed any, tradition to map the discipline of law by allocating concepts to general categories. The inquiry must instead be framed by asking whether any categories or terms remain generalizable: if so, which categories, in which circumstances and why. This is what it means to put generalizability high on the agenda of jurisprudence.

In Twining's chapter in this collection,[2] dilemmas of generalizability are demonstrated in two examples. First by considering the difficulties of applying the internationally agreed norms which form the Standard Minimum Rules for the Treatment of Prisoners, and later by considering the extent to which the term 'corruption' can be meaningfully applied around the world. These two illustrations approach the dilemma of generalizability from different directions. The Standard Minimum Rules raise the question from the perspective of international legal norms and reveal the extent to which agreements in international fora may be impossible, impractical, or simply inadvisable, to translate into domestic application. Behind this example, then, lies the question of what is achieved by establishing such norms at a highly generalized, or abstract, level – the level at which they are almost inevitably constructed. Twining's second example raises the question of generalizability from the perspective of the Western jurist: to what extent is it meaningful or appropriate to speak of a 'problem of corruption' in diverse cultural settings. The question here involves a careful inquiry into what is lost or gained or obscured by transplanting a term from one legal system to another or several others. The test then is to determine which concepts, in Twining's words, 'travel well'

---

1 'Province of Jurisprudence Redetermined' was first published in (1944) 7 *Modern Law Review* 97. It became the opening chapter in Stone's *Province and Function of Law: Law as Logic, Justice and Social Control*, Associated General Publications Pty Ltd, Sydney, 1946; Harvard University Press, Cambridge, 1950 and 1961; W S Hein, Buffalo, 2nd ed, 1968. See also Stone's *Legal System and Lawyers' Reasonings*, Stevens, London; Maitland Publications, Sydney; Stanford University Press, Stanford; Tripathi Private, Bombay, 1964.

2 This Chapter can be read as a sequel to Twining's *Globalization and Legal Theory*, Butterworths, London, 2000. It also functions as a prelude to his ongoing more comprehensive work on 'General Jurisprudence'. See also Twining W, 'Reviving General Jurisprudence' in Likosky M (ed), *Transnational Legal Processes*, Butterworths, Sydney, 2001.

and why. An answer to this in any particular case will meet the challenge he sets to make 'conceptual clarity' the precondition for other kinds of analysis.

In addition to situating the issue of generalizability differently than Julius Stone did, Twining distinguishes his endeavour from Stone's in several other areas. His inquiry has a more explicitly functional and pragmatic approach to theorizing and the intellectual tasks it involves; his view of the legal world moves beyond that of the municipal law of sovereign states and the relations between those states to encompass all levels of legal ordering 'from the very local to outer space'; and he places a greater emphasis on the complex interrelationships between normative and legal pluralism.[3]

These distinctions form the parameters of Twining's re-examination of the province of jurisprudence that is at the heart of his answer to the question of how legal theory must best respond to the challenges of globalization. Each of the other chapters in the collection takes up this challenge in some way. As a whole, the collection therefore provides a series of examples of how the project that Twining describes broadly can and must be analyzed and pursued in diverse legal settings to fulfil its mandate. The chapters relate to each other through their common engagement with the issue of generalizability: each can be read as addressing the extent to which a concept is 'travelling well'. The authors also demonstrate an engagement with functional and pragmatic theorizing, diverse spheres of legal ordering, and consideration of the interrelationships between normative and legal pluralism.

The collection is organized on two planes. The grouping of chapters reflects recurring themes in studies of globalization and also maps these themes onto the parameters that Twining establishes as those within which jurisprudence should begin to confront and address the globalization phenomenon. The existence of these overlapping planes highlights the relevance of Twining's analysis. This is not to say, of course, that the authors uniformly or unproblematically accept each of Twining's propositions. It is more appropriate to say that the collection reflects a recognition that these propositions are worth arguing over. The engagement of the chapters as a whole is therefore with one of the core concerns of

---

3 Twining also differs sharply from Stone in that he embraces a much wider understanding of the parameters of legal reasoning, while sharing with Stone an estimation of the importance of inquiring about and understanding 'lawyers' reasonings'. Twining notes that this distinction is beyond the scope of his present project. I agree with this assessment and find it mirrored in the fact that this is the only distinction Twining raises which is not taken up and illustrated elsewhere in this collection.

jurisprudence: a reflection on the place of law within society. In particular, the collection commences the work of reflection on the place of law within the increasingly interconnected globe, under the conditions grouped together by the term globalization.

Along with Twining's chapter, David Goldman's 'Historical Aspects of Globalization and Law' completes the first part of the volume outlining key themes in jurisprudence for an interconnected globe. Goldman's argument presents an historical perspective on the question of globalization and he organizes his analysis around a comparison of the two millennial revolutions and their effects on legal ordering. In doing so he tackles one of the pivotal issues of concern to globalization theorists: is globalization really a new phenomenon? Goldman's response to this is mixed. In the process of arriving at it, he engages several aspects of Twining's project. First, Goldman's work ranges over diverse spheres of legal ordering not hinged to the nation state, ranging from the ecclesiastic to cross-border commercial law. Second, he considers the question of normative pluralism as a central plank of his analysis. His conclusion that economic discourse dominates and forms the normative basis of contemporary legal ordering is key to his explanation of why some aspects of globalization can indeed be considered as 'new'.

The issue of generalizability is present in Goldman's work through his reflections on the 'grammar' of law. That is, he moves the locus of the question from particular principles which may be generalizable (his examples are the rule of law, natural justice and subsidiarity) to considering aspects of legal science, including the application, exposition and transmission of law. These can equally be cast as the mechanics of generalizability. Goldman's work is rich with exemplars from the last millennium and his argument serves to demonstrate that globalization itself may have a generalizable application.

The second part of the collection examines issues of globalization and the laws of money. The increasing financial and economic integration of the globe is one of the predominant themes in globalization literature. Whatever else globalization may be, production of Nike shoes worldwide and global currency speculation are some of its markers. Indeed, some theoretical accounts of globalization view it as an entirely economic phenomenon, in which economic ordering supercedes all other. The challenge for jurists is to consider and potentially counter this view by scrutinizing the roles which law can or does play in supporting, facilitating, resisting or preventing the economic integration which is the hallmark of globalization.

Sundhya Pahuja's analysis of international economic law shares with Goldman's work an emphasis on the normative functions of economic discourse. In surveying diverse accounts of globalization and the implications which each has for nation states and sovereignty, she calls for more considered emphasis on narratives of globalization and their performative effects. That is, their capacity to construct subject positions, some of which are within or along side the law. Pahuja's reflection on a series of studies in law and globalization point up strongly the inequalities which are fostered and reproduced by the interaction of international economic laws and globalization. She questions which perspectives are excluded in Twining's prescription for analysis of globalization and jurisprudence; and she is considerably more pessimistic than he about the continuing vitality of the Western legal canon.

One aspect of this pessimism derives from Pahuja's particular work on International Monetary Fund conditionality and trade discourse as exemplified in decisions of the World Trade Organization. Each of these inquiries, in a sense, raises in Twining's terms the question of generalizability. In each case, her conclusion is of a failure of generalizability. International Monetary Fund conditionality represents such a failure because it limits the types of economic order the Fund can respond to and therefore denies and suppresses the potential of Southern economies to differ from those of Northern donors. Similarly, trade discourse rests on a flawed foundational myth of regulatory normalcy that impedes attempts to meaningfully apply it to Southern settings without recasting and recreating colonial oppressions.

Some of these themes are echoed directly in Dimity Kingsford Smith's analysis of the regulatory regime of the International Organization of Securities Commissions (IOSCO). This analysis provides a fine example of the kind of detailed pragmatic work that Twining calls for as essential to supporting a revived general jurisprudence. Unlike the International Monetary Fund and the World Trade Organization, the IOSCO does not involve state actors as its members or sponsors. As a result, its objectives and principles cannot correspond to either hard or soft international law. Instead, they provide an important example of legal ordering which is not dependent on states. Kingsford Smith uses the insights of a legal pluralist perspective and the concept of 'interlegality' to analyze the interactions of different types of norms in the context of transnational securities regulation. Like Pahuja's, Kingsford Smith's analysis reveals stark inequities. She queries whether the IOSCO is able to achieve more than a worldwide spread of American norms and regulatory structures and queries the technocratic and anti-democratic nature of the arena. In this sense, then, her work provides another example of a failure of generalizability. While concepts may become generally applicable through the IOSCO process, this generalizability must be read as a power effect, rather than as a useful analytical conclusion. This concern echoes a prominent theme in studies of globalization, querying whether what is being globalized is simply a template of Western values and preferences.

The third part of the book takes up a further aspect of standard globalization mythology and considers its place in the law. It is taken as a given that while technologies of communication and transportation have facilitated a shrinking of the globe, people are still for the most part anchored in particular geographies. Or to express the contrast in economic terms, the mobility of capital has not been accompanied by a corresponding increase in mobility of labour. These chapters examine this question from two perspectives: first by analyzing globalizing trends within the regulation of labour in place, and then by examining how regulation of the movement of people is adapting to the challenges now facing nation states. Each of these three chapters contributes an analysis that demonstrates the resilience of legal ordering at the level of the nation state, even as they acknowledge the shifts that current trends represent for both these law-making arenas.

Jill Murray argues that labour law has followed a different trajectory than other areas of law because it has had an established international dimension for almost a century. The role of the International Labour Organization as a rule-making body, and the ways its norms have shaped rather than dictated national practice provide a crucial example for theorists of law and globalization, and an important consideration in the assessment of globalization's 'newness'. The practice of the International Labour Organization is also key evidence of the dilemmas of generalizability as states proceed to implement internationally agreed norms.

Against her elucidation of the internationalized dimensions of labour law, Murray analyzes the Ratcheting Labour Standards thesis as an example of one response by labour law scholars to concerns that globalizing trends are diminishing state capacity. Murray concludes that the Ratcheting Labour Standards proposal has been asserted without attention to the lessons of the International Labour Organization. Ratcheting Labour Standards moves its ideological focus from regulation of work to regulation of the firm itself, and in the process contributes to a commodification of labour which fits closely to mythologies of globalization. In Murray's view, this ideological shift should be resisted as damaging to workers and as overlooking the continued importance of the nation state as a relatively more 'local' unit for regulation.

Kim Rubenstein examines the twinned legal concepts of citizenship and nationality and concludes that the content of each is shifting. Citizenship, the domestic half of the couplet, is weakening as a basis for both rights entitlements and opportunities to participate meaningfully in the polity. In contrast, however, it is being transformed into a vehicle which can be used to facilitate participation in democratic rule formation activities at levels beyond the nation state, including but not limited to the international. Nationality, the parallel concept with its roots in international law, is also being slowly transformed to operate a less-restrictive, more functionally grounded basis. Rubenstein concludes that the shifts occurring in both concepts provide reasons for optimism about expanding visions of membership and inclusion in a more globalized future. Her study can be viewed as an investigation into whether the concepts of citizenship and nationality are travelling well. The response is yes, they are retaining their legal relevance in spite of shifts in the notion of state sovereignty to which they are both tied. This provides a particular caution when conducting an inquiry into the generalizability. The object of Twining's inquiry into generalizability is to provide the necessary conceptual clarity to ground further analysis. Despite 'travelling well', in terms of their resilience and widespread relevance, both citizenship and nationality are subject to some lack of clarity because of the subtle shifts they are able to contain. This study, like Twining's own analysis of corruption, suggests that concepts not only need to be tested for the capacity to reach around the globe, but also need to be pinned down in time, tied to an historical moment.

My own chapter is in some way the mirror image of Rubenstein's, analyzing laws of membership and belonging from the perspective of exclusion rather than inclusion. Examining the global array of increasingly stringent legal responses to illegal migration, I argue that nation states are, through these laws, asserting their hold on a traditional territorial version of sovereignty. Migration law is an ideal arena for testing some of the central propositions of globalization theory. In this arena, we find that the nation state is retaining its relevance through its power to exclude; to divide even its resident population into 'us' and 'them' groupings.

The issue of generalizability arises in this analysis because the notion of illegal migration is a newly minted generalizable category. There is increasing worldwide rhetoric and concern about this phenomenon, which is only in part a response to the enhanced support it receives through the technologies of travel and communication which are part and parcel of globalization. While the label 'illegal' ought technically to apply simply to any transgressor of the multitude of provisions which make up a given migration law scheme, it is instead associated with only a particular subset of transgressors. As such, the term 'illegal' acquires a life of its own – as is suggested by its transformation from adjective to noun – which is laden with stereotypes about race, gender, country of origin, and class. This stereotype of 'illegals' resonates worldwide, homogenizing the exclusions that occur at the nation state level. The term itself casts these exclusions as lawful, masking the normative significations of the law in this area.

The contrast between the two chapters is important. In the case of Rubenstein's analysis, where the issue under consideration is inclusion, globalization appears to be bringing increased and varied inclusions. In contrast, when the issue examined is exclusion, globalization appears to be escalating exclusions with a progressively simplified set of reasons for doing so. This evidence provides some support for the argument that globalization represents a working through of an inherently liberal project, replete with the universalizing tendencies which are markers of liberalism and with the need for a delineation between insiders and outsiders which liberal theory has not been able to circumvent.

The final section of the book takes up most directly Twining's call for pragmatic empirical comparative work to ground the search for generalizability. Adam Czarnota's chapter on the twinned roles of law and globalization in eastern Europe and Mark Findlay's analysis of crime in transitional cultures both provide insights into how a jurisprudence of globalization must take account of cultural locations. Each of these chapters also confronts the question of how to evaluate linkages between globalization and development, an issue that frequently arises in globalization theory. Globalization's uneven effects are in evidence here, as is the difficulty of easily assessing generalizability when its cultural context is in transition.

Czarnota's principal cautionary conclusion regards the unpredictability of legal transplants. Law and culture are interdependent, so that attempts in eastern Europe to reconstruct a legal culture by transplanting Western legal concepts are fraught with the unhappiness of Czarnota's title. As nations of the former communist bloc work to reconnect with the world economy, law is an important medium for conducting the transition. Nonetheless, the law must somehow respond both to the cultural setting into which it is transplanted, and to the past it is deployed to amend. Czarnota's work also engages the challenge Twining sets of grappling with law at levels other than that of the nation state or the international. Empirically, he tackles a politically delimited region, theoretically he queries the ability of any jurist to move beyond the nation state framework without further work in social theory to support a different analytic framework. At this juncture in time, the law in eastern Europe is struggling to respond both to forces of globalization and to the sudden removal of formerly universalizing norms within the communist world. The intersection of these two globalized perspectives provides a rich platform for study.

Findlay sets out in detail the multiple roles which comparative jurisprudence is called upon to play in confronting globalization. In setting this agenda, he provides a fully developed example of the suggestions made in Twining's chapter, a plan for conducting the work necessary to ground an analysis of generalizability. Findlay further argues that the social context of crime provides the key to its significance. The challenge that globalizing forces present from this perspective is the creation of a global social context. Globalization presents new opportunities for both crime and its control, without challenging the linkage between crime and social context. He considers the present importance of terrorism as the paradigm of a crime that must be interpreted in a global social context.

Findlay asserts that both crime and globalization present paradoxes, with the result that crime is transformed in both its local and its global settings by the shrinking of the globe. Theorizing about criminal law at this historical juncture must struggle to fit both perspectives into explanatory analyzes. Findlay takes up the questions of terrorism and corruption, among other examples. His approach to generalizability reflects the paradoxes at the centre of his analysis. Globalization itself generalizes some forms of crime, where previously crime had to be understood as entirely culturally specific. On the other hand, culture in its local variants continues to transform our understandings of crime and to render simple statements of generalizability absurd. In presenting this paradox, Findlay engages the interrelationships between normative and legal pluralism to which Twining calls our attention.

The collection makes an important step towards exploring how jurisprudence for an interconnected globe can be constructed. As a whole, the Chapters take this analysis in a variety of new and previously unexplored directions. Refreshingly, this analysis of globalization and jurisprudence does not centre itself on emerging human rights norms or the law of the European Union. Rather, it sets up analytic directions which can encompass those issues, but which retain their validity far beyond them. The work presented here provides a strong basis for analyzing other areas of the law, and for conducting the type of functional and pragmatic theorizing which Twining calls upon us to embrace.

PART I:

KEY THEMES IN JURISPRUDENCE FOR AN INTERCONNECTED GLOBE

Chapter 2

The Province of Jurisprudence Re-examined

*William Twining**

Introduction

To start with a story, based on experience, but elaborated in the form of a parable.[1] A few years ago a team of local and foreign consultants was asked to evaluate the health of the criminal justice system (including police and prisons) in an African country that was starting to rebuild after a terrible period of human and natural disasters. Under the general rubric of promoting 'democracy, human rights and good governance', their remit was to devise a strategy and set priorities for expenditure by government and a consortium of foreign donors. Part of this involved setting priorities for prisons. Seventy per cent of the prison population was on remand, often illegally. Despite the best efforts of the prison service, prison conditions were appalling. Money was short, and many of the problems seemed very intractable, if not insoluble.

It was difficult to know where to begin. The country had a newly minted Constitution (including a Bill of Rights). Legitimated and validated by an admirably democratic constitutive process, this Constitution was a source of both national pride and strong, but not universal, public support. One member of the team suggested that the first principle should be: 'Enforce the Constitution'. Brushing aside the argument that there were no sanctions against the government for non-enforcement, the team adopted this as their starting-point.

Article 24 stated: 'No one shall be subjected to any form of torture, cruel, inhuman, or degrading treatment or punishment'. Before considering complex problems of illegal detention, mixing women and children with adult males, extreme overcrowding, and forced labour, the team turned its attention to the seemingly simpler question of providing clean water or adequate food. Someone proposed that failure to provide these basic

---

* This is a revised text of the first Julius Stone Memorial Lecture delivered in Sydney in August, 2000. This lecture was written at the Center for Advanced Study in the Social and Behavioral Sciences at Stanford in 1999-2000. I am most grateful for the support and stimulation provided by staff and Fellows at the Center.

1 This is a fictitious story based on experience in several African countries.

necessities was 'inhuman' and therefore unconstitutional. This proposal met with a sceptical response.

The first argument was that there had been no local precedents interpreting 'inhuman': it was a category of indeterminate or illusory reference. To which the reply was that the local provision was derived from many international and regional conventions and standards, including the non-binding Standard Minimum Rules for the Treatment of Prisoners. To many of these documents the government was a signatory. There was accordingly a vast jurisprudence upon which to draw in interpreting Article 24, including persuasive precedents and commentaries within the same region.[2] The term 'inhuman' might be vague, but it was part of a universal principle of political morality upholding basic human needs for survival and reasonable health. From this one could infer that the government had a duty to protect the life and health of all prisoners by providing clean water, even if the government's international obligations were backed only by the moral sanctions in the tribunal of international opinion.

The next line of argument was about local conditions: 'About half of the rural population does not have clean water. Are you proposing that prisoners should be treated better than the ordinary people should? And will the test of cleanliness take into account the fact that many locals have developed some immunity to infections found in water? What about foreign prisoners, should they be treated equally?' After some debate, the team decided by a majority that the exact standard of 'clean' should be prescribed by regulation, taking into account local conditions (including costs), but not beyond a point that the water would be deleterious to health. If that meant that prisoners were being treated better than some people, that was what the Constitution, backed by international and regional jurisprudence, prescribed.

The third line of scepticism came from within the team. The economist said: 'This is sheer legalism and mischievous nonsense. What precisely are you recommending in respect of water?' 'Running water, purification, or boiling? What precisely is the test of "clean"? Standards are not self-enforcing: Who will do the testing and who will pay? How much will this cost for all prisons in the country?' 'Does the provision of clean water

---

2 A good summary of the international jurisprudence is to be found in Rodley N, *The Treatment of Prisoners Under International Law*, 2nd ed, Oxford University Press, Oxford, 1999. However, there does not appear to be much direct authority on standards for provision of food and water, and there are unsettled questions about omissions and intent in respect of 'inhuman and degrading treatment'. Some support for the team's interpretation may be found in the Standard Minimum Rules for the Treatment of Prisoners, First UN Congress on the Prevention of Crime and the Treatment of Offenders, Annex 1(A), UN Doc. A/CONF. 6/1 (1956).

have a higher priority than other claims of the prison service or the criminal justice system?' 'Are you sure that this Constitution is an institution that this country can afford?' The reply from the team was: 'The Constitution is the basic law. In interpreting terms like 'inhuman' there is leeway for taking into account local conditions and values, but it is absolute in regard to the principle that the government has a duty to treat prisoners as human beings. We are not advocating Kelsenian purity. We can tolerate some impurities so long as they do not seriously threaten health. But we reject arguments of the kind: 'Prisoners have no-right to food or clean water or freedom from torture, because we cannot afford such protections. Article 24 is part of a worldwide consensus on non-negotiable minima'.

The dilemmas in this situation are real; the issues are at the heart of legal theory. Indeed this text could be read as a *roman a clef*, incorporating phrases from several jurists. My object in starting with this tale is neither to defend nor to criticize the position taken by the majority of the team. The issues are contested. Rather, in talking about very broad, often abstract matters, I do not want to give the impression that I think that jurisprudence can be divorced from urgent, real life, historically specific problems. In talking about linking social science with the study of human values, Julius Stone wrote:

> Yet it still remains basic that this concern of jurisprudence seeks detailed empirical understanding and solution of ad hoc practical problems, and that concern with the larger more visionary enterprises ought never to obscure this truth.[3]

In private moments a jurist has two quick routes to despondency: the Palomar route and the Stone route. Italo Calvino's Mr Palomar tried to start to master the world's complexity by defining with precision a single wave.[4] This elementary task proved so elusive that he gave up, as tense and nervous as when he started, and more unsure about everything. Trying to understand a single legal phenomenon can be as discouraging as Mr Palomar's quest. An alternative route leads to the conclusion that everything that one is trying to say has been said before – and better. This has been my experience in revisiting the work of Julius Stone. I have for the past several years been struggling with a project which has successively gone by such modest titles as 'Understanding Law', 'Globalization and Legal Theory', and latterly 'General Jurisprudence'.

---

3 'Trends in Jurisprudence in the Second Half Century', 1967, printed in Hathaway BD, *Julius Stone: A Bio-Biography*, University of Texas Law School, Austin, 1980 at 30. This paper was written shortly after the publication of Stone J, *Law and the Social Sciences in the Second Half Century*, University of Minnesota Press, Minneapolis, 1966.

4 Calvino I, *Mr. Palomar*, Weaver W (trans), Harcourt Brace, San Diego, 1985 1.1.1.

In preparing for this chapter in honour of one of my jurisprudential heroes, I revisited most of Julius Stone‘s contributions to jurisprudence, and especially *The Province and Function of Law*, which had been one of my main props in the early years of teaching jurisprudence.[5] I was reminded of several of his memorable phrases: enclaves of justice; categories of illusory and indeterminate reference; the fallacy of the logical form; dangers to objectivity; leeways of choice and patterns of discourse; non-stringent reasoning; jurisprudence as the lawyer's extraversion. Then I found a piece that I had not read before and was plunged into Palomar-like despondency. This was an essay entitled 'Trends in Jurisprudence in the Second Half Century', written in 1967, but not published until 1980.[6] Here, Stone succinctly and forcefully surveyed the vast heritage of Western legal thought – formal, conceptual, normative, and empirical; winnowed out the repetitious, the ephemeral and the outdated; and then related what he considered to be worth keeping to his vision of the pressing issues for a cosmopolitan jurisprudence in the second half of the twentieth century. It is a masterly piece of cartography, sketching the landscape and contours of numerous intellectual trends and their relations, while pinpointing with uncanny foresight a wide range of issues that are still on the agenda today.[7] To make matters worse he pithily articulated some of my current concerns, dismissed others as unworthy of scholarly energy, and even advanced some ideas that I had thought were my very own.[8]

---

5 Stone J, *The Province and Function of Law: A Study in Jurisprudence*, Harvard University Press, Cambridge, Massachusetts, 1946.

6 Stone (1967, 1980), above n 3.

7 Not only did he anticipate problems that are today of pressing concern, such as interdependence, making sense of the rule of law in an unstable world, the implications of computers and other new technology for legal theory, but he also treated some much debated issues as old hat: interdisciplinarity, cultural relativism, indeterminacy, the need to integrate analytical, sociological, and ethical approaches to law. To rub it in, he reminded us that in 1912 Pound outlined an eight-point program for sociological jurisprudence which had by 1967 achieved the status of a checklist for work already proceeding with more or less success through 'massive if sporadic investigations' in 'many advanced legal orders'. Stone's assessment of the state of play in 1967 today looks rather upbeat; a more sober assessment could well lead us to conclude that hardly any of the items on the program have been systematically implemented in a sustained fashion and some have all but been abandoned.

8 A few quotations can give the flavour: Natural law should be viewed not merely as a theory of substantive justice, but rather as the cultural history of 'a vessel bearing in its ample holds a wide variety of theories of justice originating from many centuries and legal cultures'. Above n 3 at 26. Even extravagant social theorizing, like that of Talcott Parsons, can 'serve at least to loosen the hold of the truisms and commonplaces within which political philosophy has too long been confined'. Ibid at 42. Hart‘s rule of recognition 'as a working concept … still falls rather hard between the analytical and sociological stools'. Ibid at 20. 'It is no longer necessary to browbeat lawyers into

My first reaction to reading this piece, written more than 30 years ago, was: 'Why do I bother? The old curmudgeon has got there first and has said it all already'. Julius Stone's capacity for masterly synthesis and pithy apercus may provide a fast route into despondency, but he also shows the way out, reminding us 'of the time dimension that conditions all knowledge'. Situations and problems are specific and continuously in flux; all thought is provisional and frail; what was wisdom in one generation needs to be reviewed, revised and built on as the world changes. There is a perpetual job-market for jurists.

For me Julius Stone is a sort of uncle-in-the-law with some of the ambivalences that characterize such relations. I shall not presume to compare our achievements. But it is relevant to my subject to point to some important similarities in our backgrounds and general outlook, despite some very significant differences.[9] At different times, we both decided that the dominant analytical approach to law at Oxford was narrow and constricting and we found at least some of what was missing in the United States in the tradition of 'the revolt against formalism': Roscoe Pound and Harvard for Stone; Karl Llewellyn and the University of Chicago for myself. We both became loyal, but not uncritical, followers of our American mentors.[10] However, for neither of us did this involve outright rejection of the English analytical tradition: instead both have insisted that analytical, ethical, historical and sociological concerns are complementary and need to be integrated into the study of law. We both followed careers as wandering jurists in several mainly 'anglophone' countries; we shared a cosmopolitan outlook and a concern about the North-South divide; a broad vision of law; an insistence on the importance of history and social context;

---

admitting to their concern for the ethical *and* sociological imports of law, or to propagandize for interdisciplinary teamwork or the integration of all contributions to our knowledge of human society whatever disciplinary boundaries from which they come'. Ibid at 18.

9 In important respects we are very different: He belonged to a different generation; he lived through different struggles, in particular he suffered from and fought for the Jewish experience; he was a distinguished and influential figure in Public International Law; for over 40 years he wisely chose Sydney and San Francisco as his panoramic vantage points. We both were undergraduates at Oxford. We both would have chosen to read history, but for different reasons, were shunted into the study of law. My father, an amateur historian, insisted that history was a non-subject. Stone parted with his history tutor on more lofty historiographical grounds; Hawke RJK, 'Julius Stone – Humanist, Jurist and Internationalist' (1986) 9 *University of New South Wales Law Journal* 1.

10 The affinities and differences between Pound and Llewellyn are explored in depth by Natalie Hull in her *Roscoe Pound and Karl Llewellyn*, University of Chicago Press, Chicago, 1998. For some mild reservations see my review: Twining W, 'Review: *Roscoe Pound and Karl Llewellyn: Searching for an American Jurisprudence* by N E H Hull' (1999) 115 *Law Quarterly Review* 152.

and a belief that law, including jurisprudence as its theoretical part, should be concerned with the practical solution of real-life problems in specific times and places. Law is a social phenomenon; jurisprudence is in Stone's memorable phrase 'the lawyer's extraversion', examining the basics of our subject 'in the light derived from present knowledge other than the law'.[11] Extraversion and a disciplined eclecticism are not dilettantism. For jurists too have a special field of expertise and healthy inter-disciplinary relations involve reciprocity. A jurist is a lawyer and should never forget that: our discipline has as much to offer the social sciences and humanities as it has to learn from them. If some of these general ideas sound trite, it is in large part because Julius Stone made them so. He had to struggle for most of his career to be heard and to get them accepted. All of them are relevant starting-points for this essay.

The Province of Jurisprudence Re-examined

One of Julius Stone's major achievements was to redetermine the province of jurisprudence in 1944.[12] For half a century this has been the most comprehensive and coherent vision of the subject. I recently canvassed encyclopedias, writings of canonical jurists, and students' works in order to examine their conceptions, implicit or explicit, of what is variously referred to as jurisprudence, legal theory, or legal philosophy. This was rather a depressing exercise. In the past 30 to 40 years jurisprudence has developed a healthy pluralism, but it has done so at the cost of any sense of coherence. Some accounts do little more than set out the personal agenda of the author. Many are eclectic, presenting the scene as a hodge podge, an anarchy, or a somewhat random bazaar. Some are explicitly reductionist, for example, treating legal theory as a sub-branch of ethics or sociology or political economy. Most are either geographically limited – Anglo-American, Latin American, Continental European – or else geographically indeterminate, with a tendency to pay little or no attention to non-Christian or non-Western traditions. Some students' works are designed to fit traditional syllabuses for courses based on conventions that just grew without any serious attempt at intellectual coherence.

Many commentators, including some of the most sensible, doubt the value of spending time or energy on defining or mapping jurisprudence as a field of study. I have some sympathy with such scepticism and with the

---

11 Stone (1946) above n 5 at 25.

12 Stone J, 'The Province of Jurisprudence Redetermined' (1944) 7 *Modern Law Review* 97-112 and 177-92.

metaphor of a bazaar applied to our heritage of legal thought.[13] There may be little value in defining or mapping so vast and varied a range of activities in the abstract. Stone had a particular reason for doing so. Today, something needs to be said about one's conception of the field for the specific purpose of suggesting an agenda for a revived general jurisprudence as a theoretical basis for the development of a genuinely cosmopolitan discipline of law in the next decade or so, even if one's position is that this agenda should be both pluralistic and open-ended. One needs a map, but given the bewildering diversity of the current intellectual scene, maybe it should be like a weather map that identifies patterns, flows and trends rather than depicts autonomous domains with sharply defined borders.

Rather than bore you with a detailed critique of the views and assumptions of even a few modern jurists, I shall assert rather than argue that I have found nothing in recent writings to compare in breadth of vision and undogmatic good sense to Stone's attempt to re-determine the province of jurisprudence, first in 1946,[14] and again with significant glosses in 1964. So I propose to remind you briefly of Stone's vision and then to put forward a different conception, that is my picture of the directions in which jurisprudence as a collective enterprise, at least within our tradition, should move in the coming decades. Although there are important differences between our conceptions, I believe that the underlying spirit is much the same, and that the main contrasts are attributable more to differences in the situation of the discipline of law in the English-speaking world in mid-twentieth century and at the start of the Millennium.

What was Stone's vision of the Province of Jurisprudence? One of his sons, Jonathan, is reported as saying that his father was 'a mixture of anger, discipline, and a commitment to the search for justice'.[15] The start of *The Province and Function of Law* is clearly motivated by anger and frustration at the narrowness and sterility he felt about the state of academic law, much of which he attributed to 'the stranglehold' of Austinian Jurisprudence[16] in most parts of the English-speaking world. Stone lamented the marginalisation of historical and sociological jurisprudence, and, above all,

---

[13] Twining W, *The Great Juristic Bazaar: Jurists' Texts and Lawyers' Stories*, Ashgate, Aldershot, 2002. See also, Twining W, 'The Great Juristic Bazaar' (1978) 14 *Journal of Society of Public Teachers of Law* (New Series) 185.

[14] His 1944 article, above n 12, became the opening Chapter of *Province and Function of Law: Law as Logic, Justice and Social Control*, Associated General Publications, Sydney, 1946; republished by Harvard University Press, Cambridge, 1950, 1961.

[15] Quoted in Star L, *Julius Stone: An Intellectual Life*, Oxford University Press, Melbourne, 1992 at xii.

[16] Stone (1946) above n 5 at 4.

the almost total neglect of the quest for justice. But Stone's anger was disciplined and in the first chapter he made a patient and reasoned critique of all the main schemes of division of the subject in the first half of the twentieth century, including eclectic schemes, such as that of Pound, rational schemes, such as that of Kocourek, Hohfeld and Wigmore, and give-it-up attitudes which made much taught jurisprudence 'a chaos of approaches to a chaos of topics chaotically delimited'.[17] Stone believed that a systematic taxonomy of the field was important for purposes of exposition and that it needed to be based on two ideas: 'first, that jurisprudence is the examination of law in the light of other disciplines and, second, that jurisprudence must make its own classification for legal purposes'[18] rather than being a mere aggregation of relations with neighbouring disciplines in terms of 'Law and …' such as 'Law and logic', 'Law and history', 'Law and psychology'. After a rather laboured analysis, Stone eventually settled on a simple scheme that divided jurisprudence, like Gaul, into three parts: Analytical Jurisprudence; Sociological (or Functional) Jurisprudence; and Theories of Justice (or Critical or Censorial or Ethical) Jurisprudence. Stone was always careful to emphasize that these divisions were for purposes of convenient exposition, that the parts were interdependent and might combine in different ways in different enquiries. Given that important caveat, I have generally found Stone's scheme to be quite workable, even though I interpret each category rather differently from him. It reflects broad distinctions between analytical, empirical and normative enquiries without making prior commitments to either rigid distinctions between them or to a strong notion of the autonomy of disciplines.

In my view, it is not the particular taxonomy that is important. Rather Stone's achievement was to provide a usable framework that achieved four things: first, it broadened the conception of jurisprudence in a way that treated both empirical and normative enquiries as an integral part of the field; second, it challenged the conception of the heritage of Western legal thought as consisting of rival schools rather than a complex plurality of interacting lines of enquiry that had different concerns and questions at their centre. Third, it emphasized – indeed perhaps over-emphasized – the multi-disciplinary nature of legal theory; and fourth, it was capacious, flexible and open-ended, so that it did not exclude any general lines of enquiry relating to law (though it must be admitted that it has been easier to accommodate some recent developments than others into his scheme: law and economics, quite easily; law and literature perhaps less so). The phrase

---

[17] Ibid at 16.

[18] Ibid at 25.

'The Province of Jurisprudence' deliberately echoed John Austin, whom Stone accused of drawing the boundaries of that province too tightly and too narrowly, thereby excluding from consideration some of the most important elements in understanding law. Stone constructed a bold over-arching framework that encompassed a very broad range of concerns, mapped some of their inter-relations and was flexible enough to leave the door open for new developments.

Being taken for granted is one price of success. If Stone's tripartite scheme and his general conception of legal theory seem almost banal today, that is largely because his main concerns have been met: Austinian analytical jurisprudence is almost forgotten; ethical concerns occupy centre stage in contemporary legal theory; if the social dimensions of law and justice are studied rather unevenly and eclectically, at least the interdisciplinary nature of legal theorizing is widely accepted. Such has been the proliferation of different movements, fashions and paradigmlets[19] that the rich pluralism of legal theorizing around the English-speaking world still threatens to decline into a chaos of enquiries, chaotically delimited. And in reaction to this there is a real danger of different approaches being seen as deadly rivals in an atmosphere of intellectual intolerance.

Stone emphasized the need for continuously re-examining our knowledge and understandings in a changing world.[20] The landscape of jurisprudence has changed quite radically since 1967. The indexes to his great trilogy of the 1960s do not contain references to (in alphabetical order) the Amsterdam School of Argumentation, autopoiesis, communitarianism, critical legal studies, feminism, law and

---

19 I have borrowed this term from Carol Gluck.

20 Stone revisited and revised his 1944-46 formulation in the mid 1960s and again, more briefly, at various points in the last 20 years of his life. But the general outlines of his conception of the province of jurisprudence remained constant. He was remarkably prescient about problems arising from such matters as the development of computers, advances in genetics and biology, the North-South divide, global interdependence and, especially, threats to World Peace and means of lessening them. As early as 1970 he edited a book on the prospects for an International Criminal Court, Stone J and Woetzel RK (eds), *Toward a Feasible International Criminal Court*, World Peace Through World Law, Geneva, 1970. Stone's vision has almost come to fruition with the signing of the Rome Statute of the International Criminal Court, UN Doc. A/CONF.183/9 by 139 countries. Although the treaty it is not yet in force, it is anticipated that the inception of a permanent international criminal court is very near, see Schabas W, *An Introduction to the International Criminal Court*, Cambridge, Cambridge University Press, 2001 at xiii. But in the mid-1960s or even the early 1980s even he could not have foreseen such events as the collapse of the Soviet bloc, the end of apartheid, the spread of AIDS, email and the Internet, and the extreme forms of conflict in former Yugoslavia, Rwanda and elsewhere.

micro-economics,[21] law and literature, the new institutionalism, semiotics, and the various uppity post-isms like post-modernism, post-Marxism, and post-structuralism to say nothing of developments in neighbouring disciplines and the jurisprudence of The World Bank.[22]

Given the quantity and pace of such changes it does seem that the time is ripe for a re-examination of the nature and scope of jurisprudence. During the past five years I have been trying to explore some of the implications of globalization for the discipline of law and for Jurisprudence as its theoretical part. This is part of a wider project on reviving General Jurisprudence in a new form.[23] For me a central issue for a revived general jurisprudence is: how far, and in what respects, is it feasible and desirable for an English (or more broadly a common law) jurist to talk generally about any legal phenomena or issues? This applies to concepts, values, empirical facts, and various kinds of interpretive theories as well as to legal doctrines and 'solutions'. As part of exploring issues of generalizability, it is necessary to re-examine the province of jurisprudence.

In order to set a context and get down to some detail, I shall assert rather than argue for a number of positions that I have elaborated elsewhere.[24]

My standpoint is that of a jet-setting English jurist, based in London, concerned with the health of his discipline in the next ten to 20 years. The mission of the institutionalized discipline of law is the advancement and dissemination of knowledge and critical understanding about the subject matters of the discipline.[25] These subject matters include the structure,

---

21 Stone dealt extensively with some aspects of economics and law (in Stone J, *Social Dimensions of Law and Justice*, Stevens and Sons, London, 1966), but he wrote before the rise into prominence of the Chicago School of Law and Economics, which started in Chicago in the late 1950s, but did not come into prominence until later.

22 A high priority for a revived general jurisprudence is a critical analysis of the assumptions about law underlying 'the Washington consensus', the policies and programs of The World Bank, International Monetary Fund, World Trade Organization and related institutions. There is already a burgeoning literature, see, for example, Chua A, 'Markets, Democracy, and Ethnicity: Toward a New Paradigm for Law and Development' (1998) 108 *Yale Law Journal* 1.

23 The first stage of the project is reported in my *Globalisation and Legal Theory*, Butterworths, London, 2000, to which this chapter can be read as a sequel. See also Twining W, 'Reviving General Jurisprudence' in Likosky M (ed), *Transnational Legal Processes*, Butterworths, London, 2002.

24 Twining (2000) ibid, *passim*, and references there.

25 On the relationship between legal scholarship and legal education in the context of globalization see my 'A Cosmopolitan Discipline? Some Implications of 'Globalization' for Legal Education' (2001) 8 *International Journal of the Legal Profession* 23 and my 'Cosmopolitan Legal Studies' *International Journal of the Legal Profession* in which I

concepts, values, and practical operation of institutionalized ordering of relations between persons (human, legal, unincorporated, and other), not just relations within a single state or society or between sovereign states. One way of roughly characterizing these levels of relations is geographical. In terms of space they include the global, international, transnational, regional, inter-communal, municipal (nation state and subsidiary jurisdictions), sub-state local and non-state local.[26] These different levels are not simply nested in a single hierarchy of larger and smaller spaces. Rather they typically co-exist within the same geographical space and interact, overlap, and sometimes conflict in extremely complex ways. For this reason, normative pluralism, legal pluralism as part of it, and what Santos calls 'interlegality' should be among the central concerns of a revived general jurisprudence.[27]

I treat Jurisprudence as the theoretical part of law as a discipline.[28] A theoretical question is no more and no less than a question posed at a relatively high level of generality. In this usage, the terms jurisprudence and legal theory are synonymous; they include, but are much broader than, legal philosophy which refers to just one part, the most abstract part, of the broad enterprise.[29] Jurisprudence can be viewed as a heritage, as an ideology, and as the *activity* of theorizing, that is posing, reposing,

---

argue that much legal education will need to remain more rooted in the local, especially in respect of focus and detail, than legal scholarship and theory.

26 For detailed discussion see Twining (2000) above n 23 at ch 6.

27 I here deliberately side-step traditional definitional issues concerning what counts as a 'legal order' and how legal and normative pluralism are distinguished. In this context, my conception of law is broad enough to include some kinds of non-state and religious law, for example a putative *lex mercatoria*, Dinka, Islamic, Hindu, or Gypsy law, as worthy subject-matters of our discipline, but how one classifies borderline cases is not germane to my argument. Similarly, this characterization deliberately leaves open questions about the relative importance of different kinds of legal order. On general definitions of law, see Twining (2000) above n 23 at 78-80, and from 224. Commenting on the early pluralists, such as Hauriou, Renard and Santi Romano, Stone expressed caution about 'down grading' of law but commented: 'Again, law may be admitted *at present* as a distinct social control and a distinct object of knowledge, but that some one of these non-legal factors may be said to be so potent and self-sufficient that the distinctness is *destined* to disappear as social evolution proceeds' (1967, 1980 above n 3 at 40).

28 See Twining W, *Law in Context: Enlarging a Discipline*, Oxford University Press, Oxford, 1997 at ch 6 and 7.

29 There is a tendency among contemporary Anglo-American analytical jurists to confine 'Jurisprudence' to 'philosophically interesting questions' and to treat Jurisprudence and Legal Philosophy as co-extensive. A clear example of this is Leiter B, 'Is there an American Jurisprudence?' (1997) 17 *Oxford Journal of Legal Studies* 367. The view advanced here is quite different. Our differences are not merely or mainly semantic; rather they reflect divergent judgments about priorities within legal theory.

answering, and arguing about general questions relating to the subject-matters of law as a discipline. The idea of heritage emphasizes continuity. The idea of ideology links one's beliefs about law to one's more general beliefs about the world – whether or not they are systematic; and in the pejorative Marxist interpretation of the term, the notion of ideology is a healthy reminder of the close connection between belief, self-interest, prejudice and delusion. As an activity within our discipline, theorizing has several functions: constructing whole views or total pictures (the synthesizing or mapping function);[30] elucidating, constructing, and refining concepts; developing normative theories, middle-order hypotheses, and general working theories for participants; intellectual history; and, most important, critically examining the underlying assumptions of different kinds of discourse of and about law.[31] This pragmatic conception of legal theorizing emphasizes the crucial role of jurisprudence in the development of law as a discipline, although in a participant-oriented discipline it is natural, and often healthy, that practice should outrun theory.

The phrase 'globalization' is in the air and has spawned a massive, excited and somewhat repetitious literature. Ironically, that literature is quite narrow in that it focuses on a limited range of issues. This is especially the case where 'globalization' is restricted to economic matters and is associated with extreme laissez-faire ideology and increasing American and Western hegemony. I want to use the term more broadly here to refer to those trends, processes and interactions which are making the world more interdependent in many complex ways, in respect of communications, cultures, language, and politics, not just the alleged development of a single world economy

Here I want to make a partial retraction. After immersing myself in the literature, I have come to the conclusion that the term 'global' is too narrow for my purposes, because most discussions focus on a quite limited range of issues and ignore or marginalize most levels of ordering in between the world and individual nation states.

In the present context, the term 'cosmopolitan' neatly expresses both a need for boldness and a need for caution. I prefer it to two other fashionable terms, global and international, both of which are quite narrow. This may be ironic, but it is not paradoxical. The term 'global' refers to the world as a whole. Global problems and relations are literally worldwide. But law, as we have seen, refers to many other levels of ordering of

---

30 One task of general jurisprudence is to construct overviews of legal phenomena in the world as a whole, global mapping of law, but legal theory needs to be concerned with all levels of legal ordering and their interrelations, Twining (2000) above n 23 at ch 6.

31 Ibid ch 1.

relations between persons. Some of these tend to get ignored or marginalized in talk of globalization. The uneven and heady literature on 'globalization' tends either to focus on a quite narrow range of genuinely world-wide issues such as climate control or world peace or humanitarian and human rights law, or else the term is loosely extended to cover topics that belong to one or more less-extensive spheres of ordering. It is inappropriate to treat as 'global', issues concerning competition and monopoly within the European Union, or debates within Islam on banking or the status of women, yet they should be of as much concern to us today as genuinely global issues. Furthermore, globalization rhetoric tends to focus on superficialities: at this stage in history, CNN and the Internet and the problems they spawn are as superficially global as Holiday Inns – they range over wide geographical spaces, but their level of penetration is extraordinarily uneven. Some objects of globalization rhetoric are no more global than the World Series in baseball.[32]

The term 'international' is sometimes extended beyond the traditional usage of relations between states to include all levels beyond the domestic or municipal. This is illustrated by the proliferation of journals, programs and courses with the term 'international' in the title, especially in the United States. This loose extension is dangerous in two ways: first, it perpetuates the myth, still reinforced by most legal theorists, that law is only concerned with two levels of ordering: the internal legal systems of nation states and the ordering of relations between states. It is dangerously misleading to lump together such varied phenomena as Islamic law, European Union Law, *lex mercatoria*, or traditional African law under the rubric of 'international law'. We should be wary of conceding too much territory to specialist public international lawyers. International law is an institutionalized sub-culture with conceptual schemes, styles of discourse, and elongated time frames that are often not well-suited to dealing with many of the problems of, for example, Islamic law or transnational trade.[33]

The term 'cosmopolitan' is Janus-faced. According to the *Oxford English Dictionary* a 'cosmopolite' is 'A 'citizen of the world': one who regards or treats the whole world as his country; one who has no national

---

[32] I am told by American friends that the 'World Series' derives its name from its original sponsor, *The New York World* newspaper, and that only ignorant foreigners, like myself, treat it as a symbol of American parochialism.

[33] In recent years the field of public international law has expanded beyond the classical scope of relations between sovereign states to encompass such matters as the rights of individuals and peoples, international organizations, and the problems of internally displaced persons as well as transnational refugees. This expansion of Public International Law's empire is understandable, but we must beware of the territoriality of experts.

attachments and prejudices ... often contrasted with *patriot*, and so either reproachful or complimentary'.[34] This duality is repeated in legal discourse. Bentham boasted that he was a citizen of the world. David Held and Martha Nussbaum present cosmopolitanism as an ethos proclaiming loyalty to humankind as a whole and as a basis for democracy and good governance in a globalizing world.[35] On the positive side it suggests breadth of vision, tolerance, freedom from parochial limitations and attachments, a sense of shared humanity. On the negative side, the idea of a cosmopolitan lawyer can also conjure up images of carpet bagging in Bhopal, intellectual dilettantism, or a Jack-of-all legal systems, who is master of none. This negative aspect has important implications for primary legal education and training, which in my view should be informed by global perspectives, but continue to focus largely on the local.

Whatever one's interpretation of the details of globalization – strong, weak or agnostic – it clearly has important implications for the discipline of law and for jurisprudence as its theoretical part. In earlier writings I have argued that globalization presents three specific challenges to traditional legal theory:

- It challenges 'black box' theories that treat nation states, societies, legal systems, and legal orders as closed, impervious entities that can be studied in isolation;
- It challenges the idea that the study of law and legal theory can be restricted to two types of legal ordering: municipal state law and public international law, conceived as dealing with relations between nation states;
- It challenges the adequacy of much of the present conceptual framework and vocabulary of legal discourse (both law talk and talk about law) for discussing legal phenomena across jurisdictions, traditions, and cultures.[36] This last category is the subject of the last part of this paper.

These challenges all point in the direction of making law as a discipline more cosmopolitan. This in turn requires the revival of the idea of general jurisprudence.

---

34 *Oxford English Dictionary*, 2nd ed, Oxford University Press, Oxford, 1989.

35 For example, Held D, *Democracy and the Global Order* Polity Press, Cambridge, 1995, Cohen J (ed), Nussbaum M and Respondents, *For Love of Country: Debating the Limits of Patriotism*, Beacon Press, Boston, 1996. See also David Harvey's witty paper, 'Cosmopolitanism and the Banality of Geographical Evils' (2000) 12 *Public Culture* 529-64.

36 Twining (2000) above n 23 at ch 1.

Because globalization has implications for law and its study, it does not follow that what is needed is a global jurisprudence, if that means looking at law solely or mainly from a global perspective. The old nineteenth century usage of the term 'General Jurisprudence' is broader and more flexible than 'global' just because it refers to discourse about two or more jurisdictions or legal orders from the micro-comparative to the universal. Viewing law from a global perspective has its uses, not least in providing *context* and dealing with genuinely global issues. But understanding law will continue to require detailed focus on particulars at all levels.

To recap: despite significant differences in our backgrounds, situations and times, Julius Stone and I belong to the same intellectual tradition – mainstream common law or anglophone jurisprudence. His account of the province of jurisprudence in the 1940s has provided the most comprehensive and coherent picture of the field within our tradition for the last 50 years. There have been sufficient changes in the discipline of law, our intellectual milieu, and conditions in the world outside to warrant a re-examination of the nature and role of legal theorizing. Our starting-points are similar, both in our concern for the health of the institutionalized discipline of law and in our respect for our intellectual heritage. Stone's immediate concern was the dominance of a particular narrow orthodoxy, especially in England and Australia – narrow because it focused on questions of doctrine and marginalized concerns about justice and relations with other social sciences. My concern today is with developing a reasonably coherent response to the challenges to our discipline associated with 'globalization' and with the lively, but incoherent and often parochial, pluralism that characterizes the current jurisprudential scene. So the picture I want to paint, while paying due regard to the continuities and the richness of our heritage, differs from Stone's in several respects:

- It has a more explicitly functional and pragmatic view of theorizing and its intellectual tasks in respect of the enterprise of developing a cosmopolitan discipline of law.
- It starts with a picture of law in the world which moves beyond confining the subject matter of the discipline to municipal law of sovereign nation states and the relations between those states, to encompass all levels of legal ordering from the very local to outer space, leaving open as a matter for inquiry and debate questions about the relative power and importance of states and other actors. It places, for example, greater emphasis on such matters as regional ordering, the phenomena and diasporas of religion and tradition, and the ordering of

economic relations that operate largely independently of state-generated law.

- As a consequence this picture places greater emphasis on the phenomena of normative and legal pluralism and their complex inter-relations, that is on the fact of the co-existence of multiple regimes and orders within the same geographical spaces.
- It postulates the need for a revival of the nineteenth century idea of general jurisprudence, but rather than *assuming* universality or generality in respect of concepts, values, legal solutions, juristic methods, and patterns of development, it treats all generalization across boundaries as problematic. In short it places issues of generalizability high on the agenda of general jurisprudence.
- One point on which I differ quite sharply from Stone, falls outside the scope of this essay.[37] One of his main interests was legal reasoning. He usefully coined the phrase 'lawyers' reasonings', but then disappointingly confined his attention to reasoning about questions of law. I find this both narrow and misleading for two main reasons. First, in our own legal cultures lawyers do not reason only, or even mainly, about questions of law. Lawyers are involved in reasoning about facts, sanctioning, negotiation, law-making, problem-solving and so on in regard to many kinds of operations. These other reasonings and their inter-relations are as worthy of theoretical attention, and as practically important, as reasoning about questions of law. Secondly, distinctions between questions of law, questions of fact, and other questions are to a large extent context- and culture-specific. But questions about rationality, practical reasoning, and the validity, cogency and appropriateness of various kinds of lawyers' reasonings are a proper concern of comparative law and general jurisprudence and should not be confined to particular legal cultures.

The Problem of Generalization

In the last decade of the twentieth century we have witnessed two conflicting tendencies: on the one hand, a generalizing tendency that involves greater interdependence, faster and more intimate communication, diffusion, and homogeneity; on the other hand, a particularistic tendency that emphasizes difference, the uniqueness of history, culture, and identity, sometimes even cultural and ethical relativism.

---

[37] Twining (1997) above n 28 at 348-50. This theme is developed in the entry on 'Legal Reasoning and Argumentation' in *The International Encyclopedia of Social and Behavioral Sciences* (Elsevier, Kidlington, 2001) Vol 13, 8670-75.

How to proceed? Having asserted that questions of generalizability are central to general jurisprudence and a cosmopolitan discipline of law, it would be ironic if I were to propose a single method for approaching such problems. As a pluralist and an anti-reductionist I doubt whether a single methodology is either feasible or desirable. I have to date proceeded both eclectically and pragmatically by undertaking a series of exploratory soundings and case studies that may at least suggest some ways forward in developing approaches that may be helpful.

As we have seen, Julius Stone divided 'the province of jurisprudence' into three broad regions: analytical, ethical, and sociological (in which he included traditional historical jurisprudence). Here it is convenient to follow his categorization, but to give a somewhat broader interpretation to each category than he did.

Normative and Empirical Jurisprudence

Rather than attempt to survey all of this vast territory here, I plan to focus mainly on analytical jurisprudence and give some concrete illustrations of what a revived analytical jurisprudence might be like. Before doing so, let me make some brief remarks on the two other domains of Stone's 'Province' – what he called 'Theories of Justice' and 'Sociological (or Functional) Jurisprudence'. I shall argue that both of these need to be extended both intellectually and geographically.

It is now generally accepted that theories of justice are only one part of ethical or normative jurisprudence, which is more generally concerned with questions about values and law.[38] Thus it also encompasses issues about the is/ought distinction, political obligation, needs, rights, the public good, and other criteria for evaluating the health of legal orders, institutions or rules. Normative jurisprudence now occupies a firm place on the agenda, as is illustrated by the attention given to Dworkin, Rawls, Bentham, and modern critical theory. Important issues about universalism and ethics are now attracting attention, as is illustrated by the debates about cultural relativism, feminism, and human rights.[39] The main Western ethical traditions such as Natural Law, utilitarianism, Kantianism, and human rights theories have also been universalistic in tendency, but in the face of challenges from multiculturalism and pluralism, leading liberal thinkers have beaten a partial retreat into an odd kind of particularism. I have argued at length elsewhere that the geographical reach of Ronald Dworkin's ideas is

---

38 See, for example, Rawls J, 'Justice as Fairness: Political not Metaphysical', (1985) 14 *Philosophy and Public Affairs* 223.

39 A convenient introductory anthology is Wilson RA (ed), *Human Rights: Culture and Context*, Pluto Press, Cambridge, 1997.

strikingly indeterminate[40] and that Rawls has played himself into an untenable position by restricting his theory of justice to liberal self-contained national communities, when no such isolated units exist.[41] Many contemporary jurists and philosophers are concerned to try to find a middle way between dogmatic extremes of universalism and cultural relativism. As the example of clean water shows, this will often involve considering specific local issues about values in broad geographical contexts.

In discussing sociological jurisprudence Stone originally limited the phrase to 'observing and generalizing upon the effect of law upon men and men upon law'.[42] He later made it clear that he included empirical enquiries associated both with theories of legal development, including those associated with old-style historical jurisprudence, and the more general aspects of what are now called 'socio-legal studies'. Since the hermeneutic turn in legal and social theory, a more sustained interest has evolved in epistemological issues concerning description, interpretation, and explanation of social phenomena. The use of the term 'sociological' in this context tends to edge out of view other disciplines that bear on the social dimensions of law and justice. Similar objections could be made to the label 'functional jurisprudence'. Rather than Stone's terms I prefer some such label as 'empirical and interpretive jurisprudence'. I would also include under this heading not only relevant aspects of social and biological sciences, but also what may be called 'technological perspectives on law' – but that, too, must be a topic for another occasion.[43]

The relations between law and other empirical and interpretive disciplines are now among the liveliest enclaves of academic law and theoretical issues relating to these are quite well-established on the agenda of legal theory. However, focusing on globalization underlines the point that progress in reaching out beyond the boundaries of societies or nation states has been quite uneven in the social sciences and socio-legal studies. Until recently, fields as diverse as sociology of law, economic analysis, feminist jurisprudence, and even anthropology have been quite parochial in tendency and have tended to neglect transnational, regional, and intra-communal (diasporic) levels of legal ordering. That is now changing. But here, too, such enquiries need a boost from theoretical criticism and guidance. My personal belief, which is little more than a hunch, is that

---

40 Twining (2000) above n 23 at from 63.

41 Ibid from 69. See now Rawls J, *The Law of Peoples* (Harvard University Press, Cambridge, Massachusetts, 1999).

42 Stone (1946) above n 5 at 31-2.

43 See Twining W, 'The Job of Juristic Method: A Tribute to Karl Llewellyn', (1993) 48 *University of Miami Law Review* 119.

comparative legal studies will have a key role to play in exploring issues of generalizability across levels of legal ordering, but progress here is dependent upon a quite radical rethinking of comparative law in the light of globalization.[44]

Analytical Jurisprudence in a Global Context[45]

Having cleared all normative, empirical, interpretive and technological jurisprudence out of the way, let me return to our old friend general analytical jurisprudence. I want to make a plea for a revival of general analytical jurisprudence, but much more broadly conceived than its nineteenth and twentieth century predecessors.

In recent years, except in Oxford, analytical jurisprudence has generally received a bad press. This is mainly because it has been loosely equated with some particular target such as Austinian positivism, simple semantics or deductive models of legal reasoning. Julius Stone reacted strongly against certain aspects of the Austinian analytical tradition, especially its neglect of history and of ethics and various versions of 'the fallacy of the logical form'. But he made it clear that he was not reacting against analysis as such.[46] Indeed, *Legal System and Lawyers' Reasonings* has been widely recognized as a major contribution to analytical jurisprudence.

Stone's contemporary, Herbert Hart, has sometimes been treated as equating analytical jurisprudence with 'linguistic analysis', or with elucidation of abstract concepts. But Hart explicitly included as part of analytical jurisprudence the study of the form and structure of legal systems, problems of legal reasoning, problems of definition of law, and analysis of legal concepts.[47] He considered that the critical analysis of

---

44 Twining (2000) above n 23 at ch 6, at 255-6 and Twining W, 'Comparative Law and Legal Theory: The Country and Western Tradition' in Edge I (ed), *Comparative Law in Global Perspective*, Transnational Publishers, New York, 2000.

45 This section is developed at greater length in an unpublished working paper, provisionally entitled 'Have Concepts, Will Travel: Analytical Jurisprudence in a Global Context'.

46 'What was wrong with the orthodox tradition of English analytical jurisprudence from which Julius Stone has liberated generations of students was *not* that it was analytical. Nor has Stone ever suggested that was the case. What was wrong with the older tradition was rather that it approached the legal system as if it were a set of precepts and concepts suspended in time – notionally frozen, as it were, for the purposes of theoretical explication and dissection'. Blackshield A, 'Editor's Note' in Blackshield A (ed), *Legal Change: Essays in Honour of Julius Stone*, Butterworths, Sydney, 1983.

47 Hart HLA, 'Problems of Legal Philosophy' in Edwards P (ed), 6 *Encyclopedia of Philosophy*, Macmillan, New York and Free Press, London, 1967 at 264-76, reprinted in Hart HLA, *Essays in Jurisprudence and Philosophy*, Oxford University Press, Oxford, 1983 at ch 3.

assumptions and presuppositions of legal discourse was one of the main tasks of legal philosophy. Like Stone, he also emphasized that distinctions between different branches of jurisprudence and philosophy of law were matters of convenience, reflecting 'no very firm boundaries'.[48] In this view, the relationship of analytical jurisprudence to jurisprudence is similar to the relationship between analytical philosophy and philosophy in general: it gives an approximate indication of a style and approach that involves the application of a range of techniques of analysis to legal discourse and its concepts.

It is part of my general thesis that analytical jurisprudence has an important part to play in reviving general jurisprudence, but that what is needed is a much broader conception of what is involved than those of Hart and Stone and Raz.

My conception of analytical jurisprudence builds on Anglo-American tradition in respects of methods, but differs in the following respects:

- It is based on a wider conception of law, including all the levels of legal ordering outlined above;
- It focuses on a wider range of concepts than traditional analytical jurisprudence. It is not limited to fundamental philosophical concepts, such as those discussed by George Fletcher in his excellent, but eclectic book, *Basic Concepts of Legal Thought.*[49] More important it is not confined to the concepts and terms in which laws and legal doctrine are expressed and their presuppositions, such as right, duty, sovereignty, validity and so on (law talk), but extends to any general discourses about legal phenomena (talk about law), including the basic concepts of legal sociology such as group, dispute, function, process, and institution;
- It is concerned not just with individual concepts, but with *groups* of related concepts in specialized discourses, such as the discourse of public international lawyers, or about prison conditions, or contract or corruption;
- Analytical method here includes not only logical, linguistic and conceptual techniques developed by analytical philosophers, but also

[48] Ibid. But Hart revived the distinction between general and particular jurisprudence to differentiate his views from those of Dworkin in the posthumously published Postscript to *The Concept of Law*, discussed in Twining (2000) above n 23 at ch 2-3.

[49] Fletcher G, *Basic Concepts of Legal Thought*, Oxford University Press, Oxford, 1996. Fletcher's selection is intriguing: I The Legal system: The Rule of Law; Law; Rules and Discretion; Discourse. II Ultimate Values: Justice; Desert; Consent; Equality. III Morality in the Law: Morality; Efficiency; Loyalty; Consistency.

tools of analysis such as ideal types, models, metaphors, and deconstruction developed in neighbouring disciplines.[50]

- The central concern is with the development of adequate ways of talking about law across legal orders, jurisdictions, traditions and cultures – ranging from comparison of two or more contexts to genuinely global generalizations. What travels well/badly, when, why, and how?

I have started with what may seem like a rather narrow, traditional topic: conceptual and semantic issues, because these seem important preliminaries if we are to develop meaningful discourses about law that transcend particular jurisdictions, cultures or traditions. So the object is to subject the concepts of transnational legal discourse to critical examination. This is work in progress. I have started to explore what it is for a concept or group of concepts or models or frames to travel far and to travel well – that is, that it can be used with reasonable clarity and precision to describe, analyze, compare, generalize about, and explain the subject matter of our discipline across various kinds of boundaries. So far my tests of travelling far and well are mainly empirical and pragmatic: does it fit? Does it work? Can the same concepts be used with roughly the same meaning in England and Italy, or in California, Tanzania and Japan? For example, would this category or group of concepts be suitable for use in regional or global statistics, or in an international convention intended for local application in many countries, or in a genuinely comparative transnational study of some legal field or institution or set of problems? I think that these ideas need to be refined.[51]

I am sometimes asked whether I think that the term 'inhuman treatment' travelled well in relation to the problem of provision of clean water in prisons in poor countries. Clearly the term itself does not resolve the issues on its own. There is room for real disagreements about such questions as whether prisoners have a right to be given clean water when many people in the rural population do not; how far should economic considerations and priorities affect the implementation of legally prescribed human rights? Is the phrase 'torture, inhuman or degrading treatment or

---

[50] The term 'analytical jurisprudence' could be used even more widely to include the more general parts of economic, institutional, and other kinds of analysis. However, here I shall concentrate on only one aspect: elucidation of concepts.

[51] Another test of travelling well is questionnaires. A large proportion of ambitious comparative projects has been based on questionnaires, for example Rudolph Schlesinger's project on the common core of legal systems in relation to formation of contract and the major comparative studies of precedent and interpretation of statutes led by Robert Summers and Neil MacCormick.

punishment' restricted to intentional acts or does it cover negligent or reckless acts or omissions?

I think that the phrase 'inhuman and degrading treatment' did travel well in this context in that, first, it provides a framework for debating such issues; second, it provides a direct link to the idea of basic human needs; but, third, it allows some flexibility in respect of its interpretation and application in different social and economic contexts. The notion of 'degrading' similarly invokes an abstract universal principle of respect for persons or human dignity, while allowing some latitude for local economic conditions and different cultural attitudes to respect and shame.[52]

As a preliminary exploration of the usability of our stock of concepts in cross-cultural and transnational legal discourses, I undertook five preliminary case studies of groups of concepts: Hohfeld's analysis of legal rights; attempts to find a 'common core' of legal systems or a *ius commune* in contract; comparative studies of legal professions and legal education; transnational discourse about prison conditions; and the worldwide campaign against corruption.[53]

In a separate paper, I have reported briefly on the main findings of these preliminary studies and used illustrations from discourse about prison conditions and regimes.[54] Rather than go over the same ground, let me talk briefly about corruption as a concrete example of the kind of task I have in mind for a revived general analytical jurisprudence. This will also serve to reinforce the artificiality of trying to maintain sharp distinctions between different branches of jurisprudence.

Corruption

Gifts in Village Tradition: A Personal Experience

> I had to see the Chief. I was seeking permission for a geophysics experiment in Northern Ghana for which we needed to dig four holes in the ground, a hundred metres or so apart, place copper tubes in them and connect them with wires to record small electric currents thought to reflect properties in the ionosphere. My local adviser and interpreter insisted I gave the Chief a bottle of whisky. I took it out with reluctance, hiding it carefully in a brown paper bag. We sat on benches outside the Chief's hut with the people of the village gathered round. I paid my respects and explained my request as best I could. My adviser whispered, 'Give him the whisky'. 'Now', I asked, 'with all these people here?'

---

52 Consider the practical problem of not mixing men, women and children in the same cell, when most police stations in a country have only one cell.

53 A detailed report on these pilot studies will be included in 'Have Concepts, Will Travel', above n 45.

54 'Reviving General Jurisprudence' above n 23 and *The Great Juristic Bazaar* above n 13.

'Yes'. I tried to pass it unobtrusively in its paper bag but my adviser protested: it had to come out of the bag and be given so that all could see. There was a murmur of appreciation from the people, and very happy smiles on the faces of the Chief's counsellors who sat nearby.

On reflection I recognized that the transaction was the equivalent of a licence fee in a pre-literate society that kept no accounts. It differed from bribes in three ways. It was done so that all could see, not in secret. It was a benefit the Chief would share with his colleagues who were involved in the decision. It was modest in scale and did not make one person or group so wealthy as to be the envy of others. Village customs can be corrupted, but they provide no valid precedent or justification for bribery in the city.[55]

I started my exploration of the literature on corruption in the expectation that the concepts and discourse in this area would not travel well. In the 1960s in East Africa it was commonplace that words such as 'corruption', 'bribery', and 'nepotism' when applied to African contexts were ethnocentric, sententious, and neo-colonialist. Many African societies, the argument went, were communitarian and personalist, characterized by face-to-face relations involving reciprocity. One's primary loyalty was to family, clan, village or people rather than to one's employer or the state. This was not just individual loyalty, but rather part of communal membership and identity. Accordingly, to condemn such practices was a standard example of imposing Western values on African tradition. Any suggestion that African societies were corrupt, but Western societies were not, was dismissed as sheer hypocrisy – often with good reason.

At that time, Western social scientists tended to interpret corruption in similar terms.[56] They acknowledged that there was cause for concern, but criticized moralistic and universalistic approaches to the subject.[57] Such attitudes did not involve condoning or justifying what they interpreted as clear examples of bribery and dishonesty – for example a Minister demanding a large payment in relation to a competitive tender – rather they relativized the issues and warned against over-simplifying problems in this area.

---

55 Osborne D, 'Corruption as Counter-Culture: Attitudes to Bribery in Local and Global Society' in Rider B (ed), *Corruption: The Enemy Within*, Kluwer, The Hague, 1997 at 17.

56 The terms 'corruption', 'bribery', and the composite 'bribery and corruption' are sometimes used interchangeably. Here, 'corruption' is treated as the generic term, under which 'bribery' is subsumed as a central case.

57 Early commentators who took a different, typically more macroscopic, tack included Huntington S, *Political Order in Changing Societies*, Yale University Press, New Haven, 1968 and Myrdal G, *Asian Drama*, Twentieth Century Fund, New York, 1968.

Since 1970 the general tone has changed dramatically. In 1997 Dr Ibrahim Shihata, Senior Vice President and General Counsel of The World Bank, could write confidently: 'Practically all people who publicly address corruption condemn it, even though it would not exist at a wide scale without the participation of many'.[58] The extent of corruption and the seriousness of efforts to combat it are now a central indicator of 'good governance' as The World Bank, Western aid agencies and other subscribers to 'the Washington consensus' use the concept.[59] Such views are not confined to supporters of The World Bank. For example, Transparency International, a non-governmental organization based in Berlin has spearheaded a worldwide campaign against corruption and in support of national integrity systems. Commentators as different as Amartya Sen, Chinua Achebe, and John Noonan have been loud in their condemnations.[60] Noonan's magnum opus, *Bribes*, is especially harsh on the apologists who invoke tradition or culture or local values. A widespread consensus seems to have gained sway among economists, lawyers, sociologists, political scientists and public administrators that generally speaking, and especially in the long-term, the costs of corruption generally outweigh any benefits to the public interest, whether this is identified with economic growth, efficiency in government, democracy, fairness or public confidence in the legitimacy of government.

Chinua Achebe has been one of the most eloquent critics of corruption in Nigeria. In 1984, in a blistering attack he wrote: 'Corruption in Nigeria has passed the alarming and entered the fatal stage; and Nigeria will die if we keep pretending that she is only slightly indisposed'.[61]

Yet in the 1960s the same Achebe, as novelist, was famous for exploring the destructive impact of colonialism on traditional African culture and values, using 'corruption' as one of his central themes.[62]

The international campaign against corruption is impressive. Not all the supporters of the campaign would necessarily agree with some of the proposed remedies, such as deregulation, privatization, and restructuring. I,

---

58 Shihata I, 'Corruption: A General Review with an Emphasis on the Role of the World Bank' in Rider, above n 55 at 259.

59 The 'Washington consensus' here refers to the ideology that links free-market ideas about development to 'democracy, good governance and human rights'. Williamson J (ed), *The Political Economy of Policy Reform*, Institute for International Economics, Washington, DC, 1994; Kelsey J, *Economic Fundamentalism*, Pluto Press, London, 1995.

60 For example, Sen A, *Development as Freedom*, Knopf, New York, 1999; Achebe C, *The Trouble With Nigeria*, Heinemann, London, 1984; Noonan J, *Bribes*, New York, Macmillan, 1984.

61 Achebe, ibid at 38.

62 Especially, Achebe C, *No Longer at Ease*, I Oblensky, New York, 1960.

for one, admire much of Transparency International's efforts and I am persuaded that much of what is being criticized is indeed very harmful to sustainable development. But I am left with some niggling doubts about the confidence with which political corruption is treated as a single worldwide problem. Let me try to probe these a bit further in relation to the concepts and underpinnings of the discourse of the international campaign.

A Narrow Definition: Transparency International

Transparency International pithily defines corruption as 'the misuse of public power for private profit'.[63] This definition is widely used in other contexts. Taken by itself it has three questionable features:

- It focuses on the behaviour of public office-holders (O) (in bribes, on the bribees) and impliedly excludes, or at least is silent about, the behaviour of bribers and other corrupters. Other definitions more clearly include both briber and bribee.[64]
- 'Private profit' (sometimes 'private ends') suggests direct or indirect gain to the office-holder. This seemingly excludes gifts to third parties in return for a quid pro quo supplied by O. For example, gifts to political party funds, or a university, or a relation of O. Similarly, 'private profit' hardly covers standard cases of nepotism or patronage when O may be behaving out of loyalty to family or friends or may be securing his or her position in office by appointing loyal supporters (e.g. Blair's 'cronies') or merely 'doing one's job' (e.g. a university President offering the prospect of an honorary degree to a potential (anonymous) donor).
- The definition assumes a sharp 'public/private' divide. At first sight this seems to restrict corruption to government officials, but in other contexts the scope is extended to 'Persons in Positions of Responsibility', including 'representatives of the people, ... and those with authority in political, economic and civil organizations'[65] – a

63 Citing Senturia JJ, (1993) 7 *Encyclopaedia of Social Sciences*. The Sourcebook continues: 'One cannot assume that corruption always means the same thing or has the same impact or motivation. Normative statements about corruption require a point of view, a standard of 'goodness', and a model of how corruption works in particular instances'. Transparency International, *Sourcebook* ch 1. The passage continues by stressing that the focus is here on the behaviour of public officials. However, the focus gets quietly extended later in the same document.

64 For example, the English Law Commission's draft Corruption Bill covers both a person conferring an advantage and a person obtaining an advantage. The Law Commission, *Legislating the Criminal Code: Corruption* (1998, Law Com. No. 248, HC 524).

65 Transparency International *Sourcebook*, reporting a 'Morals Summit' for South Africa in Johannesburg.

much wider coverage. The public/private distinction is notoriously fragile and variable. Interestingly, the English Law Commission recommended in 1998 that, in the context of legislating against corruption, the old distinction between public and non-public bodies should be discarded as no longer having much practical significance.[66]

It appears that government officials in modern state bureaucracies are indeed the primary focus of the campaigns against 'corruption' spearheaded by Transparency International, The World Bank, and other agencies. The main target is certain kinds of financial dealing that undermine efficiency and effectiveness and deplete public funds. The arguments of economists like Susan Rose-Ackerman refer mainly to public sector corruption within 'modern' government.[67] The focus is almost entirely on bribery and extortion, and much less on nepotism and patronage, two grey areas which are much more controversial.

However, the terminology is sometimes confusing. While the main focus of Transparency International's efforts is on the public service in a 'modern' bureaucracy, it quite often strays beyond the narrow definition. For example, the extension to 'persons in positions of responsibility' cited above. Transparency International's notorious world 'Corruption Perception Index' is based on the perceptions of foreign businessmen about the extent to which they need to 'oil the wheels' in any sector, not just the public sector. Similarly, one of Transparency International's main targets is tax deductibility of foreign bribes by businesses.[68] Here the focus shifts from the bribee to the briber and is not confined to bribery of public officials. Such extensions may be perfectly reasonable, but it is by no means clear that arguments about 'public interest' apply in the same way. Thus Transparency International's definition is quite narrow and cuts out some of the most controversial areas; but in practice they quite often move beyond the confines of their own definition.

A much broader definition of corruption is to be found in Jeremy Bentham's recently published Constitutional writings. For Bentham any

---

66 The Law Commission (1998), above n 64 para 4.78 (Recommendation 2). This was linked with abolishing the presumption of corruption as no longer being important since the Criminal Justice and Public Order Act, 1994 (allowing the court or jury to draw adverse inferences from refusal to answer questions or give evidence at trial) and because it might be held to contravene Article 6(2) of the European Convention on Human Rights.

67 Rose-Ackerman S, *Corruption and Government*, Cambridge University Press, New York, 1999; and 'The political economy of corruption' in Elliott KA (ed), *Corruption and the Global Economy*, Institute of International Economics, Washington, DC, 1997 at ch 2.

68 See Twining (2000) above n 23 at ch 6.

self-interested or 'sinister sacrifice' of the public interest, any action, however trivial, which promoted the happiness of the few to the detriment of the many was political corruption. Far from being exceptional, he argued, corruption is an essential feature of representative government, because in the nature of things the interests of the rulers are in constant opposition to the interests of the ruled, except insofar as constitutional arrangements can bring about an artificial harmonization of interests. I am personally sceptical of the universalist tendency of Bentham's analysis and of some of his particular proposals, but his analysis deserves attention not least because it is based on a more coherent concept of corruption than those used in the current international campaign.[69] Of course, it would not be realistic to expect an effective transnational anti-corruption campaign to target any and every 'sinister practice'. Similar objections apply to John Noonan's essentialist and universalist analysis of corruption as a moral concept, which on close examination appears to be rooted in a specifically Judeo-Christian idea of the imitation of a God who does not takes bribes.[70] This idea seems both theologically controversial, and unsuited to transnational, multi-cultural and predominantly secular contexts of modern anti-corruption campaigns. From the point of view of analyzing 'political corruption' one of the main difficulties is establishing workable distinctions between practices that are appropriate targets for a transnational campaign and practices that may or may not be acceptable by local standards.

Emotive Terms

The literature on corruption is pervaded by an array of strongly emotive terms: corruption, bribery, extortion, kickback, racketeering, sleaze, nepotism, graft, favouritism, slush fund, barratry (*barreteria*). Others are neutral or morally ambiguous, depending on context: gift, patronage, favour, tip, loan. Some are generally neutral: reciprocity, exchange, access payment, fee, influence, premium, (*munus*, *munera*). A few may be positive (or euphemistic): take care of, look after, benefaction, subsidy, informal sector, contacts, networking, indulgence, and perhaps most significant of all, loyalty.[71]

In some legal contexts the use of strongly emotive words has a function: torture, bribe, racketeering used in legislation or as part of some

69 This section is based on Bentham's *First Principles Preparatory to Constitutional Code*, in Schofield P (ed), *Collected Works*, Oxford University Press, Oxford, 1989; Schofield's excellent analysis of Bentham's views and their contemporary significance, ibid; and Schofield P, 'Jeremy Bentham on Political Corruption: A Critique of the First Report of the Nolan Committee' (1996) 49 *Current Legal Problems* 395.

70 Noonan, above n 60.

71 Noonan is a superb source of insights into nuances in the vocabulary of bribes. Ibid.

political campaign carry a strong note of condemnation that may be appropriate. But emotive terms have some dangerous tendencies: to use such terms often prejudges a situation before it has been fully described and analyzed; it assumes that the scope of the term and the reasons for condemning it are both clear. Strongly emotive terms tend to over-inclusion or under-inclusion in interpretation of their scope. Anti-corruption campaigns and scandals often involve scapegoating and exploitation of discontents that may have other roots. For such reasons it is doubtful whether the standard language for discourse about corruption is suitable for relatively detached analysis and comparison. But the vocabulary of this discourse is so strongly entrenched in campaigns and in laws that one doubts whether it is feasible to construct a useful vocabulary for more detached analysis that has much hope of widespread acceptance.

Individual and Systemic Corruption

Closely related to the emotive vocabulary is the point that much of the language used is derived from the sphere of individual morality, yet most commentators agree that the most harmful situations of corruption are systemic. Again and again the campaigners against corruption are met with the defence: 'I had no option'. 'It's not me, it's the system'. Bentham saw very clearly that there is an important distinction between personal and systematic corruption and argued forcefully that the only solution for the latter evil is redesigning the system.[72] He even argued that in that context laws punishing individual offenders were likely to be both ineffective and unjust.[73] This is recognized in the actions of some campaigners against corruption, but not in their rhetoric, for words like 'corrupt' are rooted in individual ethics. A very clear example of the conflation of systemic and individual corruption, is the First Report of the Nolan Committee on Standards in Public Life in Britain which has been sharply criticized for adopting the stance that the maintenance of 'standards' in regard to MPs financial and other relations with outside bodies is essentially a matter of 'personal integrity' – a view that Bentham had devastatingly attacked nearly two hundred years before.[74]

---

72 For example, 'Constitutional Code Rationale' in *First Principles*, above n 69.

73 Schofield states, 'Having recognized the systematic nature of corruption, Bentham was sufficiently realistic to see that attempting to punish individual transgressors by legal means was likely to be inadequate and unjust'. (1996) above n 69 at 407.

74 *Standards in Public Life*: *First Report of the Committee on Standards in Public Life* 2 vols, (Cm. 2850, 1995). The Nolan Committee suggested that there were seven principles applying to holders of public office: Selflessness, Integrity, Objectivity, Accountability, Openness, Honesty, and Leadership. All of these are expressed in terms of individual ethics, but some – especially accountability and openness – are part of

To sum up: corruption, bribery and related concepts used to be considered strongly culture-specific. Since the early 1990s a broadly based transnational campaign against 'corruption' has gained ground. Both diagnosis and prescription are based largely, but not entirely, on the ideology of the Washington consensus concerning democracy, good governance, and human rights and on free market and related ideologies concerning 'development'. The main target of this campaign is various kinds of deviation from bureaucratic norms of impartiality, efficiency, and 'service', especially financial dealings. The focus is primarily on 'public servants' of state bureaucracies, but is rapidly being extended to the private sector. When the campaign is extended to such matters as patronage and honours or 'traditional' contexts or business cultures that place heavy emphasis on personal relationships it encounters many more grey areas, for instance in respect of nepotism, and more generally, issues of loyalty that tend to be more local and culture-specific. Thus corruption and related concepts seem to travel reasonably well in respect of the modern public sector of nation states, especially state bureaucracies, but are more problematic outside this specific context. The strongly emotive language of this discourse is more suited to individual ethics than large-scale systemic practices, is often tendentious and probably hampers detached analysis and comparison.

It is not my purpose to criticize the efforts of bodies such as Transparency International, although all such campaigns should be subject to critical scrutiny and scepticism about confident generalization. Rather it is to suggest that discourse on bribery and corruption is just the kind of area that requires the attention of a new kind of general analytical jurisprudence: corruption is perceived to be an important transnational problem; it relates to all levels of legal ordering; it involves interdisciplinary analysis and cross-cultural sensitivity; to talk about it in general terms requires precise concepts, an appropriate terminology, and coherent underlying assumptions. Here analysis involves focusing not on single abstract concepts, but rather on complex discourses or conceptual schemes; and it raises very puzzling questions about generalizability that challenge both universalists and cultural relativists. Conceptual clarity is often a precondition for other kinds of analysis. Analytical jurisprudence should not be confined to the most abstract concepts of legal and political philosophy, important as these may be. The problem of clean water with which I began was complex enough, but at least it had a clear relationship

Bentham's securities against misrule. The best criticism is by Schofield (1996), above n 69, arguing that the problem was first defined too narrowly and then misdiagnosed. On Bentham's views, see above.

to basic human needs for survival and reasonable health. The so-called 'problem of corruption' is more complex, but no less pressing. It is an area which, to echo Holmes, has too little theory rather than too much. I think that this a sentiment with which Julius Stone would have agreed.

Chapter 3

Historical Aspects of Globalization and Law

David B. Goldman

Introduction

Technologically and culturally, the commonplace observation that globalization radically affects communities of all sizes – from local to national to international – is uncontroversial. At a fundamental constitutional level, however, the Western legal tradition, in its multicultural fullness,[1] has accommodated challenges similar to those posed by globalization, rendering the contemporary legal challenges perhaps a case of déjà vu. What is surprising and unsurprising about these developments is the subject of this chapter, on the way to drawing some conclusions about how the legal issues arising from globalization might helpfully be apprehended in the present. It will be argued that the twentieth century was an apocalyptic era with consequences for a global legal science, the significance of which is only just becoming apparent.[2] These consequences will be explored by considering the historical character of transnational legal education and practice, together with the development of mercantile law and the tendencies for 'private government' and government by competing jurisdictions. Sovereignty will duly emerge as an historically contingent concept all the more demonstrable by reference to globalization.

Such an approach to globalization and law should yield an appreciation of the authority, constructed from religion, custom and technology, which has underlain law throughout Western history and which is underlying global legal developments today. Legal authority derives from a creative

---

1 In this respect, see Monateri PG, 'Black Gaius: A Quest for the Multicultural Origins of the "Western Legal Tradition"' (2000) 51 *Hastings Law Journal* 479. Although the 'Western legal tradition' may have been influenced by doctrines from outside the traditional 'West', use of the term 'Western legal tradition' will be maintained because it does describe an evolution in legal science and systematization of legal doctrines which was centred in Europe.

2 Since presenting the apocalypse notion of globalization at the Julius Stone Institute of Jurisprudence Symposium, it has come to my attention that Harold J Berman recently published an essay explicitly written in a millennial vein, although with a different emphasis: see Berman HJ, 'The Western Legal Tradition in a Millennial Perspective: Past and Future' (2000) 60 *Louisiana Law Review* 739.

tension between communities of various social characteristics and scales managing their own legal orders, whilst being subject to influence from outside legal orders. At the risk of employing a whimsical metaphor, the consequent superficial duality thought to arise between powerful (sovereign) and less-powerful (subject) orders might more meaningfully be imagined as a crystalline rock, the absence of either the universality of the rock, or the particularities of the constituent crystals inside, forcing a conceptual impossibility. Hopefully, the historical sediments dredged in the course of this chapter may quake schools of thought which: (a) portray legal norms and authority as the peculiar domain of centralized, national sovereigns;[3] and (b) portray globalization as a phenomenon without legal precedent.

Definitions

Before entertaining an enquiry into the effects of 'globalization' and 'law', these terms must first be elucidated, hopefully without too much controversy.

Definitions of 'globalization' abound. The first definition (to my knowledge) developed by a legal theorist, William Twining, is difficult to trump: he writes of 'those processes which tend to create and consolidate a world economy, a single ecological system, and a complex network of communications that covers the whole globe, even if it does not penetrate to every part of it'.[4] Other definitions abound, particularly in the social and cultural studies spheres.[5] Definitions usually become more problematic the longer they become, if only because increasing inclusion inevitably reveals omissions.[6] The simple definition of globalization that I shall offer is 'the increasing interconnections amongst things that happen in the world'.

---

3 See Franck TM, 'Theme Panel III: Multiple Tiers of Sovereignty: The Future of International Governance' (1994) 88 *American Society of International Law Proceedings* 51 at 52: 'We are emerging from that *very brief* interregnum in which we had notions of sovereignty and of unlimited independence ... and are well on our way to a systemic transformation that will *return* us to a vertical rather than a horizontal system of sovereignty' (emphasis added).

4 Twining W, 'Globalization and Legal Theory: Some Local Implications' (1996) 49 *Current Legal Problems* 1 at 2.

5 See generally Lechner F and Boli J (eds), *The Globalization Reader*, Blackwell, Oxford, 1999; Featherstone M, (ed), *Global Culture: Nationalism, Globalization and Modernity*, Sage, London, 1990; Robertson R, *Globalization: Social Theory and Global Culture*, Sage, London, 1992.

6 For an overview of the multiplex possibilities, see Santos, B de Sousa, *Toward a New Common Sense: Law, Science and Politics in the Paradigmatic Transition*, Routledge, New York, 1995 at 252-4.

Definitions of law – of what law is and is not – are legion.[7] As Professor Twining has argued, the continuities and discontinuities between law and different types of ordering can be obscured by trying to define law too precisely.[8] Without treading on too many toes, hopefully it will be accepted that law can be thought about as 'norms which, for one reason or another, achieve authority'. That authority may come from the state, the tribe, the international organization or myriad other organizations. Usually there will be some manner of hierarchy for resolving conflicts where they occur amongst these legal systems, in a stable society. Sovereignty may be said to reside in this hierarchy.

Private International Law Globalization

When the words 'globalization' and 'law' are run together in a phrase, the standard response (certainly amongst commercial lawyers) is to agitate issues relating to the law of international transactions, global financial markets, cyberspace, environmental compliance and barriers to international transactions. These issues are all of exponentially increasing currency. For the most part, they are related to unprecedented advances in information technology, tending to be concerned with questions such as, 'can the law cope with the complexities of the technology?' – for example, privacy concerns and cross-border jurisdictional issues. Adopting the demarcation of law into public and private law categories, these technology issues sound of private international law. Law is a tool for getting things done.

Public International Law Globalization

Globalization and law may also evoke thoughts of, for example, human rights law, international war crimes, and the proper domain of the United Nations. These developments impact upon – if not threaten – conceptions of the national, territorial, sovereign hierarchy for resolving conflicts between competing legal systems. Dramatic commentators predict the demise of the nation state, in the face of the transfer of national sovereignty to such structures as the World Trade Organization, the European Union

---

7 It is possible in this regard to have some sympathy with Posner's criticism of enquiries in the manner of Hart and Dworkin, which have attempted to define what law 'is' rather than what law 'does'. See, in particular, Ewald W, 'Posner's Economic Approach to Comparative Law' (1998) 33 *Texas International Law Journal* 381 at 382; and more generally, Posner R, *Law and Legal Theory in England and America*, Clarendon Press, Oxford, 1996 at 1-37. The pitfall should be avoided, however, of succumbing to what law 'does' as opposed to the richness of what law 'might be' in light of that which it 'has been', across cultures and through time.

8 Twining W, *Globalization and Legal Theory*, Butterworths, London, 2000 at 244.

and even international arbitration bodies. Neil MacCormick offers balance to such nation state doomsayers: sovereignty is like virginity, 'which can in at least some circumstances be lost to the general satisfaction without anybody else gaining it'.[9] The legal history and developments to be canvassed below support this conception of plurality. Traditionally, such matters of sovereignty are of public international law significance, with a more explicitly moral ambition, loftier than the technological or industrial advances sought to be addressed by private international law. Hunting for war criminals serves no direct productive purpose, exciting, instead, feelings of justice.

Having dealt with some definitions, attention may now turn to placing globalization and law into an historical context.

Globalization as an Integrative Concept

Although the separation of private law and public law has been embodied in law since classical Roman jurisprudence and in politics since ancient Greece, sociologically the demarcation appears overdrawn.[10] A pope can only be a pope because enough people are Catholic who believe in his authority. A king can only be a king because enough people believe in the kingship, just as a parliament can only exist because enough people believe in that institution. That is to say, public authority in the long run will be projected and must be accepted by individuals in their personal capacity; terror and absolutism tend not to endure in the West, measured against the historical standards of the time.

Perhaps the most interesting issues raised by globalization are the foundational constitutional ones that construct fundamental normative authority. These issues, upon historical investigation, are not necessarily so novel. They reflect the complex interplay of the private origins of norms and the public sanctification or objectification of those norms in such

---

9 MacCormick N, 'Beyond the Sovereign State' (1993) 56 *Modern Law Review* 1 at 16.

10 Relatively few critical observers would probably still agree with Marx's contention that the bourgeois state is a *simple* projection of the economic base, but there is an obvious connection, at least in the West, between state power and civil ordination of it, for radicals and conservatives. See Marx K, 'On the Jewish Question' in Colletti L (ed), *Early Writings*, Livingstone R and Benton G (trans), Penguin, Harmondsworth, 1975. An earlier, conservative theorist, Savigny, regarded law as a reflection of the spirit of the people and their national customs (*Volksgeist*); see Savigny FK, *Of the Vocation of Our Age for Legislation and Jurisprudence* (1831), Hayward A (trans), Arno Press, New York, 1975. Interestingly, Savigny in fact taught Marx, see Kelley DR, 'The Metaphysics of Law: An Essay on the Very Young Marx' (1978) 83 *The American Historical Review*, reprinted in Kelley DR, *History, Law and the Human Sciences*, Variorum Reprints, London, 1984. What Marx saw as a criticism of law, Savigny viewed as a virtue.

tablets as the Ten Commandments or the Constitution of the United States of America, or in more exotic civil law codes.[11] Globalization, as an enquiry into the increasing interconnections amongst things that happen in the world, inherently transcends notions of public and private international law norms. This portends a marvellous advance over the manufacture, during the nineteenth and twentieth centuries, of law as a product of the nation state, and its corollary of public international law as, at times, an ineffective matrix of rules for nation states, devoid of concerned individuals.

Present moral developments in public international law, such as human rights and free trade, are attracting personal allegiance to such traditionally public, meta-state laws. In this process, international society is becoming more of a 'society' in the true sense of the word, comprised not only of states caring about narrowly defined state interests, but also of citizens who can relate to the international order sometimes with more allegiance than they relate to the state.[12] In some such cases, citizens can compel state behaviour according to public international law treaty standards, the continued development of which may be rendering 'the moral significance of the human race ... available as a moral reality of international society, as the society of the whole human race and the society of all societies'.[13] That is not, however, to suggest a single, all-encompassing society, but rather an alternate society – a global society in a dynamic conversation with powerful ideas transcending more local societies.

Similar universal tendencies are not new to the Western legal tradition, as will be seen shortly. In the interests of discerning a pattern between universal tendencies which have presented in history, with the intention of gaining a better understanding of the present, a comparison should first be made between revolutionary events at the end of the first millennium, and, more recently in our time at the end of the second millennium.

---

11 A superb study of this sanctification or authorization process remains Ehrlich E, *Fundamental Principles of the Sociology of Law*, Moll W (trans), Harvard University Press, Cambridge, Massachusetts, 1936. For an informative introductory analysis which comprehends work by Ehrlich not translated into English, see Ziegert KA, 'A Note on Eugen Ehrlich and the Production of Legal Knowledge' (1998) 20 *Sydney Law Review* 108-126. Discussion of contemporary, general difficulties of attempting to impose norms in code form from the outside inwards – that is, from the superstate to the state to the people – can be found in Hartkamp AS, et al (eds), *Towards a European Civil Code*, Martinus Nijhoff Publishers, Dordrecht, 1994.

12 See, for example, Stychin C, 'Relatively Universal: Globalization, Rights Discourse, and the Evolution of Australian Sexual and National Identities' (1998) 18 *Legal Studies* 534.

13 Allott P, *Eunomia: New Order for a New World*, Oxford University Press, Oxford, 1990 [6.60]; see also [13.105].

Armageddon may be the starting place for this frightening but promising venture.

Apocalypse

A feeling that the end of the world is nigh appears to be helpful in establishing a new legal order. It happened at the time of what Harold J Berman considers to be the birth of the Western legal tradition, in the Papal Revolution of the late eleventh, early twelfth centuries.[14] The sensation of apocalypse also occurred in the twentieth century, on the globalized Megiddo Plains of Europe and the Asia-Pacific. Globalization encompasses the unconscious reactions and the conscious responses to this cataclysm, from which we are still reeling.

The Papal Revolution 1075-1122

At the end of the first millennium, the Catholic Church, commandeered by Cluniac monks, began to overturn centuries of corruption (for example, 'simony' – the buying and selling of church offices – and 'nicolaism' – clerical marriage into secular family patronage), mass interprovincial bloodshed, and general interference by princes and the emperor in spiritual matters. Violence had played an important role in the economy. Plunder had provided an opportunity to prosper at a time when stable trade was elusive; and law was taken to belong in private hands in the manner of the family blood feud.[15] Nonetheless, with the accession of Hildebrand in 1073 as Pope Gregory VII, a canon law based bureaucracy proceeded to develop, despite civil wars of investiture between pope and emperor (ending around 1122 in Continental Europe and 1170 in England), amidst a strengthening of European unity in the form of the crusades east, leading to relative stability in Europe.[16]

Contrary to the fourth century Augustinian notion that the world would decline until the Last Judgment, the aim of the church from the time of Pope Gregory VII became more earnestly to instigate the City of God on earth, through law, striking a constitutional balance between competing polities. Although Western communities continued to demonstrate their internecine if not suicidal tendencies, this general period in history, variously referred to as the Gregorian Reformation or the Papal Revolution, succeeding from the Cluniac reforms, must be recognized as a watershed in

---

14 See Berman HJ, *Law and Revolution: The Formation of the Western Legal Tradition*, Harvard University Press, Cambridge, Massachusetts, 1983, ch 2.

15 See Bloch M, *Feudal Society*, Manyon LA (trans), Routledge and Kegan Paul, London, 1942 at 411.

16 Berman, above n 14 at 106-7.

the evolution of the possibility through law of mass stability in spite of feudal diversity.[17]

The World Revolution 1914-1989

At the end of the second millennium, between the Turkish massacre of the Armenians in 1914 and that of the Tutsis in Rwanda at the end of the twentieth century, with the world wars in between, 150 million people were killed in conditions of terror.[18] Environmentally, the recent mass extinctions of species has led one commentator to write in terms of an ecological holocaust, and globalization as 'nothing short of the end of the world'.[19]

The years 1914-1989 (the outbreak of World War I to the fall of the Berlin Wall) contain a period in which the labyrinthine interconnections amongst things that happen in the world were accomplished from an almost global war, with global phenomena such as environmental degradation and market enlargement made possible by the technological and industrial developments which surged from the catastrophe. Legal manifestations of globalization may be considered in this apocalyptic light, such as human rights (in response to the 'barbarous acts which have outraged the

17 On the significance of this period to legal history, in addition to the work of Berman, see Tierney B, *The Crisis of Church and State 1050-1300*, Prentice-Hall, Englewood Cliffs, NJ, 1964, Part III: 'The Age of the Lawyers'. A product of this time was Gratian's *Concordance of Discordant Canons* ('the *Decretum*'), the importance of which is explored as a 'common law' of Christendom in Tierney B, *Foundations of the Conciliar Theory: The Contribution of the Medieval Canonists From Gratian to the Great Schism*, The University Press, Cambridge, 1955. See also, with references to Berman's writing on this period, Helmholz RH, 'Harold Berman's Accomplishment as a Legal Historian' (1993) 42 *Emory Law Review* 475, which contains a synthesis of material critical of Berman's view; Reid CJ Jr *and* Witte J Jr, 'In the Steps of Gratian: Writing the History of Canon Law in the 1990s' (1999) 48 *Emory Law Journal* 647. For a sociological acknowledgment of 'the constitutional invention of a "constitutional state"' at that time, see Luhmann N, *Society's Law*, Ziegert KA (trans), forthcoming ch 9. See generally Tanner JR et al (eds), *The Cambridge Medieval History 5: Contest of Empire and Papacy*, The University Press, Cambridge, 1924.

18 See Manne R, 'Looking into the heart of darkness for reprieve', *Sydney Morning Herald*, 27 December 1999 at 13.

19 Chen J, 'Globalization and Its Losers' (2000) 9 *Minnesota Journal of Global Trade* 157-218 at 159. Although he suggests (at 184) that 'neither globalization nor the economic growth it has spurred can bear all the blame for today's environmental degradation', arguably such symptoms are more directly attributable to the industrial revolution of the eighteenth century and the technology and profit-making opportunities unleashed by that phenomenon, which have grown into what is considered to be 'globalization'.

conscience of mankind');[20] the European Union (component treaties of which expound grand pacific sentiments by reference to a bloody and divided history);[21] and international movements towards free trade and environmental sustainability, implicitly premised upon Kantian ideals of peace through trade.[22] Present indications suggest the emergence of a new type of peace on a mass scale (with localized exceptions) amongst urbanized societies, counterpoising the danger of mass nuclear destruction.

Comparing the Millennial Revolutions

Spiritual belief and economy are the two key concepts that together explain not only the thematic difference between these two revolutions, but also the distinction of globalization. Economy at the end of the first millennium was, like the sovereignty of that time, 'parcellized'.[23] At the end of that first millennium, European feudal economies were fixed to the soil, narrow and parochial, whilst the spiritual belief of Christianity was universal. Faith was the cornerstone of spiritual belief – a faith in one's place in the natural order of things, and, more specifically, in salvation through Christ and obedience to Biblical laws. Contrarily, at the end of our second millennium, instead of there being one main spiritual belief, there are 'many sects, many

---

20 See Preamble, Universal Declaration of Human Rights, G.A. Res. 217 A (III), Annex, adopted on 10 December 1948. John Witte Jr writes of human rights as being a response to the World War, gulags and the Holocaust, in the absence of Christianity's second coming of Christ and an Utopia of the Enlightenment: Witte J Jr, 'Law, Religion, and Human Rights' (1996) 28 *Columbia Human Rights Review* 1 at 9.

21 The preamble of the European Coal and Steel Community Treaty (1951) resolved to seek 'broader and deeper community among peoples long divided by bloody conflicts'; the Treaty on European Union (1992) recalled 'the historic importance of the ending of the division of the European Continent'; and the Treaty Establishing the European Economic Community (1957) resolved to pool resources 'to preserve and strengthen peace and liberty'. See also Dinan D, *Ever Closer Union?*, Macmillan, London, 1994 at 20. These treaties are reproduced in full in Rudden B and Wyatt D, *Basic Community Laws*, Oxford University Press, Oxford, 1999.

22 See Kant I, 'Perpetual Peace: A Philosophical Sketch' in Reiss H (ed), *Kant: Political Writings*, 2nd ed, Nisbet NB (trans), Cambridge University Press, Cambridge, 1991; Covell C, *Kant and the Law of Peace: A Study in the Philosophy of International Law and International Relations*, Macmillan, London, 1998.

23 The term, 'parcellized sovereignty' has been coined in Anderson P, *Lineages of the Absolutist State*, NLB, London, 1974 at 19. Anderson actually suggested that the economy was not parcellized, contrary to the sovereignty of the time. The economy, he wrote, paradoxically reflected 'an organic unity of economy and polity'. In a change of emphasis from that author's usage, whilst borrowing his term 'parcellization' for its concision, the only unity of the medieval economy was its reliance upon serfdom as a universal mode of production in a regularly occurring political hierarchy. For the most part, actual medieval markets were fragmented, soil-based and territorial – therefore parcellized.

creeds, many races, many ways of education and self-expression' (even in Europe alone); whilst the only universality today appears to be in the market economy.[24] This is a profound juxtaposition by Eugen Rosenstock-Huessy.

Following from this epochal inversion of economy and spiritual belief, with economy now at the apex, the contemporary global focus upon production and consumption, and a significant proportion of spiritual belief, may perhaps reflect the completion in the secularization of religion.[25] Economy and spiritual belief have, to put it simply, swapped places, and the economy is emerging as the de facto spiritual idol of a universal, secular religion. Although lacking in the traditional hallmarks of religion at first blush,[26] the laissez-faire liberalism of the contemporary economy nonetheless rates as a dominant belief and approaches the level of a religion: it contains its share of ethics (for example, read Mill on the freedom of the individual to do anything which does not harm another);[27] ritual (for example, board meetings, corporate regulation compliance); narrative or myth (for example, read Adam Smith on the difference between humans and dogs residing in the capacity of humans to bargain with each other);[28] experience (talk to many business professionals about their education and the historical inevitability of deregulation and low tariffs for prosperity); institutions or society (look skywards in a central business district during the week and downwards on Friday nights to the bars); doctrine (review the jurisprudence of the World Trade Organization); and art (observe the mass-media domination of art and music). 'Risk management' has overtaken faith as the solace from human fears of the unknown.[29]

---

24 See Rosenstock-Huessy E, *Out of Revolution: Autobiography of Western Man*, Berg, Oxford, 1993 at 495-6.

25 On this secularization process, see, for example, Mortensen R, 'The Theory Behind Secularization' (1993) 18 *Bulletin of the Australasian Society of Legal Philosophy* 19 at 23, and, more generally, Weber M, *The Protestant Ethic and the Spirit of Capitalism*, Parsons T (trans), Unwin University Books, London, 1971.

26 The indicia that follow are taken from Smart N, *The World's Religions*, Cambridge University Press, Cambridge, 1989 at 10-30.

27 See Mill JS, *On Liberty* (1859), Penguin, Harmondsworth, 1985 at 68-9. Harms meriting interference with individual liberty, such as pornography as opposed to art or fair wage as opposed to employer freedom, are the subject of an almost talmudic or scholastic liberal discourse.

28 See Smith A, *An Inquiry into the Nature and Causes of the Wealth of Nations I*, Clarendon Press, Oxford, 1976 at 25-6.

29 On the contemporary risk fixation, see by way of introduction Giddens A, 'Risk and Responsibility' (1999) 62 *Modern Law Review* 1. See also Dimity Kingsford-Smith's analysis in Chapter 5 of this volume.

After a relatively brief period of decentralization into state power, the Holy Roman Empire of Christian believers is looking increasingly like a Wholly Mammon Empire of cosmopolitan consumers.[30] A crusade has been waged for a more integrated economy, bringing not only personal prosperity but also the relief of 'the most pressing moral, political and economic issue of the time', namely Third World poverty, the future remedy of which the evangelists contend requires further integration.[31]

The globalization of the twentieth century witnesses the faster home stretch in what has been a slow race towards a new belief system, occurring within, it would seem, universal parameters of human meaningfulness traditionally occupied by religion. What is the significance of this to law? To rephrase this very difficult question, will the millenarian, apocalyptic events at the end of the second millennium found a new, or at least differentiated, legal science as occurred at the end of the first millennium?

A Global Legal Science?

The prospect of a new legal science – a global legal science – such as that which emerged with the scholasticism of the Papal Revolution and its blending of Hebrew theology, Greek philosophy, and Roman law,[32] can only be hinted at in this paper. Suffice it to note that just as Gregorian Catholicism grew into the Anselmian spirituality of the 'faith-seeking-understanding' liberal arts curriculum, and just as secularising Protestantism flourished with earthbound Cartesian science, globalization as the increasing interconnections amongst things that happen in the world is occurring amidst Einsteinian cosmology (the relativity of time and space) and chaos theory. Intuition might suggest a connection between globalization and chaos theory, as chaos theory posits the interconnections amongst relatively distant, minute things that happen in the world, with time and space interactively overcome (or at least 'disembedded'[33] from the social world) in an approximation of Einstein's theory. Indeed, it is difficult

---

30 For some reflections on the contemporary liberal (cosmopolitan consumers) paradigm of contract by reference to Platonism and Christianity, see Wagner WJ, 'In Search of the Market's Moral Limits: Liberalism, Perfectionism and "The Bad Man" in Christian Perspective' (1994-95) 11 *Journal of Law and Religion* 535.

31 For an orthodox sermon, see *The Economist*, 'The case for globalization', 23 September 2000 at 17-18.

32 See Berman, above n 14 ch 3: 'The Origin of Western Legal Science in the European Universities'.

33 Giddens A, *The Consequences of Modernity*, Polity Press, Stanford, 1990 at 21. That is to say, time is now totally abstracted from the life cycle; and in the age of virtual video meetings, space has become abstracted from place, at 19.

to imagine that these great shifts in natural scientific thought should not have correlates in social scientific thought.[34]

How this symbolism might manifest itself in legal science can only be a matter of speculation. Universalistic, normative legal principles, transcending space and time, might be expected and indeed can be experienced, such as those contained in the United Nations Universal Declaration of Human Rights and numerous international covenants. Enshrined as a global constitutional principle might be subsidiary[35] forms of legality and their norm systems in a federally orientated, plural competition of jurisdictions, such as that emerging in the European Union.[36] Subsidiarity has rich origins in pre-national Swiss Protestantism.[37] Despite the venerability of the doctrine, subsidiarity operating in a global legal science would initially be an uncertain hierarchy,[38] a characteristic of all young federal structures. It could, though, prove a stimulant to a discourse concerned with the priority of competing interests, much as medieval conflicts between church and state were profoundly philosophical and theological adventures.

Beyond the normative value principles which might be characteristic of a legal science (such as 'the rule of law', 'natural justice' or 'subsidiarity') is the actual 'grammar' of a legal system. This aspect of legal science includes the 'making, application, exposition, and transmission'[39] of law.

---

34 See, for example, Walzer M, 'On the Role of Symbolism in Political Thought' (1967) 82 *Political Science Quarterly* 191; also Santos, above n 6 ch 2.

35 The principle of subsidiarity is premised 'on the unassailable proposition that no single level of organization is appropriate for all social functions': Trachtman JP, '*L'Etat, C'est Nous*: Sovereignty, Economic Integration and Subsidiarity' (1992) 33 *Harvard International Law Journal* 459 at 468.

36 See Article 3b of the Treaty Establishing the European Community (also known as the Treaty of Rome, 1957).

37 Switzerland's counterpart to Luther, Hudrych Zwingli (1484-1531), had launched a significant Protestant trend for local communities to claim the right to control their own affairs. See Davies N, *Europe: A History*, Pimlico, London, 1997 at 488. More recently, in an Encyclical Letter of 1931, Pope Pius XI proposed that the state had assumed too much power from the domain of smaller social units such as the family. See Wilke and Wallace, *Subsidiarity: Approaches to Power-sharing in the European Community*, cited in Charlesworth A, and Cullen H, *European Community Law*, Pitman Publishing, London, 1994 at 48.

38 'The self-reproduction of law's hierarchy, questioned for decades by legal critique, effectively breaks down under the pressures of globalization': Teubner G, 'The King's Many Bodies: The Self-Deconstruction of Law's Hierarchy' (1997) 31 *Law and Society Review* 763 at 772.

39 See Schulz F, *A History of Roman Legal Science*, Oxford University Press, London, 1967 at 1. This suggests legal science is more than just interpretation of the law believed to be in force. For a more positivist idea of legal science, see Harris JW, *Law and Legal*

Perhaps the area of legal science most open to innovation falls within the activity of codification. Codes go back even earlier than the laws of the Babylonian ruler Hammurabi (who reigned approximately 1792-1750 BCE),[40] although it was not until the eighteenth century Enlightenment, notably on the Continent as opposed to England (despite the best efforts of Bentham), that torturous attempts were earnestly made to reduce customs and case law to intricate rules which spoke for themselves, supposedly to an adjudicator who had merely to apply the law with minimal interpretation or reference to extraneous material.[41] Codification and unification of legal rules is a major characteristic of the push towards the globalization of international economic law,[42] but whether there is change in store for an already established science of codification[43] is a matter for conjecture, which to my knowledge has not been considered in the globalization literature.[44]

Indulging this conjecture, regard may first be had to the process of creating legislation and codes from norms. On the one hand is an inductive process (a pattern is found), where jurists and legislative drafters embrace the norms which they observe in society, writing them onto paper in neat forms and categories, much in the manner of cases edited and gathered into a textbook and then further abstracted into the 'nutshell' or study aid, which by this stage has become a de facto code. On the other hand may be

---

Science: *An Inquiry into the Concepts Legal Rule and Legal System*, Clarendon Press, London, 1979 at 12.

40 See extracts in Robbins S (ed), *Law*: *A Treasury of Art and Literature*, Beaux Arts Editions, New York, 1990 at 19-22.

41 See Stein PG, 'Roman Law, Common Law, and Civil Law' (1992) 66 *Tulane Law Review* 1591 at 1595-96. On the need for communities with common methods of interpretation, see Mattei U, 'The Issue of European Civil Codification and Legal Scholarship: Biases, Strategies and Developments' (1998) 21 *Hastings International and Comparative Law Review* 883. The attempt to reduce complexity by recording norms in a single place actually creates complexity generated by the interaction between text and meaning: see Luhmann, above n 17 ch 6:II.

42 On the codification of international commercial law, see, for example, Berger KP, *The Creeping Codification of the Lex Mercatoria*, Kluwer Law International, The Hague, 1999; UNIDROIT (ed), *Principles of International Commercial Contracts*, Rome, 1994; Hartkamp, above n 11; Farnsworth EA, 'The American Provenance of the UNIDROIT Principles' (1984) 72 *Tulane Law Review* 1985. On the concept of international economic law, see Kennedy D, 'The Disciplines of International Law and Policy' (1999) 12 *Leiden Journal of International Law* 9 at 44-47.

43 For an attempt to understand codification as an issue requiring exploration in itself, see Varga C, *Codification as a Socio-Historical Phenomenon*, Sándor E et al (trans), Akadémiai Kiadó, Budapest, 1991.

44 A recent contribution to the topic has maintained enquiry along the traditional divide between civil law and common law: see Weiss GA, 'The Enchantment of Codification in the Common-Law World' (2000) 25 *Yale Journal of International Law* 435.

a deductive process (a pattern is followed), where, if the legislation is to be innovative, a new formula from parliament will be imposed upon society (for example, welfare legislation).[45] Although inductive and deductive reasoning, considered as opposites in logic, can become problematic,[46] the inductive method has been more characteristic of Western legal history. In view of the numbers of treaties and international organizations which have proliferated in recent years, and the principles (reminiscent of natural law) which have been formulated concerning the political and economic rights of humans without widespread customary basis, a new emphasis on deductive legal reasoning may be anticipated – at least in the early stages until a corpus of case law develops. The primacy of teleological, purpose-based (as opposed to literalist) interpretation of European Union texts and directives[47] is testament to this deductive legal mindset, which may be expected to proliferate.

Transnational Legal Education and Practice

Moving from the abstract to the tangible aspects of legal science (insofar as this describes the making, application and transmission of law), what can be suggested without tentativeness is that legal education and practice have returned to being very cosmopolitan, as they have been in the past. One sixteenth century Dutchman studied civil law in Leyden, Paris, Orléans, Bourges, Genf, Basel and Strasbourg before returning to Holland.[48] Even earlier, educated Europe shared a similar culture. Between Edinburgh and Palermo, Mainz or Lund and Toledo, a well-bred man could be educated in any of these canon law schools and rise to success in most any European church, court or university (the closest things to medieval yuppiedom).[49] From the twelfth to the sixteenth centuries, there was a reasonably uniform structure of ecclesiastical courts throughout Europe, staffed by men with a fairly common education in canon and frequently civil law.[50]

In 1996, Professor Twining proudly wrote of the cosmopolitan and internationalist student body of the University of London, and the fact that of nearly 130 courses listed in its LLM degree, only 31 purported to

---

45 See, for example, Ehrlich, above n 11 ch 18 ('The Codification of Juristic Law').

46 See Ayer AJ, *The Problem of Knowledge*, Pelican, Middlesex, 1956 at 71-75, especially at 73. A view of the world will guide information gathering, just as the information already gathered will guide a view of the world.

47 See Joxerramon B, *The Legal Reasoning of the European Court of Justice: Towards a European Jurisprudence*, Clarendon Press, Oxford, 1993 at 251-62.

48 See Zimmermann R, 'Roman-Dutch Jurisprudence and its Contribution to European Private Law' (1992) 66 *Tulane Law Review* 1685 at 1693.

49 See Knowles D, *The Evolution of Medieval Thought*, Longman, London 1988 at 73.

50 See Robinson OF et al, *European Legal History*, Butterworths, London, 1994 at 72.

concentrate on domestic law.[51] Nowadays, the East is even interested in the traditional domestic law of the West. Japan can boast one of the strongest concentrations of Harvard Law School alumni.[52] The chairman of the law firm Baker and McKenzie has boasted of that firm's global network of offices and partners of 'different nationalities, backgrounds, religions, cultures and colours'.[53] Chinese network systems of mutual obligations – *guanxi*[54] – and similar Mexican networks of *camarillas* and Japanese *batsu* – have their parallels in the West, where family ties and social connections can be as important as academic learning.[55] Patronage, of course, has a strong history in the West[56] as well as the East.

At the level of universalism, Max Weber noted in *The Protestant Ethic and the Spirit of Capitalism* that capitalistic enterprises 'have existed in all civilized countries of the earth' – in China, India, Babylon, Egypt and Mediterranean antiquity.[57] What distinguished modern capitalism, in Weber's thought, was the degree of devotion to money and gain as the ultimate purpose, that is, as the end pursuit.[58] In this respect, an increasing proportion of urban Asia and Eastern Europe would appear nowadays to be as degenerate as the West, with similar roles for their lawyers in their societies. These cosmopolitan manifestations of capitalism have made it possible to speak of 'world history'.[59]

Sometimes it is suggested that a characteristic of modern legal education is its increasing value as a generalist degree facilitating entry into careers outside traditional legal practice, for example, in management, business or politics.[60] Many law students do not enrol with the vision of becoming practitioners. The study of law is believed to provide a solid educational background, more than ever, in an increasingly complicated society. Yet the fact that law graduates may so decide to avoid professional

---

51 Twining, above n 4 at 14-15.

52 See Dezalay Y and Garth B, 'Law, Lawyers and Social Capital: "Rule of Law" versus Relational Capitalism' (1997) 6 *Social and Legal Studies* 109 at 129-31.

53 See 'Meeting Madame Chairman', *Lawyers' Weekly*, 7 July 2000 at 15.

54 See Appelbaum RP, 'The Future of Law in a Global Economy' (1998) 7 *Social and Legal Studies* 171.

55 See Dezalay and Garth, above n 52 at 111-12.

56 For example, '[P]olitics, industry, favour, etc'. were said to promote William Cecil, 'an eminent lawyer of the society of Gray's Inn' – 'Twas not his law': Prest W, 'The English Bar, 1550-1700' in Prest W, *Lawyers in Early Modern Europe and America*, Croom Helm, London, 1981 at 79.

57 Weber, above n 25 at 19.

58 Ibid at 51.

59 Turner BS, 'The Two Faces of Sociology: Global or National?' in Featherstone (ed), above n 5 at 352, citing Marx K and Engels F, *The German Ideology*.

60 See, for example, McInnis C and Marginson S, *Australian Law Schools after the 1987 Pearce Report*, Australian Government Publishing Service, Canberra, 1994, at 23, 27-8.

admission as lawyers is a timelessly European choice. In Castile, for example, between 1570 and 1610, approximately 2,000 law graduates out of 50,000 entered practice. At about the same time in England, less than ten per cent of Inns of Court students were to practise as barristers,[61] many apparently preferring the advantage of the rich cultural experiences the Inns offered in many areas, from lectures in science to lessons in 'the courtly arts of dancing and singing'.[62]

This suggests that the present internationalism of law courses and mobility of qualifications, and a roughly similar social dynamic between lawyers and society, whilst being an important cultural artefact of globalization, is not revolutionary of itself. Nor, for its traversing of continents, would it suggest, necessarily, an untrammelled Western imperialism. Whilst there exist barriers to mutual recognition of national graduate professional qualifications[63] and there is the need for detailed focus on particulars at all levels,[64] at the level of legal science the cross-border and cross-time commonalities are often underestimated. In this respect we may say that Western legal science, using Professor Twining's terminology, 'travels well'[65] to other continents and times.

The very lively norms that underlie the seemingly timeless globalism of legal education and practice are now explored in the context of a particularly pertinent legal system – that of mercantile law – which has, and is, 'travelling well'.

Private Authority – Business Custom

Networks of mutual obligation have their own means of establishing authority and legal validity. Nowhere is this better illustrated than in the history of mercantile law. A separate body of law with derivations from classical Roman law and fairly clear systematic origins in the thirteenth century, the *lex mercatoria* has been defined as 'a set of general principles and customary rules spontaneously referred to or elaborated in the framework of international trade, without reference to a particular national system of law'.[66] It varied from city to city, but was reviewable by the time

---

61 See Ranieri F, 'From Status to Profession: The Professionalization of Lawyers as a Research Field in Modern European Legal History' (1989) 10 *Journal of Legal History* 180.

62 Prest W, *The Inns of Court under Elizabeth I and the Early Stuarts 1590-1640*, Longman, London, 1972 at 153.

63 See, for example, Twining W, 'Reviving General Jurisprudence' in Likosky M (ed), *Transnational Legal Processes*, Butterworths, Sydney, 2001.

64 As William Twining argues in Chapter 2 of this volume at 13.

65 Ibid at 33; above n 8 at 191.

66 Goldman B, 'The applicable law: general principles of law – the *lex mercatoria*' in Lew J (ed), *Contemporary Problems in International Arbitration*, Centre for

of the seventeenth and eighteenth centuries in the common law courts.[67] The famous eighteenth century English commercial law judge, Lord Mansfield, acknowledged the multinational dimensions of mercatorial maritime law[68] and William Blackstone wrote of the separate regulation of the 'extensive and complicated affairs of traffic and merchandise'.[69] Although the degrees of continuity of doctrine and national reception of the system (in its variants) are questionable, it is likely that the old *lex mercatoria* of the eleventh to sixteenth centuries continued to develop, 'even in the heyday of nationalism', as part of the law of nations.[70]

The so-called 'new *lex mercatoria*' reflects, *inter alia*, 'general principles of law recognized by commercial nations, rules of international organizations, customs and usages, standard form contracts, and reports of arbitral awards'.[71] In the past 50 years it has been subjected to rigorous worldwide codification. Notably this has been evidenced in the UNIDROIT Principles, increasingly used in choice of law provisions in contracts for cross-border transactions, for adjudication or trial before arbitral bodies.

Recall, for a moment, the inversion of economy and spiritual belief identified by Rosenstock-Huessy. Going into the third millennium, there can be surmised from the rise of market ideology, the completion of the secularization of religion (or alternatively, the deification of the market). The life and times of the *lex mercatoria* support this contention. The *lex mercatoria*, for the medieval merchants of the early second millennia, was a means for salvation of the soul, reflecting the canon law as a system of law 'based on the will of God as manifested in reason and conscience'.[72] Indeed, a prototypical transnational corporation in the form of the trading empire of the late medieval Italian, Messer Francesco Datini, carried the personal trading motto 'In the Name of God and of Profit'.[73]

The very fact that the law was being made through disputes and commercial conflict demonstrates no heavenly harmony amongst merchants. It does, however, reflect an allegiance to the redemptive potential of commerce which may be gaining momentum today, albeit

---

Commercial Law Studies, Queen Mary College, University of London, London, 1986 at 116. See also Goldman B, 'Introduction' in Carbonneau TE (ed), *Lex Mercatoria and Arbitration*, Transnational Juris Publications, Dobbs Ferry, 1990 at xvii-xviii.

67 Baker JH, 'The Law Merchant and the Common Law Before 1700' (1979) 38 *Cambridge Law Journal* 295 at 306.

68 *Luke v Lyde* [1759] 2 Burrow's Rep. 887; 97 ER 614 at ER 617.

69 Blackstone W, *Commentaries on the Laws of England*, vol I at 273.

70 See Berman HJ and Kaufman C, 'The Law of International Commercial Transactions (*Lex Mercatoria*)' (1978) 19 *Harvard International Law Journal* 221 at 273.

71 Santos, above n 6 at 290.

72 Berman, above n 14 at 339.

73 Davies, above n 37 at 442-3.

through trust in the market and not God. Although there is apparently no longer any intrinsic worth assigned to legal texts, such as was accorded to the canon law, there is observable a commitment to a process of arbitration and private, 'gentlemanly' resolution of disputes along the lines of efficiency of time, cost and maintenance of a community of good credit and honour. This takes place within a mindset of industrial progress which, according to at least one prominent legal practitioner in the field, espouses a belief in its own redemptive potential for 'peace and of stability' and the 'development of a more harmonious and peaceful world order', through a 'singular sect' of 'international business lawyers' ensconced in a 'family likeness' with 'briefcase', 'laptop computer' and 'the warmth of encounters' among 'inseparable travelling companions' aboard 'flights all over the world'.[74]

Mercantile law and its contemporary adjudication by private arbitration raise the very interesting potential for what has been called 'private government'.

Private Government

Modern arbitration centres are reminiscent of the medieval merchant judges and courts prior to reception by the territorial royal courts, perhaps with comparative degrees of patronage on some panels.[75] Respected senior practitioners and academic lawyers sit on the prestigious arbitral bodies. Leading New York and London lawyers head the charge towards universalising their jurisdictions and norms through a convergence of those laws and also the laws of other industrialized countries. In this trend, national law can even be marketed,[76] the quality of the law being more important than the source. Institutionalization of arbitration rules, for example those of the International Chamber of Commerce, provides for rules that closely resemble domestic court rules, and may be nominated in contracts. The fact that almost 90 per cent of international contracts contain an arbitration clause, and over 90 per cent of international arbitral awards receive voluntary compliance by parties, without resort to the enforcement

74 Badinter R, 'Role of the International Lawyer' (1995) 23 *International Business Lawyer* 505.

75 A successful arbitrator has described international arbitration as 'a mafia ... because people appoint one another. You always appoint your friends – people you know', and, as another expert has said, 'It is a club. They nominate one another. And sometimes you're counsel, and sometimes you're arbitrator'. See Dezalay Y and Garth B, *Dealing in Virtue: International Commercial Arbitration and the Construction of a Transnational Legal Order*, University of Chicago Press, Chicago, 1996 at 10.

76 Flood J, 'The Globalising World' (1995) 23 *International Business Lawyer* 509 at 511

mechanisms of national courts,[77] reveals the viability and authority of this private legal system. Coupled with the *lex mercatoria* as the choice of law for such contracts, arbitration emerges as a consensual, universalistic institution of global norms and values: promoters of Islamic arbitration have even argued that the *lex mercatoria* is perfectly consistent with Islamic law.[78]

Notwithstanding the commercial pragmatism of arbitration, constitutionally, and at the deep level of legitimacy, contractual arbitration mechanisms conjure a problem of logic: the paradox of self-reference. If a contract creates its own law (as opposed to being created under the law within a nominated national jurisdiction), then if the contract is impugned, the contract can be said to be without law (the paradox of *contrat sans loi*). Does this render the contract and its law therefore invalid? The problem of self-reference is largely overcome by the peer group pressure effect of abiding the resolution process to preserve livelihood by continuing to maintain the confidence of peers. Under the contract, the domestic law was disregarded by the parties in favour of a substitute law of the parties' creation, effectively allowing an impugned contract to be severed from its substitute law, leaving that chosen substitute law intact for adjudication purposes. Parties can thus be said to 'autonomize' their legal relationship.[79]

There is, in fact, an often-overlooked connection between the thus conceived autonomy of private contracts and constitutionalism. In a celebration of liberal society, Article 1134 of the Napoleonic Code exalted contracts thus: 'contracts legally created have the legal value of statutes for those who entered into them'.[80] Roman law arguably even considered the *lex contractus* as a source of law creation.[81] Contracts may therefore be considered a form of private legislation for private government – self-regulation by civil society (that is, businesses and individual entrepreneurs) as distinct from the state, adding to an international commercial law and practice which does not require the state for doctrinal legitimation or enforcement of awards.

---

77 Berger, above n 42 at 159.

78 Dezalay and Garth, above n 75 at 90.

79 Berger, above n 42 at 162. See also Teubner, above n 38 at 768-70.

80 Cited in Robé J-P, 'Multinational Enterprises: The Constitution of a Pluralistic Legal Order' in Teubner G (ed), *Global Law Without a State*, Dartmouth Publishing Company Limited, Brookfield, 1997 at 58. Undergirding the contractual statutes of private government is property. Again, referring to the French experience of early liberalism, Article 2 of the 1789 Declaration of the Rights of Man and Citizen records the preservation of property as one of the goals of any political association, property being, at Article 17, 'an inviolable and sacred right' subject to alienation under a just and prior indemnity only where legally established public necessity requires it.

81 Luhmann, above n 17 ch 2:VIII, although noting Savigny's disagreement.

Possibly, vast areas of the law are 'privatizable': privately created law, although enforceable by government, often may not require that level of state coercion,[82] although account would obviously have to be taken of consumer law and other areas of law which purport to maintain public policy (for example, by prohibiting illegal contracts) and to correct unequal bargaining (private law-creating) power. In this oeuvre of contractual law-making might even be included privately instituted environmental certification programs (for example the International Organization for Standardization's 'ISO 14000' environmental management program) which may be expected to influence, in time, not only environmental law but also tort, property, tax, information, financial, and trade law.[83] Multinational enterprises and labour law are also subject to private law-making initiatives.[84]

Private government will undoubtedly never exist in isolation, just as no state government will ever be a law unto itself, in all respects, concerning either internal domestic order or the place of the state in the external international order. Regulation has always occurred, although to varying degrees throughout time, by way of competing jurisdictions. Globalization is stimulating this facet of jurisprudence.

Government by Competing Jurisdictions

International commercial law and arbitration show that jurisdictions may live with vitality outside the state. Other jurisdictions, less independent because public interests are involved, spring to mind: the World Trade Organization on free trade and environmental concerns, United Nations committees on human rights, the International Criminal Tribunal, the International Court of Justice, and the list goes on. Although some of these

---

82 See Ware SJ, 'Default Rules from Mandatory Rules: Privatizing Law Through Arbitration' (1999) 83 *Minnesota Law Review* 703. Although public authority may always be required for a percentage of privately unenforceable arbitration decisions, this does not overcome the significant private generation and adjudication of the norms which the public authority serves. A suggestion has even been made that it would be desirable for 'modern democratic societies' to enact a contract law stipulating that providers of legal rules should be selected when the contract is drafted, or else as chosen by the initiating party, with the right to unquestioned enforcement by a state court: see Hadfield GK, 'Privatizing Commercial Law: Lessons from the Middle and the Digital Ages' *Stanford Law School John M. Olin Program in Law and Economics Working Paper No. 195*, March 2000 at 36-8. Surely, though, this would raise problems of biased 'law providers' which would require regulation by the state.

83 See Meidinger E, ' "Private" Environmental Certification Systems and American Law: Closer Than You May Think' (July 2000) SSRN Working Paper Series at 1-34 <http://papers.ssrn.com/paper.taf?abstract_id=238742>.

84 See generally, Teubner's collection at n 80

organizations struggle to live up to the idea of a jurisdiction, for example the United Nations Committee for the Elimination of Racial Discrimination (the recommendations of which the Australian Commonwealth has been dismissive), such institutions have not yet had their day. There is historical scope to imagine a time when such supranational bodies may become empowered. The constitutional history of the spiritual and secular realms may provide some guide.

Although the medieval Church was an exceedingly wealthy institution, and a body such as the United Nations not so comparatively powerful, it is possible that ideological institutions such as the United Nations could become captive to a dominant state – for example, the United States of America – similarly to alliances which have existed between the papacy and kingdoms. For example, 'the Catholic Monarchs' of Spain, Ferdinand and Isabella, presided over the Inquisition in the late fifteenth century, which of course vehemently prosecuted the cause of church orthodoxy. It is also conceivable that sovereignty could, in effect, be shared between a supranational power such as the United Nations and the state government (or the European Union and member states), drawing from the experience of the medieval 'Two Swords' constitutionalism[85] of shared sovereignty between the spiritual jurisdiction of the church and the secular jurisdiction of the prince. After the Papal Revolution, numerous legal systems existed within a realm, such as, in the secular sphere, royal law, manorial law, feudal law and mercantile law. In the spiritual domain, there was the supranational legal system of the Catholic church canon law, which broadly extended into what we would now consider to be the civil realms of wills and succession, marriage, contracts under oath, the charging of interest (usury) and the criminal law of sexual offences. Choice of jurisdiction between canon law and civil law could even be contracted.[86] Bearing in mind this precedent of distinct realms, the 'constitutionalization' of Europe, effected by the European Union through the four major legal doctrines of

---

85 Watt JA, 'Spiritual and Temporal Powers' in Burns JH (ed), *The Cambridge History of Medieval Political Thought c.350 – c.1450*, Cambridge University Press, Cambridge, 1988 at 367: To the Western Church it was in the main clear that there were two great authorities in the world, not one, that the Spiritual Power was in its own sphere independent of the temporal, while it did not doubt that the Temporal Power was also independent and supreme in its sphere ... This conception of the two autonomous authorities existing in human society, each supreme, each obedient, is the principle of society which the Fathers handed down to the Middle Ages, not any conception of a unity founded upon the supremacy of one or other of the powers. See also Leff G, *Medieval Thought: From St Augustine to Ockham*, Penguin, Harmondsworth, 1958 at 74.

86 See Berman above n 14 at 222-3. See also Reid and Witte, above n 17 at 651.

direct effect, supremacy, implied powers and human rights,[87] is not so radical. The European Union, in fact, still has some catching up to do.

Accepting the evolution of the Holy Roman Empire into the Wholly Mammon Empire (characterized by global markets), the latter may be adding a new doctrine of economics to notions of shared sovereignty pioneered by the Two Swords theory. Such an economic approach might treat the maximization of global welfare as the purpose of national choice of law legal regimes – not any sense of comity, national interests[88] or the automatic appropriateness of the authority of a territorial ruler.[89] Interesting though this possibility may be, presently it is little more than an abstract type of natural law propounded in 'law and economics' circles.

Philosophically, it is arguable that increased choice means increased freedom. When people choose what might appear at an early time to be an unconventional jurisdiction, massive social transformations can be encouraged and eventually reflected when that jurisdiction later becomes conventional. This was demonstrated around the time of the English Protestant Reformation and in the following years, by the common law assuming primacy over canon law areas of law mentioned above, such as succession and marriage,[90] and also, earlier, by the rise of the royal courts over the feudal and manorial courts.

Professor Berman has identified the hierarchy and diversity of jurisdictions as being a major characteristic of the Western legal tradition, nearing extinction in the twentieth century.[91] With the benefit of almost 20 years since those thoughts, it is now possible to say that the once arguably endangered jurisprudential species of competing jurisdictions looks set to flourish in this age of globalization. On the way to a conclusion, some suggestions may now be offered for understanding the relationship between laws and the authority which laws are capable of projecting into the state and beyond, having regard to the technology which makes possible the global interconnections amongst things that happen in the world.

---

87 See Weiler J, 'The Transformation of Europe' (1991) 100 *Yale Law Journal* 2403 at 2413-23.

88 See Guzman A, 'Choice of Law: New Foundations' (26 July 2000) UC Berkeley Public Law Research Paper No. 28, <http://papers.ssrn.com/paper.taf?abstract_id=237802>.

89 On the need for purpose or meaningfulness in law, see Luhmann, above n 17 ch 11:II: 'Again and again, attempts are made to suggest principled answers – if no longer the *will of God*, then the *maximisation of welfare*' (original emphasis).

90 For a case study of the turning point of defamation from a canon law action to a common law action, see Goldman DB, 'Canon Law Origins of Common Law Defamation, the Hunne Whodunit and Western Legal Science: An Historical Challenge for Modern Lawyers' (1996) 2 *Australian Journal of Legal History* 79.

91 Berman, above n 14 at 38-9.

Sovereignty as a Function of Technology

Sovereignty, operating within what might be termed 'the sphere of containable disruption', reflects, in an imprecise manner, the military and economic power of the day.[92] That power is, in turn, a correlate of technology. Historical claims to and failures of ownership of the seas illustrate these propositions. In the thirteenth century, Venice was the transient sovereign of the Adriatic Sea. In the fifteenth century, the Atlantic was evanescently divided between Spain and Portugal. In the eighteenth century, when the sun never set on the British Empire, England asserted sovereignty only over adjacent seas at a time when no state had the power or technological advantage to pretend to own the Atlantic, nor a city the impudence to claim the Adriatic. Beyond the nineteenth century, it became an acknowledged principle of international law that maritime sovereignty was limited largely to inland and territorial waters – defined (upon reflection, not surprisingly) in technological terms by the three-mile rule – the reach of the cannon ball from the shore[93] and the symbolic technological limit of the sphere of containable disruption. There appears to be a pattern: as soon as economics, military power and technology increase power, an opposing force seems to increase the disruption which undermines the power in the first place.

Pursuing this hypothesis, some speculation may be permitted as to the relationship between sovereignty and technology, by reference to the law of spying from outer space, contrasted with the law of aerial espionage. The reasonable and not altogether cynical view should be open that international law permission to spy from outer space (at least in peacetime)[94] has been forthcoming because there is simply nothing foreseeable which can be done to prevent it from occurring. Reconnaissance flights over sovereign territories are a different story. Concerning such flights it was, for example, always within the realm of possibility that the U-2 photo reconnaissance spy plane (which spearheaded early Cold War United States reconnaissance over the Union of Soviet Socialist Republics) would pass within the reach of USSR defences. That matter came to a head when, on 1 May 1960, the USSR was finally able to

---

92 See generally Kennedy P, *The Rise and Fall of the Great Powers: Economic Change and Military Conflict from 1500 to 2000*, Unwin Hyman, London, 1988, for an excellent analysis of the relationship between military power and economic fortune.

93 See Harvard Law Review Association, 'Note: National Sovereignty of Outer Space' (1961) 74 *Harvard Law Review* 1154 at 1160-1.

94 See Scott RG, 'Territorially Intrusive Intelligence Collection and International Law' (1999) 46 *Air Force Law Review* 217 at 219.

intercept the high-flying intruder.[95] The extreme altitude at which the U-2 had been able to fly had been beyond the USSR's real sphere of containable disruption for many years, but not outside the possibility of containment some time in the future. On the contrary, the toleration of spying from outer space appears to be accepted in law because it is completely outside any nation's realistic hope for its sphere of containable disruption. The reach of the sovereignty applied by nation states to their spheres is dependent upon what is technologically feasible.

Even the rise (and eventual decline) in recent centuries of the nation state is inconceivable without the prior technology of 'precisely demarcated territories' made possible by developments in cartography, particularly in the sixteenth century, in what has been termed the 'territorialization of social relations'.[96] Similarly, the invention of the printing press and its connection in the sixteenth century of fellow readers into particular language fields, fertilized the nationally imagined community.[97] With such technology comes increased strength inside the designated sphere of containable disruption, balanced by an opposing threat of military and normative invasion from other spheres.

Normative invasion may be in the form of new ideas being spread by a revolutionary movement, internally; or from the outside, by customs of another realm or state (for example, the various strains of Protestantism in the sixteenth century or communism in the twentieth century). It may even take the form of a permeating language such as English[98] or the Latin of the Holy Roman Empire. The system of nation states had evolved, by the twentieth century, as the paradigmatic unit of governance, for their ability to be internally regulating and rigid enough externally to protect the interior. Weak states are weak because they lack the technology[99] to fortify against military and normative invasion. Yet no technology nowadays appears sophisticated enough to fortify a nation state against the dominant trends of globalization, whether considered, for example, as the largely

---

95 See Wright Q, 'Legal Aspects of the U-2 Incident' (1960) 54 *American Journal of International Law* 836.

96 Deterritorialization reflects a trend from status to locus, mirroring Maine's model of the movement from status to contract-based society, for example from kinship, common interests and customs to the fact of shared territoriality): see Ford RT, 'Law's Territory (A History of Jurisdiction)' (1999) 97 *Michigan Law Review* 843 at 845, 872.

97 See Anderson B, *Imagined Communities: Reflections on the Origin and Spread of Nationalism*, Verso, London, 1991 at 44.

98 See Crystal D, *English as a Global Language*, Cambridge University Press, Cambridge, 1997.

99 See van Creveld M, *The Rise and Decline of the State*, Cambridge University Press, Cambridge, 1999 at 378.

macroeconomic criteria of 'the golden straitjacket',[100] or the micro-economic golden arches culinary colonialism demonstrated by the McDonald's hamburger hegemony.

Sovereignty is premised upon being able to contain disruption, which, in the midst of incredible technological innovation, is threatened by the exploding interconnections amongst things which happen in the world – that is, globalization. The consequence of globalization is a decline in sovereignty, otherwise expressed as a decrease in the potential to contain disruption in a given space.

Despite the disparity between medieval and contemporary technology, it is the deducible reality of both historical periods that there is an absence of any one single power or technological tyrant able to contain disruption and, obversely, a multiplicity of viable legal systems opting to fill that void.

Conclusion

> Vanity of vanities, all is vanity ... There is nothing new under the sun ... There is no remembrance of former things, nor will there be any remembrance of things that are to come by those who will come after.[101]

With the remembrance of former things, discernment may arrive as to whether there are actually new things under the sun, overcoming the amnesiac presumption that challenges such as globalization are necessarily novel. Remembrance can overcome vanity, as history can endow, with meaning, the accomplishment of a phenomenon such as globalization.

Although historical parallels do not prove anything of themselves,[102] they have hopefully aided, for present purposes, investigation into the extent to which jurisprudential thought needs to be amended to accommodate the challenges of globalization.[103] Some valuable lessons for the legal future may be learnt from history:

---

100 Friedman T, *The Lexus and the Olive Tree: Understanding Globalization*, Harper Collins Publishers, London, 2000 at 105. The 'golden straitjacket' includes: private-sector-driven economic growth, low inflation, price stability, decreasing state bureaucracy, balanced budgets if not surpluses, eliminating and lowering tariffs on imported goods, removing restrictions on foreign investment, reduction of quotas and domestic monopolies, increasing exports, privatising state-owned enterprises, deregulating the economy, eliminating government corruption, and allowing citizens a choice of pension options.

101 Ecclesiastes 1:2-3, 9,11, *The Bible: Authorized King James Version*, Carroll R and Prickett S (eds), Oxford University Press, Oxford and New York, 1997.

102 See Galtung J, *The European Community: A Superpower in the Making*, Allen and Unwin, London, 1973 at 187.

103 Tully has asked a similar question in relation to the degree to which constitutionalism has to be amended to recognize cultural diversity. See Tully J, *Strange Multiplicity: Constitutionalism in an Age of Diversity*, Cambridge University Press, Cambridge and

- Key aspects of the Western legal tradition, such as competing jurisdictions and transnational legal science, are being revived. Twentieth century technology and industry have thrown territorial sovereignty back into the boxing ring with other jurisdictions.
- Progress is inevitable after periods of crisis and apocalypse, and law is crucial to the reasonableness of that enterprise. Progress to one person is regress to another. It is vanity to praise one direction and blame the other, without recognising the struggles of either in a systematic, principled manner. An historically accurate constitutional law offers that possibility.
- Cooperation at the national and international levels will not be accomplished by cold legal systems and formalities. Inquisitions and world wars bespeak the passions and shifting spiritualities and ultimate concerns that underlie fundamental legal challenges such as globalization. Legal systems that ignore these passions do so at the peril of missing out on the increased effectiveness of laws that are believed in, rather than simply coerced.
- Legal norms and social authority do not come from one place. Although a proposition may ultimately be 'legal' or 'illegal', it is so by reference to different legal or normative systems that compete for priority in the prevailing discourse of authoritative norms.[104] In William Twining's terms, 'black box' theories of closed legal orders and systems are under challenge.[105]
- Humanity is fickle. To name but a few nationalities, French, English, German, American and Japanese children, formerly the bomb targets of opposing parents, now trade like the best of friends. Although this is nothing new, the scale is. Historical consciousness can help to overcome such vanity and, where appropriate, use peace to capitalize on capitalism.

The radicalness of a development can be measured by the lack of its commonality with things past. Constitutionally, it has been shown, globalization is manifesting significant ancestral traits of the Western legal tradition. Nonetheless, despite the historical commonalities, globalization

---

New York, 1995 at 17. He concludes that there are significant antecedents for diversity in the history of political science (at 184).

104 Along these lines, see Cover R, 'The Supreme Court 1982 Term Foreword: *Nomos* and Narrative' (1983) 97 *Harvard Law Review* 4 at 5, 'Every prescription is insistent in its demand to be located in discourse – to be supplied with history and destiny, beginning and end, explanation and purpose'.

105 See above n 63 at 13. This is a major theme in the collection of essays in Twining, above n 8.

also represents an encounter with the hitherto unseen worldwide destruction of humans and environment, and unprecedented attempts and prospects for turning these lamentable circumstances into something constructive.

A more sophisticated legal science appears to be the principal prospect – a science which might draw upon more and more sources of norms which integrate the technology of ever more complicated legal rules, discourses of morality, and wisdom from historical reflection.[106] In this respect, the multiplicity of phenomena passing under the trendy modern banner of 'globalization' may be considered revolutionary, together with the overall repercussions for law. In the twenty-second century, schoolchildren may well consider these matters in their studies of 'the World Revolution' or 'the Global Revolution'.

---

[106] On the desirability of integrating rules with morality and history, see Berman HJ, 'Toward an Integrative Jurisprudence: Politics, Morality, History' (1988) 76 *California Law Review* 779, reprinted in Berman H, *Faith and Order: The Reconciliation of Law and Religion*, Scholars Press, Atlanta, 1993.

PART II:

GLOBALIZATION AND THE LAWS OF MONEY

Chapter 4

Globalization and International Economic Law

Sundhya Pahuja[*]

It was six men of Indostan
To learning much inclined,
Who went to see the Elephant (Though all of them were blind),
That each by observation, might satisfy his mind.

The First approached the Elephant,
And happening to fall
Against his broad and sturdy side, At once began to bawl:
'God bless me! but the Elephant is very like a wall!'

The Second, feeling of the tusk,
Cried, 'Ho! what have we here?
So very round and smooth and sharp? To me 'tis mighty clear
This wonder of an Elephant, is very like a spear!'

The Third approached the animal,
And happening to take
The squirming trunk within his hands, Thus boldly up and spake:
'I see,' quoth he, 'the Elephant is very like a snake!'

The Fourth reached out an eager hand,
And felt about the knee.
'What most this wondrous beast is like is mighty plain,' quoth he;
'Tis clear enough the Elephant is very like a tree!'

The Fifth who chanced to touch the ear,
Said: 'E'en the blindest man
Can tell what this resembles most; deny the fact who can,
This marvel of an Elephant, is very like a fan!'

The Sixth no sooner had begun
About the beast to grope,
Than, seizing on the swinging tail, that fell within his scope,
'I see,' quoth he, 'the Elephant is very like a rope!'[1]

---

* I wish to thank Richard Joyce for his assistance in the preparation of this chapter.

1 Taken from a poem called, 'The Blind Man and the Elephant' by Saxe JG based on an Indian folk tale from the Panchatantra. The inspiration for the idea of using this parable in the context of globalization came from the preface by Fredric Jameson, in Jameson F and Miyoshi M (eds), *The Cultures of Globalization*, Duke University Press, Durham and London, 1999 at xi.

It is trite to observe that there is currently a proliferation of work dealing with globalization. However, despite this profligate usage, globalization remains an elusive term.[2] Indeed, as a concept it can often seem rather like the elephant in the above parable. Intuitively, we have a sense that there is something there, but depending on where one tries to take hold of it, it seems like a completely different creature. Obviously, we cannot stretch this metaphor too far, for where the elephant does have a definite shape and certain existence, globalization is amorphous and is far from a unified whole. However, despite its slipperiness, in my view it is crucial for a writer attempting to deal critically with globalization to try to articulate what the concept means to her. Without an attention to definitional issues in this instance, I believe that 'globalization' has a tendency to move and morph in meaning, so that any critique presented is so general that the word 'globalization' is really synonymous with nothing more precise than 'contemporary'. Indeed, if as many, including Twining,[3] argue, 'globalization' calls for new approaches, we surely need to consider what the concept means and to which of its particular effects we are referring before we can consider why new approaches are called for. Only after this can we begin to explore what sort of approaches might be useful. This is especially true when we consider that, because of its conceptual sweep, globalization often promotes a tendency to take for granted that which should be the very subject of close questioning.

Thus in this chapter, I wish to consider some of the ways in which we might define globalization and to outline the ways in which my current work is relevant to those interested in the concept of globalization and what it means for the study of law. In teasing out these threads, I will draw comparisons and highlight contrasts with the recent work of William Twining on globalization and legal theory.[4] In particular, I will address two

---

2 A search of the leading law, economics and social sciences databases, including Lexis, Westlaw, ABI/Inform Global and Reuters Archives, reveals that the term 'globalization' seems first to have appeared in journals of economics and management in the mid-to-late 1970s and in law journals from the early 1980s. The term was used rarely until the early 1990s. Since then, its use in academic and journalistic writing has steadily increased, however, this increased use has, perhaps predictably, failed to result in the crystallization of its meaning.

3 See, for example, Twining W, *Globalization and Legal Theory*, Butterworths, Hampshire, 2000, ch 1.

4 For this purpose, the texts I have considered are: Twining (2000), ibid; Twining W, *The Province of Jurisprudence Re-Examined: Problems of Generalization in a Global Context*, Inaugural Julius Stone Address 2000, given at the University of Sydney Law School on 24 August 2000, see Twining, this volume, Chapter 2; William Twining, *Reviving General Jurisprudence*, paper presented at Julius Stone Symposium on

themes which respond to Twining's call for an increased attention to the notion of 'generalizability' and the need to examine norms and concepts which, as he puts it, 'travel well'. In my view, such calls demand an exploration not only of the norms or concepts themselves, but also of the discourses in which they are situated, for the twin discourses of globalization and law are powerful elements in their own right. Each contains entrenched views about the world which exclude and undermine other ways of looking at it. I characterize such a study as the examination of the broader regulatory practices that order globalized practices, within which the operation of formal law takes place.

A study of the regulatory practices at work in any given site, will produce different conclusions in different places. However in this chapter, I will argue that certain themes do emerge. The first is the way in which old oppressions are reproduced in new forms, and second, the normative role played by economic discourse. In this chapter I will discuss the ways in which my work has shown that these themes have played out in various contexts. Each of the examples I will give demonstrates, in a sense, the failure of generalizability in that arguably, it often seems to represent a kind of universal arrogation of the particular, and to that extent, shows that we must exercise considerable caution in any approach to that concept.

Wall, Spear, Snake, Rope, Tree or Fan?

Globalization is an evocative term. It conjures up images of flows of people, of ideas, of information and of capital moving around the world at an ever-increasing rate. To me, its appeal to the popular imagination is largely intuitive because it seems to capture a sense of the 'now', or what distinguishes the imagined realities of today from those of 150, or even 20 years ago. To many, the term is a resonant way of encapsulating myriad variations on what one might call the 'global village' theme along the lines of: Chinese/Italian/Indian woman, lives in Australia, wears a Swiss watch, eats croissants for breakfast, sushi for lunch, Thai food for dinner, watches CNN and the BBC, works for an international firm, travels overseas regularly, does Latin dancing in her spare time and so on.[5] In other understandings, globalization encapsulates the transformations taking place in the global economy. These transformations have several facets including the increased speed of capital movements,[6] technological advances which

---

Globalization and the Universalization of Legal Norms at the University of Sydney Law School on 24 August 2000, copy on file with author.

5 An undercurrent of this can be found in Twining, above n 3, ch 9: Epilogue, particularly section 1 entitled, 'Mr. Palomar in Paolo Alto'.

6 See, for example, Piciotto S, 'Introduction: What Rules for the World Economy' in Piciotto S and Mayne R, *Regulating International Business*, 1999, 1 at 1; Saskia Sassen,

make international communication faster and easier,[7] the new ease and speed with which people and things can move around the globe,[8] and the conjunction of all these factors. And these processes, which in some senses might be called 'global', have local effects, just as local developments impact upon the global.

On one level, I share the view of Anthony Giddens, to whom Twining refers, who argues that, in globalization, what we are seeing is an 'intensification of worldwide social relations which link distant localities in such a way that local happenings are shaped by events occurring many miles away and vice versa'.[9] I also agree with commentators who argue that in considering this intensification, we should pay attention to the distinctions between these two different directions in which the flows move. As Boaventura de Sousa Santos puts it, when we are considering the interaction between the local and the global, we need to distinguish between 'globalized localisms' and 'localized globalisms'.[10] The former refers to local phenomena that have been spread and transplanted, such as McDonald's or CNN. The latter refers to the local effects of what might be called 'global' phenomena such as the establishment of Free Trade or Export Processing Zones in countries such as Mexico or India in response to global trade and capital flows.[11] This distinction is similar to the distinction drawn by Roland Robertson who considers that the dynamic of

---

Cities in a World Economy, 1994 at 2-3; Pettman JJ, 'Globalization and the Gendered Politics of Citizenship' in Yuval-Davis N and Werber P (eds), *Women, Citizenship and Difference*, Zed Books, London, 1999 at 208.

7 Sassen, above n 6 at 65.

8 See, for example, Appadurai A, *Modernity at Large: Cultural Dimensions of Globalization*, University of Minnesota Press, Minnesota, 1997 at 28.

9 Giddens A, *The Consequences of Modernity*, Polity Press, Cambridge, 1991 at 64.

10 Santos B de Sousa, *Toward a New Common Sense: Law, Science and Politics in the Paradigmatic Transition*, Routledge, New York, 1995 at 263.

11 The examples Santos gives include free trade enclaves; deforestation and depletion of natural resources to pay foreign debt; touristic use of historical, religious or natural treasures; ecological dumping; conversion of the object of agriculture from sustainability to export; and the ethnicization of the workforce, ibid at 263. See also, Buchanan R, 'Border Crossings: NAFTA, Regulatory Restructuring, and The Politics of Place' (1995) 2 *Indiana Journal of Global Legal Studies* 371; Coombe R, *The Cultural Life of Intellectual Properties: Authorship, Appropriation and the Law*, Duke University Press, London 1998. Whilst the localized globalism/globalized localism distinction is a useful one to be drawn, we need to be careful that what we consider to be 'globalisms' which are localized are not simply extraversions of a particular wealthier state or group of states.

globalization is 'the twofold process of the particularization of the universal and the universalization of the particular'.[12]

Although these definitions do go part of the way in teasing out some of the particular characteristics of globalization, I have a sense that there is something lacking from such characterizations. This remains the case even if we combine several of them to produce a composite and complex picture. My sense is that what is absent from the picture is an attention to the narratives of globalization. These narratives have come along with this intensification of social relations and are part and parcel of them. That is, I have a sense that the narratives themselves have a performative effect and must therefore be considered to be part of what we might call the phenomenon of globalization itself.[13]

One thing the many characterizations of globalization have in common is that they all have implications for the state. Contemporary economic transformations captured under the rubric of globalization and the many stories we tell about them all call into question the capacity of the state to make laws, the nature and meaning of 'sovereignty' and how governance of the global economy is effected. Some theorists herald and others lament these transformations as bringing about a 'withering away' of the nation state,[14] yet others rejoice in the emancipatory potential of a new global civil society and the potential for new forms of democratic participation, such as internet democracy and culture jamming.[15] However, none of the stories paint a full picture, nor do they capture the complex and often contradictory articulations between states, law and the myriad processes within the global economy. Because of the oversimplifications of the place of the state in the stories we tell about globalization, it is useful to ask questions about what is happening to the state in particular sites. Thus paradoxically, in order usefully to ask how global governance is being effected we must resist the temptation to take only a 'global' approach and focus as well on the

---

12 Robertson R, *Globalization: Social Theory and Global Culture*, Sage, London, 1992 at 177-8.

13 On this question, see generally Gibson-Graham JK, *The End of Capitalism (as we knew it): A Feminist Critique of Political Economy*, Blackwell, Oxford, 1996, and Morris M, *Ecstasy and Economics: American Essays for John Forbes*, emPress, Sydney, 1992.

14 For examples of theorists who herald the withering away of the nation state, see Freidman T, *The Lexus and the Olive Tree*, Farrar, Straus, Giroux, New York, 1999, and Ohmae K, *The Borderless World: Power and Strategy in the Interlinked Economy*, Harper, New York, 1990. For an example of a scholar who is more circumspect, but still considers the withering of the nation state to be a real phenomenon, see Strange S, *The Retreat of the State: The Diffusion of Power in the World Economy*, Cambridge University Press, Cambridge, 1996.

15 For an example of an organization that views itself as utilizing this potential, see 'Adbusters: The Culture Jammers' Website' at <http://adbusters.org/home/>.

different ways in which global processes are being articulated in particular contexts.

The Elephant in a Law Shop?: Globalization and My Work[16]

My work is relevant to those interested in questions of globalization because my focus is on governance and transformations to the global economy in the context of International Economic Organizations. International Economic Organizations such as the World Trade Organization, International Monetary Fund and the World Bank, play a key role within processes of globalization and are important sites which both produce and are shaped by narratives of globalization. The particular questions in which I am interested in relation to International Economic Organizations are questions about what role these organizations play in the ways in which global governance is effected.

This raises the central question of what role law itself is playing in global governance, or, put another way, where law is located in the global economy. In asking this question, we need to go beyond a consideration of formal law (by which I mean law emanating from the state directed at either the domestic or international planes) and ask questions about how things get done, or how things happen, and this means extending our focus from just formal law to what we might call broader 'regulatory practices'.[17] This is somewhat akin to Twining's observation about the specific challenges which globalization presents to traditional legal theory. In particular, Twining points out that globalization 'challenges the idea that the study of law and legal theory can be restricted to two types of legal ordering: municipal state law and public international law…'.[18] I share Twining's conviction that globalization presents such challenges, and I also share his tentative prescriptions (following Santos) about the possibility of legal pluralism helping us to find ways out of the 'black box'.[19] However, as well as what we might call the 'extra-legal' or 'quasi-legal' rules to which our attention is drawn by legal pluralists,[20] we must also pay attention to the broader regulatory practices, including discursive practices,

---

16 This title alludes to the idiomatic expression 'like an elephant in a glass shop', which is an Arabic expression equivalent to our 'bull in a china shop'.

17 I owe the suggestion of this phrase to encompass this idea to Professor Ruth Buchanan, Law School, UBC. For the use of a variation of this term, see Buchanan, above n 11.

18 Twining, Chapter 2 this volume.

19 Twining (2000), above n 3 at 252. See generally, Santos, above n 10.

20 Twining usefully situates legal pluralism within a broader normative pluralism that encompasses all norms, rules and customs in operation to regulate behaviour in a particular site. See Twining (2000), above n 3 at 231-3.

associated with global processes if we are to understand something about the ways in which global governance is effected.

Approaching the Elephant – My Work Thus Far

A study of what is actually happening at the level of the particular, that is a study of the regulatory practices at work in any given situation, will produce different conclusions in different sites. However, certain themes do emerge. Two themes which have emerged in explorations undertaken in my own work have been, first, the ways in which old oppressions are reproduced in new forms, and second, the normative role played by economic discourse. In discussing the ways in which these themes have played out in various contexts, I will focus on three recent projects, one of which was in progress throughout 2001-2002.

Each of the projects engages with formal legal rules of international economic law. However, each also tries to explore the broader regulatory practices which are enabled by, but which extend beyond those rules. After tracing the two themes through the three recent projects, I will briefly outline one final project which brings together some of the ideas explored in this chapter. That project is an upper-level law course I have developed in collaboration with Ruth Buchanan[21] called 'Globalization and the Law' which tries to encourage students to think critically about the way governance is effected in the global economy.

Theme One: White Elephant or Red Herring?

The first theme we find in analyses of the regulatory practices of international economic institutions is the extent to which old forms of oppression reappear in new guises, often clothed in the tales of globalization. The project in which this theme first made an appearance in my own work focuses on the regulatory practices of the International Monetary Fund in the context of the Fund's conditionality[22] and the South.[23] The genesis of this project was an attempt to unpack just one of the

---

21 This project is a course taught simultaneously at Melbourne University and at the University of British Columbia in 2001-2002. Students in each place have real classes, as well as virtual role-play exercises and dialogues in which they collaborate with students in both cities. The project was funded by a *Universitas 21* collaborative multi-media grant through Melbourne University and UBC. The course is being taught in this way for the first time this year.

22 'Conditionality is a portmanteau word that encompasses all the policies that the Fund wishes a member to follow so that it can resolve its problems consistently with the articles'. Gold J, *Conditionality*, IMF Pamphlet Series No 31, Washington, 1979.

23 The binary on which the assumption of 'the South' rests, can, with varying degrees of accuracy, variously be described as South/North, Third World/First World, developing states/developed states, poor countries/rich countries, debtor nations/creditor nations,

series of processes that are intimately connected with processes of global economic integration. In my view, it is particularly productive to juxtapose a study of conditionality with Professor Twining's call for a reinvigoration of the study of the generalizability of norms. This is because conditionality, and the wide-ranging package of legal, social and economic reforms which it delivers to those countries subject to International Monetary Fund intervention could be said, in some senses, to represent an attempt at generalizability on a grand scale.

The project began with the production of a kind of genealogy of the legal development of the Fund's conditionality as it applies to the South.[24] I considered this necessary because of the distance between the Fund's original role and what it has become. At its inception, the Fund was set up to maintain stable exchange rates between industrialized countries. Its role shifted such that it is now associated with development financing and economic restructuring in the Third World.[25] As set out elsewhere,[26] some of the transformations were caused by Fund practice, some by an amendment to the Fund's Articles of Agreement,[27] and some by the responsive actions of other institutions. The transformations both expanded the regulatory and financial functions of the Fund and gradually increased its role in the business of providing finance for the Third World.

However, when I began to trace this genealogy, I discovered that most legal commentators focus on the Mexican debt crisis of 1982 as the

---

industrializing states/industrialized states. Each pair of descriptors is imbued with its own assumptions about the nature of the states on each side of the divide. None of the descriptors can encompass the whole of the matrix of inequalities, political divisions, economic disparities and cultural chasms which divide those we characterize as being on one side of the line or the other. However, they each draw imaginary lines in similar, though not identical, geographical locations. I hesitate to use these terms, not the least because of their geographical inaccuracy. By using them here I do not wish to endorse the construct, however they do capture some sense of where the 'divide' falls. Using this binary conveys some sense, not only of the wealth and poverty on each respective side of the slash, but of the specific American/British/European-ness of the putative 'North'. See generally Head I, *On A Hinge of History: The Mutual Vulnerability of South and North*, University of Toronto Press, Toronto, 1992. Each of these binaries has its inadequacies, however, for the purposes of this essay, I will not engage with the problematics of the various constructs and will use the various terms largely interchangeably.

24 Pahuja S, 'Technologies of Empire: IMF Conditionality and the Reinscription of the North/South Divide' (2000) 13 *Leiden Journal of International Law* 749 at 759-81.

25 Carreau D, 'Why not Merge the International Monetary Fund (IMF) with the International Bank for Reconstruction and Development (World Bank)?' (1994) 62 *Fordham Law Review* 1989 at 1990.

26 Pahuja, above n 24 at 759-81.

27 *Articles of Agreement of the International Monetary Fund*, 22 July 1944, 60 Stat. 1401, T.I.A.S. No. 1501, 2 U.N.T.S. 39 (entered into force 27 December, 1945).

crystallizing moment at which the Fund became involved in the business of providing finance to developing countries.[28] Beginning the story at the moment of the debt crisis tends to disregard the political and economic conditions which gave rise to the Fund's involvement and the extent to which the use of International Monetary Fund conditionality assumed its early importance in relation to sovereign, rather than Fund, lending. Additionally, the prevailing version of the story pays insufficient attention to the shift, which occurred at around the same time, in Fund policy towards the enforcement of conditionality from an emphasis on strict compliance to consultation and surveillance.[29] It is this shift I wish to discuss in relation to the first of our two themes.

Since its inception, the Fund has taken what I have called an 'informational turn'.[30] When the role of the Fund shifted from exchange rate monitor between industrialized states to one that managed the business of financing the South, its tasks also shifted qualitatively and began to revolve around information gathering and surveillance of the South.[31] Making visible this shift signalled a need to adopt methods of analysis that centred on information or knowledge construction.[32] In other words, it suggested a need to pay attention to the discursive functions of Fund conditionality.

Such an analysis differs from mainstream analyses of globalization because the focus here is on a different kind of power. In mainstream analyses, what we often find is an attention to power exercised through economic coercion or by military intervention and so on: what one might call a kind of 'guns and money' approach. Such analyses are important, however my project is somewhat different to these. The type of power I have explored in this project is a more insidious and less obvious kind of power. The form of power I am interested in is the power to create or preclude certain possibilities and practices through the representational frameworks used in the production of information about the South. The particular narratives which are the subject of this project are the inscribed

---

28 See, for example: Lichtenstein C, 'Aiding the Transformation of Economies: Is the Fund's Conditionality Appropriate to the Task?' (1994) 62 *Fordham Law Review* 1943; Malloy M, 'Shifting Paradigms: Institutional Roles in a Changing World' (1994) 62 *Fordham Law Review* 1911; Carreau, above n 25.

29 Pahuja, above n 24.

30 Ibid at 759-81.

31 In my argument, this shift happened in three ways. The first was the way in which the IMF was drawn into lending to the South, the second was the shift in IMF policy relating to the enforcement of the conditions attached to its finance facilities and the third was the shift in the juridical nature of the Fund's powers. Ibid at 759-81.

32 Ibid. See also, Ericson R and Haggerty K, *Policing the Risk Society*, University of Toronto Press, Toronto, 1997, ch 4.

products of the International Monetary Fund, produced in the exercise of its information gathering and surveillance functions in relation to the Third World, and more particularly, those produced in response to the Asian Debt Crisis.[33]

So, I began by trying to map some of the representational frameworks operating in the inscribed products of the Fund. And in this process, the first of our themes became apparent. That is, many echoes emerged within these contemporary texts of some of the particular attitudes or fears about the Third World that informed, and to some extent facilitated and justified, the colonial project. In turn, the discursive mechanisms deployed in response to these fears reproduced those used during moments of overt imperialism of North over South.

The resonances lie in two particular fears in relation to the Third World which underlie both International Monetary Fund discourse and those representational practices and mechanisms identified by post-colonial scholars as in existence during moments of imperialism.[34] These fears may be characterized respectively as the 'fear of entry', and the 'fear of exit'.[35] I have described them in detail elsewhere, but it is clear that both these fears hinge on the fear of difference.[36] The existence of those fears generates particular discursive mechanisms, or technologies, which are directed at allaying the fears. In turn, the discursive structures in place are shaped by the existence of the fears. Thus arises the highly problematic situation in which the range of any outcomes that might be possible as a result of Fund intervention in the Third World is shaped largely by anxieties about that world. Because these discursive mechanisms resonate with certain mechanisms employed by the former colonial powers to govern the 'oriental' colonies, I have called these discursive strategies 'technologies of colonial governance'.[37]

In addition to the problematic extension of the colonial continuum into the post-colonial era, the discursive strategies used by the Fund also reveal two other features of the Third World which are perceived as problematic

---

33 The first part of the article is a genealogy of the conditionality of the Fund which traces the inception and expansion of the Fund's information gathering and surveillance powers, which in fact were not part of the Fund's original brief: Pahuja, above n 24 at 759-81.

34 See, for example, Guha R, 'The Prose of Counter-Insurgency' in Guha R and Spivak GC (eds), *Selected Subaltern Studies*, Oxford University Press, New York, 1988 at 45.

35 Pahuja, above n 24 at 784.

36 These seemingly contradictory fears resonate with Catherine Dauvergne's engaging insight about the way in which liberalism's tendency toward increasing inclusion necessarily produces a commensurately enlarged field of exclusion. See Dauvergne, Chapter 8 this volume.

37 Pahuja, above n 24 at 796-803.

by the First World. Because these features are perceived to be problematic, they also require discursive strategies to accommodate them. Paradoxically, it appears that both of these problems arise from what might be termed the 'post' in post-colonial. The two problems are the problem of sovereign equality and the problem of democracy. But even though these problems are new, the technologies used to manage them are again highly resonant with those used in the colonial era.[38]

Because the strategies are responding to the fear of difference and are attempting to normalize that difference, the consequence of the first of our themes, that of old forms of oppression reasserting themselves in new guises, produces a highly problematic outcome. Using these technologies of colonial governance to manage the Third World precludes the possibility of real difference, and limits the range of possible outcomes of International Monetary Fund intervention in the Third World and in particular, limits the Fund to imagining and producing only a particular kind of international economic order. Thus in this, we find an instance in which we see played out, the power to create possibility, or perhaps more importantly to preclude possibility. In this example, what is precluded is the possibility of difference, and in particular, difference in economic, social and political models.

The constraints for the Third World inherent in the imposition of Western epistemologies made visible by examining the discursive practices of the International Monetary Fund leads me to be cautious about Twining's responses to globalization and his call for an increased attention to generalizability to find those norms and concepts which 'travel well'. In this respect, I am reminded of Foucault's characterization of the 'technique of travelling' as 'a political enterprise of exercising power and an enterprise of curiosity and acquisition of knowledge …'.[39] Particularly challenging to me is Twining's suggestion that we revisit 'the canon' to produce an appropriate conceptual tool box for jurists to grapple with questions of globalization. For example, as I understand it one of the key challenges he identifies is the need to construct a conceptual framework and metalanguage of legal theory that can transcend legal cultures.[40] Whilst this does raise some useful possibilities, in that it might steer mainstream Anglo-American and Australian jurisprudence away from an overt rejection of the sustained study of other legal orders, it also suggests the possibility

---

38 Ibid at 803-10. See also Pahuja S, 'Postcolonial Approaches to International Economic Law' (2000) 13 *The Hague Yearbook of International Law* 123.

39 Foucault M, 'Truth and Juridical Forms' (1996) 2 *Social Identities* 327. I owe this reminder to Fitzpatrick P, *Modernism and the Grounds of Law*, Cambridge University Press, Cambridge, 2001 at 163.

40 Twining (2000), above n 3 at 53.

of a new, very subtle form of imperialism in that perhaps we would be reconstructing our own eyes, better to gaze upon the other.

This is particularly worrisome when such a call goes hand in hand with the processes of globalization which Twining himself leaves largely unmentioned, such as the dominance of the West in International Economic Institutions which have the power to reconstruct economic systems in the South,[41] the massive indebtedness of the South which facilitates this, the growing inequality of wealth between North and South and the terms of trade between South and North.[42] In a way, highlighting the positive, intercultural exchange aspects of globalization and then arguing that we need in a sense, a legal theory to go with them, carries hidden dangers which cannot be revealed unless we also focus on the huge inequalities which are also part of these processes. I agree with Professor Twining about the need to develop tools for comparing both law and lawyers in a sociological sense across cultures,[43] but again, I am wary that the appropriate place to find such tools is in the canon, or that such a study can proceed in the absence of an attention to the discursive power of the narratives in which those conceptual tools are embedded.

Professor Twining spends little time considering non-mainstream theoretical traditions such as feminist jurisprudence. He points to the fact that critical legal theory for example, is parochial in its own right (in that it focuses entirely on the United States). However, what is interesting to me is that the 'alternative' theories to mainstream jurisprudence could, in a sense, be said to have been generated in response to the exclusions in mainstream theory.[44] This is certainly true of feminist theories, many of which would argue that mainstream theory has played a critical role in perpetuating and maintaining gender inequality.[45] Therefore, if one is aiming to '[meet] the

---

41 See, for example, Chossudovsky M, *The Globalization of Poverty: Impacts of IMF and World Bank Reforms*, Zed Books, London, 1997.

42 For a discussion of the indebtedness of the South, see ibid. For a discussion of the inequality in trade, see Brown BS, 'Developing Countries in the International Trade Order' (1994) 14 *Northern Illinois University Law Review* 347. For a discussion of the impact of the North's control of intellectual property rights, see Shiva V, *Stolen Harvest: The Hijacking of the Global Food Supply*, South End Press, Cambridge, 2000.

43 Twining (2000), above n 3 at 54.

44 There are numerous examples of this phenomenon which include: Crenshaw K et al (eds), *Critical Race Theory*, The New Press, New York, 1995; Williams P, *The Alchemy of Race and Rights*, Harvard University Press, Cambridge, Massachusetts, 1991; Naffine N, *Law and the Sexes: Explorations in Feminist Jurisprudence*, Allen and Unwin, Sydney, 1990.

45 Again, there are many examples of this concept. See, for example, Boyd S (ed), *Challenging the Public/Private Divide: Feminism, Law and Public Policy*, University of Toronto Press, Toronto, 1997; Naffine, above n 44.

challenges of globalization'[46] and respond to changes in the global economy which effectively bring more diversity into our lives, why return to a canon from which so many have shown that they are excluded? I would argue that in this context, globalization is less a break in a continuum than it is part of it, and theories which pay attention to difference are the ones to which we should turn in the first instance to equip our evolving conceptual tool boxes.

Theme Two – The Power of Economic Discourse

The second theme that emerges in a study of the regulatory practices of international economic institutions is the normative role played by economic discourse in the 'rules' of international economic law. Economic discourse is central to almost all popular narratives about globalization. One site and body of rules that is particularly shaped by economic discourse is the World Trade Organization and the rules of international trade. This influence is key in the ways in which trade rules play a role in global governance and is visible in two of my recent projects, the second of which is work in progress.

The power of economic discourse is perhaps best illustrated in the first project that considers the ways in which economics, as part of dominant narratives of globalization, animates the operation of international trade rules to produce certain normative outcomes.[47] In particular, this work explores the way in which the relationship between trade law and what might be called 'social concerns' is mediated within trade discourse. That is, the way in which the relationship between trade law and human rights, or trade rules and environmental rules is constructed to exclude human rights or the environment from the purview of international trade.[48]

The project starts from the observation that human rights, labour standards and environmental concerns are continually excluded from the scope of international trade law. It asks why, despite ongoing attempts to link human rights and environmental standards to trade agreements, these rules continue to operate in 'two solitudes'[49] with few inroads being made by those promoting 'social' concerns even though the link between international trade and the conditions in which many people live and work

---

[46] Twining (2000), above n 3 at 89.

[47] Pahuja, S, 'Trading Spaces: Locating Sites for Challenges within International Trade Law' (2000) 14 *Australian Feminist Law Journal* 38.

[48] See ibid.

[49] Langille B, 'Labour Standards In The Globalized Economy' in Segenberger W and Campbell D (eds), *International Labour Standards And Economic Interdependence*, International Institute for Labour Studies, Geneva, 1994 at 330.

is clear.[50] My conclusion is that one of the key processes by which political contestation is excluded from trade discourse is through that field's links to economics. Because of the way in which economic discourse is privileged in comparison to other, for example political, discourses,[51] the myth that regulation is advisable only to the extent necessary to remove 'market distortions' is able to continue. In addition, the depoliticising effect of trade law's characterization as largely economic is compounded by trade law's centrality to globalization discourse and myths of inevitability that are frequently associated with that story.[52]

---

50 We know, for example, that trade liberalization is directly related to the appalling work conditions of women in clothing and footwear sweat shops all over the developing world, see for example, 'The Debate over Sweatshop Monitoring', *Journal of Commerce*, Tuesday March 4 1997; to women in the maquilladoras on the US/Mexican border, see for example, Human Rights Watch Women's Rights Project, *Mexico: No Guarantees, Sex Discrimination in Mexico's Maquiladora Sector*, Human Rights Watch, New York, August 1996; to children in Huandong Province in China making toys for the Western market, see, for example, Chan A and Senser R, 'China's Troubled Workers' (1997) 76 *Foreign Affairs* 104. The list goes on. Stories about conditions of workers in the Third World and the interconnectedness of this with trade appear almost daily in the international news. In addition, one source of much information on the conditions of workers in the Third World is the Third World Network. Some of the pieces produced by the Third World Network include; Raghavan C, 'Asian female migrant workers require protection, says ILO'; Rajalakshmi TK, 'Sita and her daughters: Women Workers at an Indian Export Processing Zone'; Sakanond B, 'Double Whammy for Women'; Daorueng P and Yamin K, 'Women: Last in, first out'; Oliveros T, 'Impact of New World Trade Regime on Peasant Women in the Philippines'. All of these articles are available at <http://www.twnside.org.sg/title>. See also; Williams P, 'Disorder in the House: The New World Order and the Socioeconomic Status of Women' in James SM and Busia A (eds), *Theorizing Black Feminisms: The Visionary Pragmatism of Black Women*, Routledge, New York, 1993 at 118.

51 Brodie J, 'Shifting the Boundaries: Gender and the Process of Restructuring' in Bakker I (ed), *The Strategic Silence: Gender and Economic Policy*, Zed Books in Association with the North South Institute, London, 1994 at 56. Ben Fine has argued that 'the relationship between economics and other social sciences is currently undergoing a change. Economics is aggressively seeking to colonize the other social sciences by extending its methods to them, treating non-economic or non-market relations as if they were economic'. Fine B, 'Neither the Washington Nor the Post-Washington Consensus: An Introduction' in Fine B, Lapavitsas C and Pincus J (eds), *Development Policy in the Twenty first Century: Beyond the Post-Washington Consensus*, Routledge, New York, 2001 at 8.

52 Discursively, I would argue that the depoliticizing effect of international trade law's characterization as economic is compounded by the way in which globalization is presented as inevitable; political decisions having been replaced by economic ones, see for example; Saul JR, *The Unconscious Civilization*, Penguin, Melbourne, 1997 at 2. An example of this is found in a speech given by British Prime Minister Tony Blair: 'You have no choice, this is inevitable ... These forces of change driving the future don't stop at national boundaries, don't respect tradition. They wait for no one and no nation. They

As part of this first project, I urge those interested in bringing social concerns into the trade debate to draw tools from feminist theories directed at bringing the politics back into the private sphere.[53] In my view, we need to find spaces within trade theory to challenge the myth of regulatory normalcy that posits that there is a baseline norm from which all market regulation departs. This would open up trade law to political contestation, so that those involved are at least forced to acknowledge and defend the politics inherent in particular kinds of trade regimes. I argue that one such site is the subsidies debate which cannot really be usefully conducted without a recognition that the entire regulatory framework of a state can be thought of as either a positive or negative subsidy depending on how it compares to another state with which it trades.[54]

My second project on the rules of international trade in which we see the power of economic discourse is being developed at the same time as this chapter. In a way, it is a kind of 'flip side' of the first project. In the first project, I considered the ways in which narratives of globalization, and in particular the economic myths associated with those stories, shape the normative effects of trade rules. In contrast, this second project builds on that idea, but also explores the idea that trade rules themselves have normative effects beyond their apparent legal scope because of their discursive functions. In other words, this project asks questions not only about the way in which trade rules govern the resolution of disputes, but also about the way in which they construct their subjects. The form in which these questions play out is in considering how concepts of sovereignty are constructed in the decisions of the panel and appellate bodies of the World Trade Organization.

The World Trade Organization, like other International Economic Organizations, is a site that is deeply implicated in complex ways in narratives of globalization. It is particularly relevant to my broader project about global governance for two reasons. The first is that there is a particular kind of normativity imbricated within the 'rules' of international

---

are universal'. Quoted in Bunting M, 'The New Cold War Comes to Seattle', *The Age*, 30 November 1999 at 15.

53 Pahuja, above n 47 at 44.

54 Ibid at 47-9. For example, if a state were to subsidize the cost of cars by direct grants to the automotive industry, that would clearly be a positive subsidy. However, if the automotive industry was excused from complying with occupational health and safety rules, or if taxpayers were to bear the environmental costs associated with automotive manufacturing processes, this could amount to a similar financial benefit to the company and have a similar effect on the cost of the cars. It would also be a (negative) subsidy compared with the costs incurred by a putatively efficient competitor, which had to bear its own environmental costs, or bear a certain standard of occupational health and safety costs.

trade law which is consonant or sympathetic with neo-liberal economic theory.[55] The second is that the World Trade Organization Dispute Settlement Body is increasingly accepted as a forum in which certain kinds of conflicts between states are negotiated.[56]

What we find then in the shape of the dispute settlement body is a strong and strengthening body where an increasing range of conflicts is being negotiated, including conflicts between state 'sovereignties' and more importantly, between differing conceptions of sovereignty. And because of the particular kind of normativity embedded in trade rules, what this means is that the dispute settlement body presents us with a site in which the notion of sovereignty is being remade in a way which, in my view, is consonant with the perceived needs of the market.

However, the context of this project also takes us back to an exploration of our first theme which is to consider the different and competing ways in which global flows are described and constructed and the ways in which these narratives create or deny possibilities for democracy or justice or indeed, reproduce or transform old forms of oppression. In this context, it is not only the normativities embedded within trade rules which result in sovereignty being constructed in a particular way, but also the way in which doctrines of sovereignty have been constructed in the past, or have come into being. Tracing such constructions reveals that the delimitation of sovereignty according to market need, or if you like, this 'economization' of sovereignty, is not new for the South, but is new for the North.

Certain commentators have argued that the colonial encounter was essential to the production of the modern notion of sovereignty.[57] Scholars such as Antony Anghie compellingly delineate the development of doctrines of sovereignty, and reveal the extent to which sovereignty doctrines were imbricated with the 'civilizing mission' of colonialism.[58] Such work then goes on to consider the ways in which this civilizing mission continues to inform both doctrines of sovereignty, and international law more broadly and to ask what impact this continuum has on the

---

55 See, for example, Tarullo D, 'Logic Myth and the International Economic Order' (1985) 26 *Harvard International Law Journal* 533.

56 See for example, Abbott F, 'Challenges Facing the WTO from the US Perspective', paper given at the First Joint Meeting of the Australia/New Zealand Society of International Law and the American Society of International Law, Sydney, 26 June 2000.

57 See for example, Anghie A, 'Finding the Peripheries: Sovereignty and Colonialism in Nineteenth Century International Law' (1999) 40 *Harvard International Law Journal* 1.

58 Ibid.

South.[59] What I am doing is building on the insights of such scholars about the discursive functions of sovereignty doctrines in relation to the South to ask questions about the effects of such constructions on the North.

The steps in this argument are as follows. We begin with the insights outlined above, that doctrines of sovereignty have served to construct, and continue to construct the South. As well as being deeply involved with the civilizing mission, this construction, according to some scholars, has taken a notably economic turn, finding its limits in the needs of commerce.[60] We then turn to the insight of post-colonial scholars more generally that in the European epistemology, self is always defined by reference to the other.[61] The question I am then interested in asking is, what effect does the construction of the other (the South) have on construction of the 'self' (the North), in the context of the production of sovereignty?[62] In other words, if we accept the fact that sovereignty has been constructed in particular ways as a result of the colonial confrontation and the need to contain and govern the South, and we also accept that those constructions continue to be imbricated in contemporary notions of sovereignty, then what effects does that have on the North? These effects arise in the context of the North being subjected to dispute resolution proceedings that involve constructing or interpreting sovereignty. From my preliminary exploration of this question, I would suggest that what we can see is partly an instance of the ways in which the construction of the other will come to have its own performative effects on the possibilities for the ongoing construction of self.[63]

One key aspect of this project that I have just begun to consider is what the implications of this might be. This again takes us back to our first theme that is to consider whether one aspect of globalization is the repackaging of old products. In this case, the 'old products' in question are certain technologies of colonial governance that are reproduced through the

---

59 See, for example, Thomas C, 'Neo-Victorianism and the Ideology of Globalization', paper given at *New Scholarship in International Public and Private Law*, workshop organized jointly by the Association of the Alumni of the Academy and the European Research Center of Harvard Law School, The Hague, 22 & 23 July, 2000. Copy on file with the author.

60 Work currently being done in this area includes; Beard J, *The Art of Development: Law and Order in the Global Economy* (working title), PhD thesis in progress, Law School, University of Melbourne.

61 This is of course, somewhat of an oversimplification. For greater detail on this point, see Prakash G, 'Introduction' in Prakash G (ed), *After Colonialism*, Princeton University Press, Princeton, New Jersey, 1995 at 3.

62 On the question generally of how the construction of other effects the construction of self, see Bhabha H, *The Location of Culture*, Routledge, London, 1994 at 1-9.

63 Ibid.

workings of the World Trade Organization. However, what is new is that those technologies may now be being reproduced in relation to the North.

My approach to this question has been to begin to undertake close readings of panel and appellate body decisions of the World Trade Organization Dispute Settlement Body in order to analyze the ways in which sovereignty is framed by these bodies. Initial readings of the 'Shrimp/Turtle' case,[64] a case in which the defendant state was the United States, reveal that in that case, the approach the panel took towards the notion of sovereignty was one which the bounds of sovereignty were defined and confined by the needs of the market.[65] As I have already mentioned, this seems to be part of that continuum in which sovereignty may always have been constrained to some extent by the needs of commerce, but this ruling also signals a shift in which the sovereignty of the North may be being economized by the World Trade Organization in the same way that the sovereignty of the Third World was economized even as it was ostensibly given at the end of the imperial period. This to me illustrates the idea that the construction of 'the other', and concepts such as sovereignty through which that construction occurred have, in a sense, come back to haunt the North. So, in a way the oppressive quality embedded in notions of sovereignty is reasserting itself in an unexpected context.

We see here the conjunction of the two themes outlined at the start of this chapter as coming out of an exploration of the regulatory practices of International Economic Organizations. It may be that one theme assists and reinforces the other. In relation to the discursive functions of International Monetary Fund conditionality raised above, the re-emergence of the technologies of colonial governance is facilitated by the way in which those technologies are imbricated in economic discourse and globalization's most powerful myths about development and progress.[66] In the second example, in the context of the World Trade Organization, the dominance of economic discourse facilitates the re-emergence of technologies of colonial governance, even in unexpected contexts, such as the (re)construction of sovereignty in relation to the states in the North.

---

64 *United States: Import Prohibition of Certain Shrimp and Shrimp Products*, WT/DS58/AB/R, 12 October 1998.

65 Pahuja S, 'Embedded Normativities and the Dispute Settlement Body of the WTO', paper given at the First Joint Meeting of the Australia/New Zealand Society of International Law and the American Society of International Law, Sydney, 26 June 2000, copy on file with author.

66 See, for example, Tarullo, above n 55.

Conclusions: The Elephant in the Classroom

In conclusion, I wish to raise one final project which is a course taught simultaneously at the University of Melbourne, Australia and the University of British Columbia, Canada in which students in the two places each have real classes but also have virtual classes and communication facilitated via the web. The course, called Globalization and the Law, was designed jointly by me and Professor Ruth Buchanan of the University of British Columbia[67] and the objective of the course is to encourage students to think critically about processes of globalization and their relevance to law.

In a sense, what we are trying to do is encourage students to look for, or locate, law in the global context. One aspect of this is a consideration of the changing role of the nation state in the production of law. If we are looking for possibilities for regulation, from controlling migratory flows to capital flows, to corporate conduct, to currency trading neither domestic nor international law paints a complete picture of the ways in which these things are, or might be, regulated. Indeed, the dichotomy habitually drawn between these two sites of law making is often a false one and ignores the fact that both national and international law are both focused only on the state as a site of law making, the international plane being an extraversion of the national.[68] Because of the paucity of this picture, we need to ask more carefully where law making takes place and how it takes effect. As I mentioned earlier in this chapter, the answer to this question is often different and contradictory depending on where one looks. This variety of possibilities means that we need to use a number of case studies to consider what regulatory practices may be in operation at any particular site. In considering those practices, we need to go beyond simply looking at formal or state-based law.

This endeavour is not dissimilar to Twining's project of encouraging students to question what they mean by law through the exercises outlined in *Globalization and Legal Theory* entitled 'Normative and Legal Pluralism and Non-state Law' and 'What Counts as a Legal Order'. In these exercises, students are forced to trouble or 'problematize' what they understand to be meant by 'law' and to take a broader view of the regulatory frameworks which can be classed as forms of law or legal

---

67 The course is based loosely on an earlier course of Professor Buchanan's design called 'The Regulatory Impact of Globalization' offered at the University of British Columbia.

68 Or indeed, the national being a necessary introversion of the international. On this point, see generally, Fitzpatrick, above n 39. Twining also makes this point in his recognition that international exchanges came first and necessitated the creation of nation state. Twining (2000), above n 3 at 7.

ordering. Though the projects are alike in this respect, Professor Buchanan and I go beyond a consideration of the extra legal or quasi-legal forms embraced by legal pluralists to consider other regulatory practices at play such as discursive practices. We also wish to encourage students to ask what effect the stories of globalization have on the ways in which global governance takes place.

The course is constructed in modules, and each module focuses both on asking not only what the law is in a given context, but also on how things actually get done. Each module contains one or two case studies focused on sites of particular relevance to global governance. Examples of modules include:

- Module 3: Trade and Investment Agreements as Regulatory Regimes;
- Module 4: People and Borders: Labour and Migration in the Global Economy;
- Module 5: Reinscribing the North/South Divide; and
- Module 6: Contesting Globalization.

In order to illustrate the method followed in the course, I will outline Module 3, on trade and investment agreements, which touches on some of the issues already raised in this Chapter.

In Module 3 we ask students to focus on the rules governing trade disputes in international law. As well as looking at the rules themselves, we also ask them to consider the shifting and complex relationships between international legal orders and domestic legal systems. We try to unpack with students the understandings that underpin these agreements and legal rules. In this module, we do this by looking at two case studies. The first is the Shrimp/Turtle decision of the World Trade Organization dispute resolution body,[69] the second is the Metalclad decision heard under the investor protection provisions of the North American Free Trade Agreement.[70] In each of these cases, the locus of decision making, is moved from the local to the international because of the agreement. However, as Twining points out, there is no neat, consistent nesting of hierarchies[71] being produced by global transformations and if we look elsewhere, we see different alliances arising between regional, national and international levels of governance.

After a consideration of the relevant rules and the relationships between the national and international forms of ordering in this example, we then lead students to consider the ways in which the disputes are transformed

---

69 Above n 64.

70 *Metalclad Corporation v United Mexican States* (ICSID Case No. ARB(AF)/97/1), 30 August 2000.

71 Twining (2000), above n 3 at 231.

when they cross national boundaries and become disputes subject to the relevant international body. This point relates to one of the themes drawn out earlier in this chapter about the relevance of economic discourse. In this instance, this relates to the ways in which environmental disputes, for example, about the questions of dumping toxic waste in a particular area, or conservation methods aimed at protecting endangered sea turtles are transformed into economic disputes about investor protection (Metalclad) or non-tariff barriers to trade (Shrimp/Turtle).

These examples show that the bare rules themselves provide us with little information about how a dispute will be resolved in a given instance, and in turn, even less about the role played by a particular international regime in the ways in which global governance is effected. In order to determine how such disputes will be resolved, or what role a particular organization plays in global governance, we need to tease out the understandings, assumptions and underpinnings in operation in relation to a particular regime. In the constitution of these underpinnings, stories of globalization also have a part to play and we must also pay attention to those narratives and their effects.

Using this case-by-case approach, we help students to unpack various regulatory practices at work in the global economy. This helps to give them a sense of the economic transformations taking place, where the continuities with old practices and oppressions might lie and how to find the place of law in processes of globalization. As discussed above, these questions not only inform the course, but also play a central role in my own approach to questions of globalization.

Thus we share much in common with Professor Twining, his understandings of globalization and the transformative effects processes commonly united under that rubric potentially have for the processes of law and law making. The major point of departure is that we urge scholars in the area to go beyond asking questions about the possibility of finding generalizable norms and concepts, or those which 'travel well', to considering the discourses of which current or proposed laws (as usefully reconceived in broader terms by Twining and Santos) form part. In our view, any such study needs to be attended by an exploration of what normativities might be embedded within those concepts and laws and what possibilities those normativities might produce and preclude.

Chapter 5

Networks, Norms and the Nation State: Thoughts on Pluralism and Globalized Securities Regulation

*Dimity Kingsford Smith**

Introduction

Today we often refer to crashes in the financial markets as a 'financial market meltdown'. This metaphor got a lot of play in the year 2000 crash of 'dot.com stocks' and in the aftermath of 11 September 2001. The implications of both of these events reverberated from Wall Street throughout the exchanges of the rest of the world. Using the metaphor of nuclear catastrophe in connection with financial crashes is, however, more than just another example of market hype; rather, it captures a number of purposes I have in writing this chapter.

The first is to point to a relationship already noticed by others between the interconnectedness of contemporary financial markets, and recent thought on the nature of 'risk'. Worldwide financial markets are really networks of national markets, each interconnected and capable of transferring instability (even locally caused) to the others. This interconnection is simultaneously a transnational phenomenon, and an interconnection between markets in different types of financial instruments. Like a nuclear accident, a dip in one market can set off a chain reaction in others, the repercussions of which it is difficult to predict. Writers on globalization have identified this interconnection of man manufactured risk, spreading in a web from a local incident, as a leading feature of the globalization phenomenon.[1] As David Nelken puts it, globalization is 'a further stage in the lifting out of social relations from local contexts of

---

* I am grateful to Caroline Bradley, Frances Hill, Michael Froomkin and other participants at the Law and Society Association meeting in Miami, Florida in 2000, for their comments. Also to William Twining for his comments at the Julius Stone Institute Symposium in 2001 and to Ian Enright, Catherine Dauvergne and anonymous referee for their thoughts on this final version of the chapter. I am also indebted to Jade Harkness and Elaine Miller for research assistance.

1 Giddens A, *Runaway World*: *How Globalization is Reshaping Our Lives*, Routledge, New York, 2000 at 22-32.

interaction and their restructuring across time and space through symbolic tokens such as money, media and expert systems'.[2]

This distribution of risk has been given as one of the justifications for the development of 'networks' of norms, often cast in the form of principles, which are formulated and promoted by transnational regulatory organizations such as the International Organisation of Securities Commissions (IOSCO). These networks of financial regulation exist in the zone between international law (that is, between nation states, strictly speaking) and national legal systems – they are best characterized as transnational, though occasionally they may be accurately described as truly global. By global, I mean that the networks have both formal and substantive reach across the globe, rather than operating only across borders between actors in a relatively small number of countries. Braithwaite and Drahos, in analysis and theory building at the end of their enormous empirical inquiry of global business regulation, argue 'that the globalization of regulation has ushered in the rule of principles ... The rule of principles (meaning that regulatory contests are fought at the level of principles) is, as we have demonstrated, the empirical reality of global business regulation'.[3] So the second purpose of this piece is to explore the institutional origins and the legal nature and effect of the network of principles issued by transnational financial regulatory organizations, with particular focus on IOSCO.

Although these networks of regulatory principles are influential, they are by no means the only norms acting on securities intermediaries and customers in the course of cross-border transactions. Such intermediaries and customers are also acted upon by a myriad of other norms: national laws, some with extraterritorial effect; rules of professional and industry associations; clauses of standard form contracts invariably used in such transactions; and associated practices. How, in a world of such legal complexity, with such interaction of rules, principles and other norms, is it possible to sketch a framework to understand this polyphonic legal environment? How do all these norms of various provenances relate to each other? What does it say about regulation in the global age that some of these transnational norms seem to have no visible means of support from the authority of either states or international law strictly understood?

Legal pluralism supplies a framework from which to make a start in answering these questions. Legal pluralism is a view of law that takes

---

2 Nelken D, 'The Globalization of Crime and Criminal Justice' (1997) 50 *Contemporary Legal Problems* 251 at 258.

3 Braithwaite J and Drahos P, *Global Business Regulation*, Cambridge University Press, Cambridge and New York, 2000 at 531.

account of principles, practices and other law-like patterns of behaviour that do not emanate from legal institutions or processes. It recognizes the wide variety of pressures or influences that can direct behaviour into regular and identifiable patterns that are functionally similar to law in their operation and effect. Legal pluralism also accepts that rules, principles and other norms emanate from other sources than the state, and that the participation of the state is not essential for the creation of law-like relations. In other words, pluralism extends the gaze of law to a wider field than rules authorized by the state.

By raising the social fact of the many types of norms that affect social behaviour, pluralism invites the question: 'How do all these different norms inter-relate?' What effect do informal rules and patterns of behaviour have on state law and vice versa? Although I employ it in a context dramatically different from that in which it was originally observed, I suggest that Boa de Sousa Santos' concept of 'interlegality'[4] helps to explain interactions of different types of norms in many contexts, including cross-border securities regulation. 'Interlegality' provides a concept through which to identify the nature and effect of interrelationships in the transnational world. For example, William Twining suggests that interlegality might be explored through identifying different types of norms (principles, rules, practices, etc.), 'agglomerations of norms' (systems, codes, etc.) and examining what already well-considered intersections might add, for example between rules and principles, primary and secondary rules.[5] Of course, no framework can provide all the answers. But the following thoughts on pluralism and globalized securities regulation identify some of the power effects which may be at work in the creation of norms of transnational or global securities regulation. They also reveal possible difficulties with the legitimacy of transnational securities regulation and the need to consider wider representation in the creation of such norms. So a third purpose of this piece is to examine, through the prism of legal pluralism, the operation, nature and effect of the wide variety of norms which may influence a transnational securities transaction.

I have used the word 'global' in the title and often throughout. This is more to signal the connection of the issues I raise with the concerns addressed by recent legal and socio-legal writing on the globalization phenomenon, than to suggest that securities regulation has a truly global reach. The great disparities between economies in the development of financial systems make it more accurate to speak of cross-border securities

4 Santos B de Sousa, *Toward a New Common Sense: Law, Science, and Politics in the Paradigmatic Transition*, Routledge, New York, 1995.

5 Twining W, *Globalisation and Legal Theory*, Butterworths, London, 2000.

transactions as transnational.[6] As regulation follows the money, most securities regulation will in practical terms also be transnational, although on paper it may appear to be truly global. Often global financial markets are referred to as if they are inevitable and ubiquitous. They are certainly not inevitable but are partially the creations of the deregulatory policies of nation states. They are also not ubiquitous. When even telephony is not ubiquitous, it is not sensible to speak of securities markets, which rely so heavily on telecommunications and information technology, as global. Even in countries like Australia, which have embraced technology quickly and where share ownership is widespread, cross-border trading is carried out in urban enclaves by relatively few people. As in most arenas, globalization is more fragmented here, too, than is often apparent. As Giddens puts it, '[globalization] is highly uneven in its consequences'.[7] It is important to recognize just how fragmented and uneven it is, since the empirical evidence about its reach is very thin indeed. The operation of cross-border securities and financial regulation is no exception.

Globalization of Systemic Risk and Market Meltdown

Although a relative newcomer to the world of ideas, globalization has already spawned a huge body of literature spanning sociology and social theory, economics and political science, international affairs and latterly, law and legal theory.[8] Of particular relevance to regulation of financial markets is the intersection of ideas on globalization with those surrounding the notion of living in the 'risk society'.[9] Giddens' idea that globalization is 'an intensification of worldwide social relations which link distant localities in such a way that local happenings are shaped by events occurring many miles away and vice versa'[10] suggests that we are exposed to risks from which in the past we were insulated because of time and space. But risk is not an unalloyed menace; it is very often accompanied by

---

6 For example, although the members of IOSCO represent 99 per cent of the world's capitalization and its principles are therefore on paper truly global, in practice there is little information about the degree to which these are implemented, and in any case the vast majority of cross-border securities business is done between actors in New York, London, Frankfurt, Paris, Tokyo, Toronto and Sydney.

7 Giddens, above n 1 at 4, 15.

8 See, for example, Braithwaite and Drahos, above n 3; Twining, above n 5; Giddens, above n 1.

9 Giddens A, *The Consequences of Modernity*, Polity Press, Cambridge, 1990; Beck U, *Risk Society: Towards a New Modernity*, Sage, London and Newbury Park, California, 1992; Power M, *The Audit Society: Rituals of Verification*, Oxford University Press, Oxford and New York, 1997; Lupton D (ed), *Risk and Sociocultural Theory*, Cambridge University Press, Cambridge and New York, 1999.

10 Giddens, above n 9 at 64.

dramatic innovation, and therefore its regulation is always a difficult balancing act. As Giddens again explains, 'risk here is double-edged. Risk is closely connected to innovation. It isn't always to be minimized; the active embrace of financial and entrepreneurial risk is the very driving force of the globalizing economy'.[11]

The revolution in communications, along with the liberalization of national regulation of financial markets, has resulted in an explosion of trading between market centres in mainly Western countries, linking economies and currencies. As Harvey points out, communications have contributed to 'that process of annihilation of space through time that has always lain at the centre of capitalism's dynamic ...'.[12] It is as a result of this 'annihilation of space through time' that collapses and crashes in a market centre in one country are transmitted to markets in other parts of the region or other countries. Trading between markets occurs so constantly, and so quickly, that information about events that initially involve mainly local actors quickly assumes significance in other markets. 'We face risk situations that no one in previous history has had to confront ... many of the new risks and uncertainties affect us no matter where we live, and regardless of how privileged or deprived we are. They are bound up with globalization ...'.[13] The dramatic reach of this risk is illustrated by the experience of the beneficiaries of the social security fund of Gabon. Their retirement funds were invested in the Bank of Credit and Commerce International that became insolvent, leaving the citizens of Gabon wondering what they had worked for all their lives.[14]

Not only are different countries and regions connected through trading and information flows, but markets in different interests are interconnected, spreading the initial contagion into other sectors. So for example the year 2000 crash in high-tech stocks registered not only in the markets for securities in their shares, but also in related derivatives markets. What is more, the initial crash can manifest itself in different ways in the markets it subsequently affects. The crash of high-tech stocks registered in the Australian economy by a dramatic downward price adjustment in equity prices, but also in a significant drop in the value of the Australian currency.[15] This point serves to illustrate one aspect of the

---

11 Giddens, above n 1 at 3.

12 Harvey D, *The Condition of Postmodernity*, Blackwell, Oxford and Cambridge, Massachusetts, 1989 at 293.

13 Giddens, above n 1 at 3.

14 Braithwaite and Drahos, above n 3 at 105.

15 'Watch out for chain reaction', *The Australian Financial Review*, 1 May 2000, at 31; 'Nervous markets brace for sell-off', *The Australian Financial Review*, 17 April 2000, at

interconnectedness of globalization: when risks do eventuate, it is difficult to predict how they will manifest themselves. This adds to the difficulty of anticipating them through international regulation or other cooperative means, and in a way augments the risks associated with international financial meltdown. The above features of globalization are often used to justify the networks of transnational financial regulation exemplified in the IOSCO principles.

Transnational Regulatory Norms for Securities

The regulation of global securities markets has been described as 'a quilt of national systems',[16] and to a considerable extent this is so. This of course brings with it all the difficulties of the extraterritorial effects of national regulation, evident both in resistance to extraterritoriality when nations are thought to have overstepped their jurisdictional bounds,[17] and in attempts by regulators themselves to cut back the reach of their own laws so as not to bring the inadvertent activities of foreign nationals within those laws. So for example, the Australian Securities and Investments Commission 'targets' its supervision and enforcement activities at offers of securities that are directed to Australian investors. As long as other offers contain the appropriate disclaimers, the Australian Securities and Investments Commission is not concerned that Australian investors can access them through the Internet.[18] Despite regulatory policies like this, there is still considerable overlap between national systems and the obvious problem of conflicting standards and requirements.

In other areas of cross-border activity this overlap and dissonance of standards might be dealt with through treaties, that is, through international law strictly so called. But at the international level, there are virtually no treaties that have as their purpose the regulation of securities. Rather, through the activities of IOSCO, regulation through transnational principles has evolved. These principles are a mixture of standards and guidelines intended by IOSCO to encourage convergence in the form and content of national laws and the policies behind their administration. These transnational regulatory norms lie between the national and the

---

1; 'The revolution of American booty', *The Australian Financial Review*, 17 April 2000, at 55.

16 Sheng A, Chairman of the Hong Kong Securities Exchange Commission, address to the 25th Annual Conference of IOSCO, Sydney, 18 May 2000.

17 Braithwaite and Drahos, above n 3 at 214, 153, 156-7.

18 For example, in Australian Securities and Investment Commission *Interim Policy Statement 162 – Internet Discussion Sites*, 15 August 2000, paras 44-5 and Australian Securities and Investment Commission *Policy Statement 107 – Electronic Prospectuses*, 10 February 2000, paras 18-19.

international, and their juridical nature is little considered. The following section is devoted to understanding the nature and effect of these transnational regulatory norms and how they relate to national laws and other transnational laws.

IOSCO Principles: Between International Law and the Nation State

Traditionally, bilateral treaties between states have been the source of obligations in international law, and multilateral treaties can be construed as a series of bilateral relationships. The doctrine of *pacta tertiis* associated with treaties protects non-parties to a treaty from having the treaty imposed on them. Other obligations of international law, strictly so called, can be made only by public international organizations substantially comprising states.[19]

Braithwaite and Drahos argue that there has been relatively little effective global regulation of securities markets in comparison with other globalized industries.[20] It is true that there has been little activity between states directly, in the form of international treaty making. This is possibly because treaties are unwieldy instruments of regulation, and because the US has historically been uncomfortable with the idea of compromising its own regulatory standards for securities.[21] With the US markets accounting for about 40 per cent of the world's capitalization, there is little to be gained by a treaty to which the US is not a willing party. It is also true that there is no obvious public international organization, substantially comprising states, from which we might expect instruments of public international law such as conventions to govern securities.

The decline in the use of closed diplomatic methods for the resolution of international issues, and the rise in public institutional arenas for international debate, mean that many parties other than states are able to express a legitimate international concern about a wide range of issues.[22] Even the modes of international law strictly so called are adapting. Instead of the more rigid bilateral treaty model or the use of conventions, restraints and standards are formulated within international organizations through formally non-binding instruments such as Resolutions and Codes of Conduct. These make it difficult for a state to claim non-party status, as it can for a treaty to which it is not a party. The adoption of standards and

19 For the sources of public international law see Brownlie I, *Principles of Public International Law*, 5th ed, Clarendon Press, Oxford, 1998 at ch 1.

20 Braithwaite and Drahos, above n 3 at 156.

21 Ibid ch 9; for example, in relation to accounting standards, see Hunt I, 'It's a Small World After All: The SEC's Role in Securities Regulation Globalization' (1999) 51 *Administrative Law Review* 1105.

22 Chinkin C, *Third Parties in International Law*, Clarendon Press, Oxford, 1993 at 1-5.

statements of principle in this more informal way, as Chinkin points out, 'operates to create expectations as to future behaviour between members of the international community in a wider setting than treaties; there has been a move towards developing normative standards being expressed in "soft law"'.[23]

In this process of widening the scope of public international law, non-governmental organizations (NGOs) of individuals and corporations[24] have become influential, in both policy making and the supervision of implementation of internationally agreed regimes.[25] Generally NGOs participate in international dialogue by advocating new ideas or principles and arguing for changes in existing international regimes. NGOs can be particularly effective in this if they are able to mobilize international public opinion, or to engage 'mass publics', as Braithwaite and Drahos have put it.[26] Some NGOs, such as Greenpeace and Amnesty International, have been so influential in the international arena that there have been calls for a recognized legal status for NGOs, accompanied by a regulatory framework to constrain their behaviour.[27]

Instead of more formal modes of international lawmaking, transnational organizations of national financial regulators have developed in the financial domain, and these organizations work towards convergence of national standards by negotiating, promulgating and to some extent supervizing broad principles of financial regulation applicable in both worldwide and domestic financial markets. The most prominent of these is the Bank for International Settlements, which has most famously developed and disseminated capital adequacy and liquidity standards for banks.[28] Much less well known is the International Association of Insurance Supervisors.[29] Most relevant to this paper is IOSCO.[30]

Considering IOSCO's international status, it is clearly not an NGO. These are usually constituted by private individuals or associations of

---

23 Ibid at 3; Chinkin, C 'The Challenge of Soft Law: Development and Change in International Law' (1989) 38 *International and Comparative Law Quarterly* 850.

24 Amerasinghe C, *Principles of the Institutional Law of International Organizations*, Cambridge University Press, Cambridge and New York, 1996 at 10.

25 Nowrot K, 'Legal Consequences of Globalization: The Status of Non-Governmental Organizations under International Law' (1999) 6 *Indiana Journal of Global Legal Studies* 579; Willets P (ed), *Pressure Groups in the Global System*, St Martins Press, New York, 1982.

26 Braithwaite and Drahos, above n 3 at 497-501.

27 Nowrot, above n 25 *passim*.

28 See <www.bis.org>.

29 See <www.iaisweb.org/framesets/inter.html>.

30 Sommer A, 'IOSCO: Its Mission and Achievement' (1996) 17 *Northwestern Journal of International Law and Business* 15-29; see also <www.iosco.org>.

individuals, although states may be members too. Rather, IOSCO is composed of independent securities commissions and self-regulatory organizations. More particularly, IOSCO does not agitate for causes and agendas in other international organizations – if anything, it is more like an international body, being itself the institution which promulgates transnational regulatory principles. In transnational securities regulation there is not much NGO activity, and as already pointed out, there are no obvious public international forums for securities regulation. The most important exception to this general absence of NGOs is the International Accounting Standards Commission, which sees IOSCO as one of the main forums for its activities. This Commission has recently reached agreement with IOSCO, with the latter consenting to adopt its standards[31] after sustained opposition by the US.[32] Accounting standards are fundamental to the operation of disclosure, the foundational technique of securities regulation.

As well as not being composed of states, strictly speaking IOSCO is also not a public international organization because it was not established by international agreement between states under international law,[33] but incorporated by an act of the Quebec Parliament. In this it is similar to the Bank of International Settlements, which is established under Swiss law and hence is classified as a private international organization. Despite the strict classification, functionally, both IOSCO and the Bank of International Settlements perform roles on the transnational stage which are very similar in kind to those of public international organizations. This point may be made particularly strongly in relation to IOSCO, which, while not constituted by states, does have state regulatory authorities as its voting members. Further, even its affiliate membership of self-regulatory organizations (generally associations of private individuals, firms or corporations) often has a considerable element of public regulatory responsibility and stands in substitution for a fully public commission or government department.

Given this relative vacuum in public international law securities regulation, and the limits on the extraterritoriality of state law, IOSCO

---

31 Braithwaite and Drahos, above n 3 at 159; agreement between IOSCO and IASC reported at IOSCO 25th Annual Conference, Sydney, 15-19 May 2000.

32 The US has advocated the use of its domestically created FASB standards; see Hunt, above n 21.

33 Amerasinghe, above n 24 at 8-10; Armstrong D, Lloyd L and Redmond J, *From Versailles to Maastricht: International Organisation in the Twentieth Century*, St Martins Press, New York, 1996; Bennett AL, *International Organizations*, Prentice-Hall, Englewood Cliffs, New Jersey, 1984; Schermers H, *International Institutional Law: Unity within Diversity*, Nijhoff, The Hague, 1980.

assumes importance as the main source of transnational norms for securities regulation. IOSCO's principles do not have the status of public international law, nor are they truly international 'soft law', as 'soft law' is usually understood to be established through the resolutions of conventions and public international organizations.[34] I will, however, argue that the IOSCO principles, which are a prominent and important variety of transnational regulatory norms, do share many of the juristic purposes and characteristics of 'soft law'.[35]

To summarize: IOSCO lies between the national and the international, and adds a new type of actor to the sphere of international relations. Its principles add a new level of legal norms between international law and national law. IOSCO and its principles imitate international law and organizations in aiming for collective action on a worldwide level. But the principles do not have the force of international law; instead they assume authority by a myriad of mechanisms. These mechanisms, typical of the globalization phenomenon, disrupt the traditional levels of international relations and national sovereignty, interacting with both and also with the multitude of other norms at the transnational level.[36] Before moving to consider this complex interaction – or 'interlegality', to use de Sousa Santos' term – it is helpful to consider the nature of the IOSCO principles in isolation for a moment.

The IOSCO principles, not being a recognized part of international law, are more akin to what Picciotto and Jayasuriya call 'network governance'.[37] These global webs of regulation do not depend on treaties or public international organizations, but on informal connections (in international

34 'Only states have the capability to internationalize a subject matter. Persons cannot do so. For this reason it may be said that international formulations of standards by non-governmental organizations such as the ICC are not soft law. They do not show the desire of states for collective action', Gruchalla-Wesierski T, 'A Framework for Understanding Soft Law' (1984) 30 *McGill Law Journal* 37 at 60.

35 Chinkin, above n 23; Gruchalla-Wesierski, above n 34; Riphagen W, 'From Soft Law to Ius Cogens and Back' (1987) 17 *Victoria University Wellington Law Review* 81; Schachter O, 'Recent Trends in International Law Making' (1992) 12 *Australian Year Book of International Law* 1; Bothe M, 'Legal and Non-Legal Norms: A Meaningful Distinction in International Relations?' (1980) 1 *Netherlands Year Book of International Law* 65.

36 See text surrounding n 61 below.

37 Picciotto S, 'The Regulatory Criss-Cross: Interaction Between Jurisdictions and the Construction of Global Regulatory Networks', in Bratton W et al (eds), *International Regulatory Competition and Coordination*: *Perspectives on Economic Regulation in Europe and the United States*, Oxford University Press, New York, 1996 at 89, 92-8; Jayasuriya K, 'Globalization, Law and the Transformation of Sovereignty: The Emergence of Global Regulatory Governance' (1999) 6 *Indiana Journal of Global Legal Studies* 425 at 448.

law terms). In the most straightforward instance the principles are implemented through national legislative and administrative authority, the regulatory network adhering through local action to various points around the globe. The standards are formulated at relatively high levels of abstraction in comparison with most domestic regulatory rules, allowing autonomy of action and choice of implementation strategy by the national regulator that is part of the network. In this way, the IOSCO principles are 'nationalized' or 'localized' on a transnational and sometimes even global basis.[38]

It is axiomatic among securities lawyers that the IOSCO principles have no legal effect and are 'voluntary', 'sanctionless' and 'unenforceable'; indeed, it is part of the ideology of securities regulation that this is so.[39] From this perspective, which sees a complete unity between law and the state, it is argued that the principles only have legal effect if they are incorporated into national law by a formal act of a sovereign state.[40] However, this is only part of the picture. Early writers on globalization and law identified a kind of 'anational' law that, as Giddens put it, exists in 'relative insulation' from the state.[41] In asserting that orders such as the *lex mercatoria* exist as global law and independent of national authority, Teubner argued that there had come into being a new 'living law of the world'.[42] This new 'living law'... 'is nourished not from stores of tradition but from the on-going self-reproduction of highly technical, highly specialized, often formally organized and rather narrowly defined, global networks of an economic, cultural, academic or technological nature'.[43]

---

38 Twining W, 'Globalization and Legal Theory: Some Local Implications' (1996) 49 *Current Legal Problems* 1 at 3.

39 Braithwaite and Drahos, above n 3 at 157.

40 This is done by a number of means, including incorporation through legislation, etc. As the IOSCO principles are not rules of international law (strictly so called), the rules for reception of international law in the national jurisdiction in question are not obviously imperative.

41 Giddens, above n 9 at 70.

42 Teubner G, 'Global Bukowina: Legal Pluralism in the World Society', in Teubner G (ed), *Global Law Without a State*, Dartmouth University Press, Aldershot and Brookfield, USA, 1997 at 7. Although not published until 1997, an earlier version of this essay was delivered at the London School of Economics as a public address in 1991 and so was one of the early contributions on the nature of global law. The term 'living law' is an obvious reference to the work of Eugen Ehrlich, one of the earliest socio-legal theorists to observe and propound the existence of normative orders other than those of the state, although he did so in relation to orders that were sub-national, not supra-national. For more detail, see Cotterrell R, *The Sociology of Law*, Butterworths, London, 1984 at 29 ff.

43 Teubner, above n 42 at 7.

From the account of the organization and constitution of IOSCO that is provided below, it will be noticed that it fits well with this description. For example, there is within IOSCO a community of like-minded, highly technically able securities regulators and lawyers, whose opinions are very influential in the creation of the principles. Also, Teubner identifies as leading characteristics of this new 'living law of the world', or global law, that it operates despite the absence of formal sanctions and that its rules are rather indeterminate. The second proposition clearly applies to the IOSCO principles.

The first proposition requires empirical investigation. Before we can accept the proposition of securities lawyers that the principles are voluntary or unenforceable, we need a great deal more evidence about how, when and why they are used. For a start there is no evidence of the degree to which, or whether at all, IOSCO principles are relied on in international securities arbitrations, which are virtually entirely private. There is no evidence collected about reliance on the principles in the negotiation of transactions or the drafting of documents, nor the settlement of disputes arising from them. Nor do we know the degree to which the IOSCO principles are considered in the development of standard form agreements and relevant industry association rules. We do not even know very accurately the degree to which they are formally incorporated and administratively acted upon in the national laws of many IOSCO states. In other words, from a socio-legal perspective there is no novelty at all in the idea that norms such as the IOSCO principles may be largely self-executing and, from the internal standpoint of their addressees, impose a sense of obligation.[44]

We now have two opposite positions. On the one hand it is argued the IOSCO principles are ineffective unless they are authorized by the action of a nation state. On the other, it is asserted that there is a developing 'anational' system of law that compels compliance without the authority of the state. Perhaps unsurprisingly, the passage of more than a decade since these early views on globalization were expressed has led to a more complex middle position. It is one that neither excludes nor demands the presence of the nation state. The formations of law at the transnational level vary greatly, some showing more state involvement, some greater insulation from the state. In all cases it is necessary to adopt 'the method of

---

44 An excellent account of this is given in Twining W, *How to Do Things with Rules*, Butterworths, London, 1999 at ch 3; Schauer F, *Playing by the Rules*, Oxford University Press, New York, 1991; Hart H, *The Concept of Law*, Clarendon Press, Oxford, 1961; Black J, *Rules and Regulators*, Oxford University Press, New York, 1996. This has also been observed in empirical studies: Bardach E and Kagan R, *Going By the Book: the Problem of Regulatory Unreasonableness*, Temple University Press, Philadelphia, 1982, *passim*.

detail'[45] and to analyze in context. This will often show that state law in the global world is fragmented and intricately interwoven with sources and types of law that do not depend on nation states for their authority. Without having the empirical evidence to know exactly, this seems to be the case with securities regulation. And for understanding these changes, legal pluralism and the concept of 'interlegality' would seem to be helpful.

Pluralism and Transnational Regulatory Norms

William Twining reminds us that we need to distinguish between different patterns and levels of relations, and between the various actors in the globalized world.[46] To this point we have considered the international and the national levels but have identified in detail only one source of transnational norms: IOSCO principles. In fact the picture of cross-border securities regulation is infinitely more complex than just the IOSCO principles. To make sense of this complexity, we need an approach that takes those conditions as its starting point, and for this, normative pluralism and its subset legal pluralism are very apt.

Pluralism and Decentred Regulation

Some writers suggest that globalization diminishes the power of states, that there is a decline in national sovereignty.[47] 'End of the state' thinking has been a prominent theme of post-modern predictions of the end of modernity, the nation state being a leading feature of modernity. From a different political perspective, advocates of neo-liberal agendas also anticipate the end of the state, through programs of 'rolling back the state' and 'small government', deregulation and privatization. While neo-liberals would replace the state with market relations, some post-modernists look to more utopian visions of radically democratic socialism which seek inspiration from local communities, especially those which have been marginalized or repressed by the centralized state.[48] While the prescription varies dramatically, the 'end of the state' diagnosis of both neo-liberals and post-modernists generally includes as a causal factor the external pressure exerted on the state by global forces.

It is true that states and the municipal law they create can no longer be considered in isolation from outside influences, legal or otherwise.[49] As we

---

45 Twining W, 'Pericles and the Plumber', in Twining W (ed), *Law in Context: Enlarging a Discipline*, Oxford University Press, New York, 1997 at 63.

46 Twining, above n 38 at 5.

47 Ohmae K, *The End of the Nation State: The Rise of Regional Economies*, Free Press, New York, 1995.

48 Santos, above n 4.

49 Twining, above n 38 at 7.

have already seen, the international networks of markets in securities and finance have national and local effects that are difficult for any one state either to predict or control. But in fact the question of whether states are losing their sovereign rights to legislate and govern in an interdependent world is complex and reflexive.

To begin with, states create markets as much as markets create (or diminish) states.[50] The transnational regulators such as IOSCO are a response to deliberate national policies of deregulation and the abolition of interest and exchange rate controls in the late 1970s and early 1980s.[51] If states were to reimpose interest and currency controls, global markets would shrink overnight. The role of national states in constituting transnational regulatory networks is also crucial. The IOSCO principles depend in part on national legislation and reciprocal arrangements between national regulators that are accountable to national governments.

'End of the state' thinking has also been evident closer to home, in critiques of domestic state centred law and regulation. This has led to consideration of decentred forms of law,[52] and growing understanding of the limits of state-centric regulatory techniques.[53] State regulation or 'command and control' approaches have been caricatured (at times unfairly) as legalistic, under- and over-inclusive, expensive to enforce, and lacking legitimacy with the subjects of regulation.[54] Of course these criticisms are not valid in all circumstances, and 'command and control' regulation still performs valuable if often admonitory functions. However, there is a broad consensus among those who study regulation that effective regulation has to embrace approaches that persist independently of and even despite the state.

---

50 Esping-Anderson G, *The Three Worlds of Welfare Capitalism*, Polity Press, Cambridge, 1990 at 79. Nelken, above n 2 at 262, raises a similar question, asking whether globalization constitutes crime, as much as crime is an effect of globalization. This question is also analyzed by Findlay in Ch 10 of this volume.

51 Giddens, above n 1 at 14-17.

52 Gunningham N and Grabosky P, *Smart Regulation: Designing Environmental Policy*, Clarendon Press, Oxford, 1998 *passim*; Black J, 'Decentring Regulation: Understanding the Role of Regulation and Self Regulation in a "Post-Regulatory" World' (2001) 54 *Current Legal Problems* 105, and 'Critical Reflections on Regulation' (2002) 27 *Australian Journal of Legal Philosophy* 1; Kingsford Smith D, 'Decentred Regulation in Online Investment' (2001) 19 *Companies and Securities Law Journal* 532.

53 Ayres I and Braithwaite J, *Responsive Regulation*, Oxford University Press, New York, 1992.

54 Baldwin R and Cave M, *Understanding Regulation: Theory, Strategy and Practice*, Oxford University Press, Oxford and New York, 1999 at 35; Bardach and Kagan, above n 44 *passim*.

By contrast, 'decentred' regulation involves 'governing at a distance'. Instead of the state-initiated, cause and effect, 'one technique fits all' approach of 'command and control', decentring describes and even advocates an approach in which the state is only one actor of several. It anticipates that the interaction of state and non-state entities will sometimes mutually strengthen the regulatory purposes and goals, and at other times paradoxically undermine them. It accepts that the sources of law and regulation in any context are plural, and both state and non-state in origin. Decentring also treats complexity as a normal feature of any regulated situation: the motivations of those subject to regulation will be neither identical nor consistent, and the circumstances and motivations of other non-state actors will also be changeable. In particular, complexity is a natural result of various actors having different information,[55] compounded by their interpreting things differently depending on their regulatory standpoint.[56]

At a national level, like much else about decentring, the forms of regulation in which it appears are variable, and exhibit decentredness to differing degrees. So for example, the various forms of self-regulation may be thought of as moving away from state-centric 'command and control', introducing non-state actors to a greater degree. There are numerous examples of self-regulation in financial markets.[57] As Julia Black has noted, 'self-regulation' has developed a range of meanings.[58] It is most widely understood as a reference to neo-corporatist arrangements in which industry associations or professional organizations take on regulatory functions. Often self-regulation that seeks to co-opt or compel associations or interested groups is complemented by the adoption of codes of conduct, sometimes as a condition of membership, but more often than not voluntarily. Voluntariness extends to adhering to codes of conduct or to the findings of dispute resolution schemes, undertaking education programs, and voluntarily disclosing information and warnings. Voluntary arrangements are reasonably common in securities markets, often within or adjacent to state regulation.

---

55 Black, above n 52.

56 Ibid; Twining, above n 45 at 49-53; Kingsford Smith D, 'Interpreting the Corporations Law: Purpose, Practical Reasoning and Public Policy' (1999) 21 *Sydney Law Review* 161.

57 For example, the Australian Stock Exchange, the Self Regulatory Organisations, which previously existed under the Financial Services Act 1986 (UK), and the National Association of Securities Dealers in the USA.

58 Black, above n 52; and Black J, 'Constitutionalising Self-Regulation' (1996) 59 *Modern Law Review* 24 at 25-9.

What, you may ask, does all this have to do with globalization and transnational norms of securities regulation? The point of the digression has been to show how thinking is already developing within *national* boundaries towards understanding the descriptive reality and normative attractions[59] of a more decentred and plural approach to regulation – an approach that does not always envisage law with the state at the centre and does not require the state as a prerequisite to legality and legal effect. The state is not absent from the picture, as it will and should remain an important source of legal and other norms. Rather, the point is to recognize the normative and/or legal significance of values, principles, codes, guidelines and rules which emanate from sources other than the state.[60]

In the case of transnational regulatory norms, the state is not absent but is definitely decentred. There are multiple non-state sources of norms that act on transnational investment intermediaries and their customers. Obviously there are the IOSCO principles and with the convergence of banking and securities products, many securities intermediaries may also be within the principles of the Bank for International Settlements. The same point may be made in relation to the authority of the International Association of Insurance Supervisors in relation to the hybridization of securities and insurance products. But even these clearly non-state sources of transnational principles are only the more formal tip of the cross-border iceberg.

In the same regulatory space, acting simultaneously is a myriad of other norms of various degrees of legality. Depending upon the nature of the financial instrument or parties involved, the transaction may be influenced by any or all of the professional rules and practices of the International Swaps and Derivatives Association, International Bond Dealers Association, the Code of Ethics of the International Bar Association, more recently the Common Code of Conduct for Lawyers in the European Community[61] and similarly internationalized professional codes in the accounting,[62] banking and actuarial professions. In some transactions codes of ethics or conduct of a more general nature may apply, at least at the level

---

59 For further consideration of the benefits and limits of decentred regulation see Kingsford Smith, above n 52.

60 As, for example, is done by Griffiths J, 'What is Legal Pluralism?' (1986) 24 *Journal of Legal Pluralism* 1; Arthurs H, *Without the Law: Administrative Justice and Legal Pluralism in Nineteenth-Century England*, University of Toronto Press, Toronto, 1985 *passim*; Macdonald R, 'Metaphors of Multiplicity: Civil Society, Regimes and Legal Pluralism' (1998) 15 *Arizona Journal of International and Comparative Law* 69.

61 In relation to the latter two, see Arthurs H, 'A Global Code of Ethics for the Transnational Legal Field' (1998) 1 *Legal Ethics* 59.

62 The standards of the International Accounting Standards Committee.

of world's best practice. So for example, the OECD Guidelines on Corporate Governance or international labour law or human rights guidelines may have normative weight in particular circumstances. The advent and growing popularity of ethical and socially responsible investment gives some impetus for such guidelines to be taken seriously.

Finally, standard form agreements[63] may be adopted by parties and supply a set of rules governing some connections with third parties appurtenant to the agreement.[64] In a national context it might be objected that because contracts are enforced by the state they are not good examples of pluralism at work, but in a transnational context this objection has much less force. Although international financing and securities issuance agreements routinely contain choice of law and forum clauses, the fact is that they are almost never litigated. To default or litigate is to be excluded from the small group of repeat players who make up the market. Instead, disagreements are settled by compromise, according to a growing body of custom, practice and agreed interpretation surrounding significant clauses in the standard form contracts. In this and in the privately constituted international securities arbitrations that are now used to settle disputes in cross-border securities issues, there are the beginnings of a transnational *lex financiera* – a body of private legal norms virtually universally accepted but having no obvious foundation in public authority. In fact, many of the items in this very long list of sources of norms or law that might touch and affect a transnational securities transaction could be said to have no obvious foundation in public authority, whether national or international strictly so called. It will by now be clear that decentring of the state and recognition of the plurality of sources of law and other norms has obvious application to transnational securities regulation.

Instead of the 'end of the state' it might be more accurate to describe the domestic and global pressures decentring the nation state as moving towards a rearticulation of the state. There are a number of theoretical positions that recognize the fragmentation of the nation state and the changing nature of law constituting it. All move away from the predominant view that law is coextensive with the nation state. Communitarians see transnational changes as unsettling the nation state and opening up regions and other sub-national groupings or communities as a prism through which to reassess law. This is not to return to ideas of

---

63 For example, eurobond issue and underwriting agreements, and in particular swap agreement standard forms.

64 For example, the terms of bonds issued to bondholders by eurobond syndicates are set by the agreements between the syndicate members, to which bondholders are not parties.

traditional community,[65] but as Roger Cotterrell puts it, a move to 'a diversity of social collectivities, commitments and systems of interests, values or beliefs, coexisting, overlapping and interpenetrating'[66] in contemporary contexts. Although it may be possible to explore the nature of law in supra-national as opposed to sub-national groupings through communitarian thinking, this theoretical framework lacks the more obvious applicability of two alternatives: governance theory and legal pluralism.

Within national legal systems, governance theory has been central in the analysis of domestic decentred law discussed above.[67] In short, governance involves a translation of the purposes and objects of the state into the myriad mechanisms of self-regulation, voluntary action and other technologies of governance such as data collection and analysis. Often regulation emanates from private organizations; governance theory contemplates a variety of sites of government, not all of which are obviously supported by state authority. In embracing private action within state purposes and law, governance theorists contemplate a decentred state as fragmented, complex and extending further than the reach of obviously governmental institutions. Viewed in this light rather than in 'end of the state' terms, the influence of the sovereign state may have increased rather than diminished.

In the transnational arena, Jayasuriya argues that sovereignty has not been eroded; rather, as in the national sphere, it has been transformed into a more complex notion. This 'complex sovereignty'[68] is part of a regime: 'a set of implicit or explicit principles, norms, rules and decision-making procedures around a particular set of issues' in a policy area.[69] As national deregulation, international communication and the symbolic value of money have detached markets from territorial boundaries, national laws have also detached governmental functions from the centralized state. These are then transferred either to the market (usually under state

---

65 That is, not 'Gemeinschaft' closely knit by proximity and practices: see Kamenka E and Tay A (eds), *Law and Social Control*, E. Arnold, London, 1980 *passim*.

66 Cotterrell R, 'A Legal Concept of Community' (1997) 12 *Canadian Journal of Law and Society* 75 at 78; Cotterrell R, *Law's Community: Legal Theory in Sociological Perspective*, Oxford University Press, Oxford University Press, New York, 1995. The idea of community has been applied in a diversity of contexts, including business and corporations: Selznick P, *The Moral Commonwealth: Social Theory and the Promise of Community*, University of California Press, Berkeley, 1992; citizenship and nationhood: Krygier M, *Between Fear and Hope: Hybrid Thoughts on Public Values*, ABC Books, Sydney, 1997.

67 Rose N, *Powers of Freedom: Reframing Political Thought*, Cambridge University Press, Cambridge and New York, 1999.

68 Jayasuriya, above n 37.

69 Krasner S (ed), *International Regimes*, Cornell University Press, Ithaca, 1983 at 2.

supervision) or to independent state organs such as securities commissions.[70] Jayasuriya argues that it is bodies such as securities commissions that exercise sovereignty in this semi-detached way, as they are positioned to mediate between the global and the national.[71] In this light, IOSCO can be seen as governing at a distance for the nation state, performing, in a decentred fashion, a classic state role of lawmaking.

That brings us to legal pluralism. As has occurred with the idea of community in contemporary communitarian theory, legal pluralism now extends beyond an interest in traditional societies and ethnographic studies of law, and is applicable to law in contemporary society.[72] Like both communitarian and governance theory, legal pluralism seeks to explain the nature and effect of law that emanates from sources other than the state. It too investigates the local, the informal, and the rules of groups that seem to have no obvious basis in state authority.[73] Legal pluralism is a part of a larger normative pluralism which tries to understand those practices, conventions and norms that are virtually universally complied with but have no obvious source in, connection with or sanction by legal institutions or processes.[74] While this focus enriches the descriptive sociological content of law, it has led to criticisms of legal pluralism as being incapable of defining its own subject matter;[75] that unless legal pluralism can specify where general social norms end and legal norms (or law) begin, then the theory lacks analytical power – everything collapses into a general category of 'social control'.[76] But as Teubner points out, 'It has proved hopeless to search for a criterion delineating social norms from legal norms'.[77] Instead it may be more productive to think, as Cotterrell does, about the shading between law and norms from other social fields along a spectrum of

---

70 This has been particularly noteworthy in relation to the wave of laws to separate central banks from government, for example in the UK and Australia in the last five years.

71 Jayasuriya, above n 37 at 437.

72 Merry S, 'Legal Pluralism' (1988) 22 *Law & Society Review* at 869-74; Twining, above n 5 at 83-5; Roberts S, 'Against Legal Pluralism: Some Reflections on the Contemporary Enlargement of the Legal Domain' (1998) 42 *Journal of Legal Pluralism and Unofficial Law* 95.

73 Arthurs, *Without the Law*, above n 60 *passim*, especially at ch 1; Griffiths J, 'What is Legal Pluralism?' (1986) 24 *Journal of Legal Pluralism* 1 *passim*; Merry, above n 72.

74 Twining, above n 5 at 83.

75 Teubner G, 'The Two Faces of Janus: Rethinking Legal Pluralism' (1992) 13 *Cardozo Law Review* 1443 at 1448-52; Tamanaha B, 'A Non-Essentialist View of Legal Pluralism' (2000) 27 *Journal of Law and Society* 296.

76 Teubner, ibid at 1450, especially note 26.

77 Teubner, 'Global Bukowina', above n 42 at 13, although he does suggest the binary relation 'legal/illegal', which I do not adopt.

legality.[78] This allows the development of pluralist theorizing without it getting stuck on threshold questions of definition.

In the global or transnational arenas, pluralism has obvious application to the multitude of networks, norms and laws of nation states that potentially have an impact on cross-border transactions as described above. Pluralism also treats as unexceptional the ever-present fact of global and transnational norms that do not emanate from and are not enforced by the state. Further, the fact that there are various types of norms – principles, policies, rules, practices – and that they have differing degrees of legality is also something that pluralism explicitly recognizes. In short, legal pluralism promises an analytic framework that grapples with the complexity of transnational networks, norms and rules, and recognizes their heterogeneity. The important question now is: in what ways can a pluralist approach to this transnational field illuminate our understanding of the interaction of these various networks, norms and rules?

Transnational Regulatory Norms and 'Interlegality'

The diversity of values, principles, policies, guidelines and practices that might govern a transnational securities transaction brings us to an enquiry into how to make sense of this bewildering forest of competing norms. One important idea that has developed in pluralist thinking is that of 'interlegality', first articulated as such by Santos.[79] The essence of pluralism is, of course, that there may be more than one type or source of law applicable in the same time and space. The modes of coexistence of potentially simultaneously applicable orders have been noticed previously.[80] But Santos's concept of 'interlegality'[81] captures in detail the complexity and dynamism of interrelations between different legal orders. Santos describes interlegality as follows:

> the conception of different legal spaces superimposed, interpenetrated and mixed ... We live in a time of porous legality or of legal porosity, multiple networks of legal orders forcing us to constant transitions and trespassings. Our

---

[78] Cotterrell, *Law's Community*, above n 66 at 36. Twining also makes this point in *Globalization and Legal Theory*, above n 5 at 85-6.

[79] Santos, above n 4 at chs 3, 4, 5 and 7.

[80] See, for example, Moore's idea of 'semi-autonomous social fields', in Moore S, *Law as Process: An Anthropological Approach*, Routledge, London and Boston, 1978. This question is reviewed by William Twining in *Globalisation and Legal Theory*, above n 5 at 85. The ways plural regimes have been thought to interact is also discussed by Roberts, above n 72 at 101-2; Arthurs, *Without the Law*, above n 60 at ch 6, especially. at 177-83.

[81] Santos, above n 4, especially at 473.

legal life is constituted by an intersection of different legal orders, that is, by *interlegality*.[82]

Santos derived the concept of interlegality from his observations of the interaction of state law and non-state rules and practices observed by community organizations and individuals in the illegal squatter settlements of Brazil. There the state law declared the squatter settlements (*favelas*) illegal but nonetheless in practice mostly tolerated their existence. Within the squatter settlements informal rules and practices developed administered by community organizations. These constituted a well-understood system of 'entitlements' to a variety of 'interests' in property in the *favelas*. Santos' observations of disputes under this non-state system allowed him to identify the modes of interrelationship between the state and non-state regimes.

An important feature of interlegality in Santos's work is recognition of the influence of the state on the forms and processes of non-state sources of law or norms, even those latter sources which the state views as illegal, strictly speaking.[83] As Santos observed sometimes the non-state system mimics, borrows or adapts from the state.[84] At other times it inverts the legal concepts used by the state, possibly through the use of legal fictions.[85] At others still, there is a feedback effect in which concepts originating with the state are partially transformed through their use in the non-state system and reabsorbed in this changed condition back into the state legal system. The non-state system may also define itself against the state system by omission, for example by consciously not acting in an area that the state occupies.[86] More generally, the non-state authorities might seek to persuade recalcitrant subjects of the authority of their system by threatening to invoke the official law. This might be done either by threatening to withdraw the services of the non-state functionary, leaving the dispute to the less tender mercies of the official law, or by calling on the authority of the official system to corroborate the authority of the unofficial, where this option is available.[87] In short, the unofficial system operates to some extent on the reflected authority of the state law or 'in the shadow' of state law.

While others have observed that non-state orders mirror or are imagined against the template of state law,[88] this is not to say that they have

[82] Ibid.
[83] Ibid at ch 3 *passim*, especially at 160-1, 164-76, 228-30, 232-40.
[84] Ibid.
[85] Ibid at 176-80.
[86] Ibid at 162.
[87] Ibid at 218 and 224.
[88] Macdonald, above n 60 *passim*.

no independent forms, nor that they do not have different substantive norms. Throughout the presentation and analysis of the empirical portion of his argument, Santos is at pains to point out that 'selective borrowing of legal formalism' from the state[89] is what he observed and that the informality of the non-state procedures remained important. Further, despite these borrowings, the non-state system maintained some substantive norms that were quite unlike or even at odds with those of the state law.[90]

Santos uses the interaction between state and non-state law as his source in developing the idea of interlegality. However, the whole tenor of his argument makes it clear that interlegality will be found between non-state orders *inter se* and even observed between different modes of state law. This means that interlegality could be usefully applied to the intersection of any of the myriad of principles, rules and practices that apply to transnational intermediaries and their customers. Not only is interlegality apt to show the legal analytic nature of the relations between legal orders, but, as Santos demonstrates from interpretive discussion of his own empirical research, it may also reveal the motivations of legal actors and the power relations between them. Santos' research suggests that the power effects arise through the possibility of the state's physical coercion of those living by the non-state law. Although the Brazilian authorities tolerated the *favelas*, occasionally they razed them, reminding the occupants of their informal and contingent tenure. By contrast (as will be evident in the next section), power differentials in transnational securities markets arise from disparities of market size and sophistication. They are also created from the overwhelming resources and depth of technical expertise that Western securities regulators and securities lawyers bring to the committees of organizations such as IOSCO and to transnational securities transactions. We now turn to an examination of these power effects in relation to the creation and dissemination of the IOSCO principles, and their interrelation with other transnational norms of securities regulation.

'Interlegality' and Transnational Securities Regulation in Practice

In this section I explore in a preliminary fashion an intersection between different legal orders, which occurs regularly in transnational securities practice. I use the concept of 'interlegality' in an attempt to tease out how those orders might interact. I will concentrate on the intersection of nation state rules and the IOSCO principles. There are of course many other

[89] Santos, above n 4 at 238.

[90] Ibid at 233-4, 238.

interactions to be explored: between the IOSCO principles and the rules of international professional associations; between the IOSCO principles and the clauses of standard form transnational contracts; between these norms themselves without the IOSCO principles; and more besides. Here there is space to investigate only one possibility, but in the current state of transnational securities regulation, interaction between national laws and IOSCO principles is likely to be one of the most frequently occurring types of relation. I do not attempt to gather up and analyze any case law that might be relevant. Instead I sketch out what I think would be the major interlegalities, and hope that will provide guidance for a more-detailed account on another occasion. To begin with it is necessary to consider the context in which the IOSCO principles are created.

IOSCO: the Institutional and Legal Structure

For more than 25 years IOSCO has developed, negotiated, and persuaded its members to adopt a range of objectives and principles for the regulation of both worldwide and national markets in securities and financial products such as financial derivatives. Domestic legislation and protocols for cooperation have been established in line with these principles, such as the protocol establishing the system of Memoranda of Understanding for cooperation and information sharing between national securities regulators.

As we have seen, IOSCO is established not by international agreement between states, but by agreement between what are usually independent commissions or government departments charged with securities regulation. IOSCO's members are also commissions and government departments, not states. The organization has 110 members that regulate 99 per cent of the capitalization of world securities markets.

IOSCO has three classes of membership: ordinary, associate and affiliate. Ordinary members are either governmental regulators of securities markets, or a self-regulatory organization if there is no public authority. Ordinary members have one vote, and are members of the President's Committee that meets at the Annual Conference of the Organisation. The President's Committee approves motions that become the resolutions of IOSCO. The Objectives and Principles of Securities Regulation were adopted in this way. The ordinary members of the President's Committee elect nine of their number to the Executive Committee, the standing governing committee of the organization. Associate members are market authorities in subdivisions of a country where the national regulator is already a regular member. Although they are members of the President's Committee, they have no vote and are ineligible for membership of the Executive Committee. A self-regulatory organization or an international body, with an appropriate interest in securities regulation, is eligible for affiliate membership. This level of membership confers no membership or voting rights in relation to either the President's Committee or the Executive Committee. A self-regulatory organization that is an affiliate member may belong to the SRO Consultative Committee, which is consulted by other IOSCO committees in relation to the market effect of proposed resolutions and other departures. The organization is financed by an annual contribution of its members that is currently set at US$6750.

In addition to these organs, IOSCO also has a Technical Committee made up of 16 representatives of securities authorities that regulate the larger and more-developed markets. The Technical Committee determines its own membership, procedures and agenda. It operates through five standing Working Groups, each with a mandate in relation to particular issues of securities regulation. The Working Groups make recommendations to the Technical Committee, which in turn presents them to the Executive and President's Committees for formal adoption by the organization. The Emerging Markets Committee performs a role similar to that of the Technical Committee in relation to issues facing emerging and developing markets. There are also four Regional Committees that meet to deal with regional issues.

Interlegality between IOSCO Principles and Nation State Rules

In what follows I use some of the dimensions of interlegality identified by Santos to consider the interrelations between the IOSCO principles and national law. The contexts in which Santos made his observations of thc modes of interlegality are both literally and metaphorically a world away from transnational securities regulation. However if the concept of interlegality has any explanatory power independent of the context in which it was originally observed, and I think it has, then it should be possible to draw some conclusions from its employment in such a radically different context.

Interlegality through imitation: One of the leading features of the empirical work which led Santos to the concept of 'interlegality' is the degree to which the non-state system imitated the official or state law. This was so even though the state gave only conditional recognition to the legality of the non-state law, and sometimes withdrew that recognition in an arbitrary fashion.[91] It is true that the non-state system had some very important, substantively different norms and was generally more informal in its processes. But there was a substantial degree of imitation or adoption and

[91] By destroying the squatter settlements, Santos, above n 4 at 236.

also a kind of symbiosis in calling on the authority of the state law to bolster the authority of the non-state system.

Although the context is very different, it is not difficult to see similar patterns in the development of the IOSCO principles. Most of the substantive norms in the principles are derived from the securities regulation regimes of developed Western economies, notably those of the members of the IOSCO Technical Committee. In particular, in following the securities regulation schemes of Western countries, the IOSCO principles place great importance on disclosure, and on associated prohibitions such as insider trading. In developed markets there is an established 'equities culture' and investors are typically professional or middle class and comparatively well informed. Regular disclosure of high-quality information has developed against that background.

In contrast, members from emerging markets have less-experienced investor populations. Elevating disclosure in such a context may be less beneficial than, say, merit regulation where the regulator approves a financial product in the light of the investors to whom it is to be issued. As a merit approach may result in the prohibition of some products, it may also be a cheaper form of regulation than disclosure and may require less regulatory expertise to administer,[92] which can be beneficial in emerging markets. Replication of Western patterns of securities regulation in the IOSCO principles strongly implies a power effect – one enjoyed by the more-developed economies through their greater depth of technical knowledge and longer experience, and their membership of IOSCO's Technical Committee. This globalizes Western economy standards: those of the US and other developed markets.

Imitation of national approaches is also likely in the interpretation of the IOSCO principles as well as in their creation. Interpretation of IOSCO principles is likely to occur at a variety of sites and from a variety of standpoints, as is the case with national laws. I discuss this further below. For the moment it is sufficient to observe that as the principles are not part of international law there is no sense in which their interpretation develops as part of that body of law in a formal sense. The most influential interpreters of the principles are likely to be the IOSCO Committees responsible for developing the 'know-how' that leads to distillation of the principles, assessment of their operation, and the introduction of amendments. The Technical Committee, constituted by members from advanced markets and led by the US, is the most powerful of these. As Braithwaite and Drahos observe, we should not overlook:

---

[92] It should be remembered that it has been less than four years in Australia and not many more in the UK since merit regulation in relation to unit trusts was abandoned.

> [the] importance of what goes on in countless little technical committees at international organisations and more so in voluntary standard-setting bodies … These are crucial sites of epistemic community-building … their importance is in both the incremental construction of regimes and epistemic communities of the regime-builders.[93]

Indeed, one of the reasons for the weight that is accorded to the IOSCO principles is that they are created and promoted by a community of experts, though these are experts in securities markets at a particular stage of development and with particular values. Given the diversity of economic structure and stage of development that characterizes IOSCO members, the promotion of a particular vision of securities markets and their regulation as authoritative is important to the development and promotion of the principles. As we know from the literature on interpretive communities, there are no shared rules without shared patterns of judgment or normative action,[94] and it is around the creation and maintenance of these that the interpretive community in the committees of IOSCO operates.

It is true that the agenda for the creation of principles is led and promoted by members from advanced economies, and few countries have the regulatory depth of the advanced markets. But the large membership of the Emerging Markets Committee of IOSCO is an important counterpoint to the agenda setting of the advanced economies, and part of the dialogue of interpretation and creation of an interpretive community within IOSCO. The liberal democratic values that are transmitted through the market-oriented agenda of the advanced member countries are never rejected; they are modified, or more time is required by the emerging market members for implementation. An example of this is the implementation of the IOSCO protocol for Memoranda of Understanding for information sharing and cooperation between IOSCO members. In a fashion reminiscent of non-state law adopting the values of the state system that Santos observed, the non-state IOSCO principles reflect many of the values of the advanced economies, despite the diversity in economic structure and development which characterizes IOSCO member economies. This level of agreement about the principles and their underlying values is no doubt greatly enhanced by the epistemic community of technical expertise and opinion constituted in IOSCO committees.

Interlegality through incorporation and convergence: As we have just seen the IOSCO principles tend to imitate the securities laws of the developed

---

93 Braithwaite and Drahos, above n 3 at 503.

94 Black, *Rules and Regulators* above n 44 at 16; Fish S, *Doing What Comes Naturally: Change, Rhetoric and the Practice of Theory in Literary and Legal Studies*, Duke University Press, Durham, North Carolina, 1989 *passim*.

economies. Interlegality between the IOSCO principles and national laws may also be seen through incorporation and convergence. Mostly this is likely to have the greatest impact on the securities laws of countries other than Western economies. In turn, over the long term, this may lead to greater convergence in securities laws.

The IOSCO principles, having sometimes taken years to negotiate, are at a high level of generalization and abstraction. They provide overall direction and policy (or purpose) and they carry foundational regulatory values such as transparency, manifested in disclosure regimes. What Christine Chinkin says of 'soft law' is also true of the IOSCO principles – both are 'intended to construct and program development'[95] in a convergent direction. The IOSCO principles both cause change and are consequential upon it. They cause change by supplying values and policy justifications to support legislative changes at national level. As Nelken points out, implementing global regulation can serve as a means by which national regulators augment their resources and [re]legitimate themselves.[96] They are consequential upon change in that they respond over time (in further rounds of revision) to new market circumstances and regulatory changes in the national systems of economies with leading securities markets.

There are of course limits to the interpenetration of national securities law through incorporation and convergence. Broadly expressed principles like those of IOSCO are excellent vehicles for the specification of interests and values. They are much less good for the technical or precise jobs of law such as specifying passage of title or risk; these are left to national regimes. So in the all-important details of rules, there may be significant diversity. The broad way in which the IOSCO principles are expressed allows for the coexistence of some different regulatory approaches or priorities. This may be necessary to accommodate the variety in IOSCO members' economic structures and stages of development. At least for an adjustment period, principles drawn at a high level of abstraction can accommodate diversity, though they do create expectations that emerging markets will eventually converge with the standards of developed markets.

Even when action includes steps to incorporate IOSCO values and policies into national law, it is unlikely that there will be a direct correspondence between the IOSCO principles and member state law or even close convergence. In the most straightforward instances (probably those of Western economies), adjustments may be made to national securities regulation through legislation, administrative rules, and policy

---

95 Chinkin, above n 23 at 853.

96 Nelken, above n 2 at 256. Such relegitimation could lead to program invigoration and new impetus for institution building.

justified by reference to the principles. Other instances are likely to be less straightforward, for a number of reasons. To begin with, it may be that the level of expertise and resources available domestically simply means that the standards in the IOSCO principles cannot be met in practice even if part of the formal law. Then, there may be a myriad of political, cultural and technical reasons why global generality is lost in the translation to the domestic realm. Finally, of course, there are IOSCO members that just do not implement the principles at all. This indicates that although global standards may establish a general trend of convergence, it is likely to encompass convergence of various kinds. Unlike the more direct incorporation from state to non-state systems observed by Santos, the diversity of circumstances of the nation states receiving the IOSCO principles means that the results of interlegality are more difficult to observe and classify. Overall, however, anecdotal evidence suggests that many IOSCO members adopt the principles as legal norms that obligate them to action in a particular direction. They raise expectations and it may be difficult to resist political or moral claims made on the basis of the principles, even if they are not formally incorporated into national legal systems.

Interlegality through interpretation: Direct legislation or administrative rule making, though the most straightforward, are not the only modes of interlegality between the IOSCO principles and nation state securities regulation. A complex interaction between the principles and domestic legal rules can occur through processes of interpretation. This is not new, as in the domestic arena we often see interaction between law and soft law such as guidelines, the latter giving substance to the meaning of the former.[97] The same effects might be observed in the operation of IOSCO principles with national laws. For example, in a national tribunal, a party (perhaps a regulator) may argue that a 'black box' legal concept such as 'reasonableness' or 'efficiency' might be given meaning by reference to the IOSCO objectives and principles. The principles may also be made concrete either domestically or transnationally through their adoption by parties to securities contracts, or in international securities arbitrations. They may even underpin arguments through the doctrine of estoppel.[98] In all these examples the IOSCO principles clearly interweave with other national or even transnational laws, with real though oblique legal effect. The interpretive opinions and arguments of the IOSCO committees are likely to be an authoritative source of interpretive material in this process.

97 Kingsford Smith D, 'The Regulation of Life Insurance and Superannuation Investments in Australia' (1993) 21 *Australian Business Law Review* 9-42.

98 Gruchalla-Wesierski, above n 34 at 63.

Conclusion

Although the idea of interlegality encourages us to consider the detailed ways in which different types of law interrelate, 'the complexity of current interactions ... is such that in some instances the two levels are so interconnected as to make it impossible to distinguish their respective determining conclusion'.[99] This threatens to be the case with transnational financial regulation, and it is a problem much exacerbated by the lack of empirical evidence about how networks, norms and national laws in this area work in fact. But at least interlegality lets us see the general directions that might be followed and leads us to some preliminary conclusions.

Pluralism and Interlegality

The first thing that a pluralist approach to transnational securities regulation shows us is the multitude of the norms in the transnational space in which transactions are undertaken. Recognizing this social fact may lead on to seeing the characteristics of different types of norms. The IOSCO principles are open textured and sanctionless (though not ineffective) and serve purposes different from those of national securities laws. The former adjust expectations and guide convergence of rules and practices. The latter have a narrower focus – they determine rights and duties, effect the passage of property and other technicalities, and often impose sanctions. In addition the pluralist lens allows us to see the myriad of other norms, such as those arising from standard forms, association rules and codes of practice, and to identify their juridical nature more precisely.

In particular, a pluralist approach emphasizes that we cannot look only to formal national and international sources of law, and that we must investigate the transnational level of regulation in a number of dimensions. First, as I have already suggested, there is a huge program of empirical investigation of the different networks, norms and rules and those they act upon in the transnational field. We know very little about the operation of even something as prominent as the IOSCO principles, let alone less well-known norms. Until we know how these different orders work, we simply cannot say, for example, that norms such as the IOSCO principles have no legal effect without the support of nation state authority. A pluralist perspective enlivens us to the possibility that law is not coextensive with the nation state.

That leads us to an investigation of a second dimension of transnational securities regulation. A pluralist approach not only helps to separate and

[99] Santos B de Sousa, 'State, Law and Community in the World System: An Introduction' (1992) 1 *Social and Legal Studies* 131.

identify the nature and effect of the multiplicity of rules that make up global securities regulation, but to recognize the ways they inter-relate – their interlegality.

We have considered three interlegalities between a state and a non-state system. IOSCO principles may be considered non-state law because strictly speaking, IOSCO has no international or sovereign lawmaking capacity. We have observed the degree to which IOSCO's principles reflect the values and interests of the nation states that dominate its Committees. In fact, the opportunity for state influence of the non-state system here is arguably greater than it was in Santos' research, where the actors in each system were different. At IOSCO members wear two hats: they are at once authorities in their state law system and the authors of the principles which are part of the transnational network. To the extent that the IOSCO principles replicate national laws, this amplifies their authority, as they acquire additional legitimacy through being seen to be effective in existing securities regimes.

But we cannot leave the question of interlegality here. We have examined the relationship between the IOSCO principles and national law because it corresponds most closely with Santos' example, is the most accessible and because I suspect it occurs numerically more often than many others. However, Santos' discussion of interlegality makes it clear that the concept applies to interrelations between legal orders other than state and non-state. So future research on transnational securities regulation should consider both non-state orders *inter se* and also state pluralism – that is, different orders within the state.[100] The former means considering the interoperation of the IOSCO principles with the rules of professional and industry associations, clauses of standard form contracts, and perhaps also international codes of conduct on various topics. The latter, state pluralism, could help us understand the operation of a more complex state in the transnational field. For example, as I discuss further below another way to think about the interlegality between IOSCO principles and nation states is as state pluralism, with IOSCO seen as part of a more complex or extended state, rather than an autonomous transnational body.

The second dimension of interlegality we examined operates through incorporation of IOSCO principles into national laws. This is what might be called the second part of a 'two-step interlegality'. While Santos observed a single-step relation between state and non-state orders, the IOSCO example involves interrelation between the laws of (Western) nation states and IOSCO, and onwards to the national systems of IOSCO members generally. For all the reasons we have already identified, the

[100] See for example, Arthurs, *Without the Law*, above n 60 *passim*.

second step – the incorporation of the IOSCO principles into national law – is likely to produce variety within a general trend of convergence. There are likely to be variations between the forms of national rules but also a growing generality in that the rules will be about the same topics, such as disclosure, for example. Further, even though the precise rules are very likely to differ between states, the underlying principle will be embedded in complex state rules and not easily removed.[101] Further revisions may bring the national laws closer and closer to the IOSCO model. In the leading essay in this collection, William Twining argues for a re-examination of the possibilities of general jurisprudence or the universalization of norms in a global context. He suggests that we reconsider whether there are any concepts of general application – any that might have at least a core of universal meaning recognizable and applicable across various boundaries: state, social, economic and political. With inimitable pith he asks, 'Are there any legal concepts which "travel well"?'. Although we need more research to know for sure, I suspect that in transnational securities regulation, concepts like transparency and disclosure 'travel well' and that the interlegalities of imitation, incorporation and convergence between the IOSCO principles and national laws is one of their main means of transport.

Interlegality through interpretation is the final intersection between the IOSCO principles and national securities laws we considered. Interpretation is the central point in the operation of rules, and continues the process of their creation. Interpretation is fundamental to, and perhaps the only mode of control in, 'soft law' circumstances. It is the dynamic aspect of any rule or principle. It is where change is introduced from the conditions on which the rule operates, and where internal changes occur, such as changes in the scope or the operation of the rule's internal parts.[102] Not only may interpretation cause a coincidence of meaning in rules and concepts between state and non-state systems, in the transnational arena it may also influence the development of interlegality between non-state orders *inter se*. For example if negotiating parties interpret a term in a standard form contract by reference to the meaning given to it in the IOSCO principles, there will be legal effects in the absence of direct state authority, though not entirely without its influence.

---

101 One has only to recall the attempts to abolish the doctrine of *ultra vires* in company law to understand how much more difficult it is to remove rules than to add them.

102 Black, *Rules and Regulators*, above n 44 at 13

The Regulatory Implications of Pluralism and Interlegality

What is the significance of pluralism and interlegality for the state's role in securities regulation? As we have seen, there are convincing views, even at the national level, that the state has been decentred. This is emphatically not an 'end of the nation state' view, but one that sees the state in a more complex relationship with non-state orders. The nation state is not in retreat, but the lines between the public and private spheres are blurred, and functions previously discharged by clearly public means may now be undertaken by non-state entities. Self-regulation of securities markets provides a stock example. Globalization adds decentring at the supra-national level to decentring at the national level. The implications of pluralism and interlegality for securities regulation at the transnational level really depend on the extent to which state influence can be seen in non-state rules and practices.

So, on the one hand, governance theorists might argue, as Jayasuriya does, that organizations like IOSCO are an extension of a more complex state, governing at a distance. On this view we should expect to see functions usually undertaken by the state discharged at the transnational level under the auspices of non-state organizations. We should expect more informal legal modes, and indeed the IOSCO principles are less formal in their creation and less direct in their legal effect than national legislation or international law. Nevertheless the principles have a considerable degree of legitimacy. They are seen as models for national laws and are incorporated into the legislation and administrative rules of national securities regimes. They may also supply guidance in the interpretation of national laws, contractual terms etc. in a variety of situations which we have already canvassed. In these ways IOSCO and its principles function in a fashion which is regulatory and state-like, though at a distance from the state.

By comparison, a pluralist reading of IOSCO and its principles would emphasise the tendency of state systems to influence non-state ones. Through interlegalities we should expect to see the non-state system imitating the state, which is the case with IOSCO. Alternatively the relationship between the state through its securities regulators and IOSCO could be seen as one of state pluralism. This involves different modes of action by the state itself, some such as IOSCO more informal than others such as national securities regulators.

Whether we adopt a pluralist or governance theory explanation, either way, we may surmise that the state can still be influential in regulation, even in transnational circumstances. Until there is good evidence to the contrary, we should resist the twin views that rules only have effect when they are part of national law, and that the regulation of global markets is entirely outside the power of states. What we require is much more investigation of how this can be done effectively, when it works best, how it compares with the treaty process, and so on. Clearly, the role of the state in the transnational or global world, and the implications of this for regulation of cross-border securities, requires much more thought.

Legitimacy of Transnational Regulation and the Rule of Law

In the course of his reflections on the possibilities of a 'living law of the world',[103] Teubner remarks that 'global laws will probably remain in a diffuse but close dependency upon their respective specialized social fields with all their attendant problematic side-effects of which strong exposure to outside interests and a relative weakness of due process and the rule of law are important examples'.[104] Concerns about lack of autonomy have also been expressed in relation to decentred regulation of nation states. There it has been suggested that legitimacy through autonomy must be weighed in the balance with legitimacy arising from effective regulation. Law can lack legitimacy because it does not serve its perceived purpose, despite having the imprimatur of parliamentary due process and satisfying the (contested) ideal of the rule of law. The problem with decentred law is that although it may be effective, its more informal creation and administration opens it to the perception of bias in favour of influential groups and absence of procedural natural justice.[105] In the above quote, Teubner extends these reservations to the global or transnational field.

With decentred regulation at a national level, the diagnosis has generally been the selective imposition of due process and the conventions of the rule of law – 'constitutionalising' decentred regulation of various types, as Julia Black describes it. Could this be done for transnational networks and norms? What, if anything, does pluralism have to say about this aspect of non-state legal orders?

In fact the nature and the central interests of legal pluralism mean that this question does not seem to have been one of first priority. Pluralism is first a social fact, and only secondarily a program.[106] It has been intent on

103 Ibid.

104 Teubner, 'Global Bukowina', above n 42 at 8.

105 Perceptions which may well be justified, for example, the unwillingness of National Association of Securities Dealer's disciplinary panels to punish market makers for breaches in relation to the NASDAQ Small Order Execution System and National Association of Securities Dealer's 'turning a blind eye' to the tendency of NASDAQ market makers to quote prices only in even eighths (and not odd eighths): Jennings RW et al, *Securities Regulation*, Foundation Press, New York, 1998 at 105-6.

106 As Harry Arthurs puts it, pluralism 'is a program as well as a paradigm', Arthurs, *Without the Law*, above n 60 at 191. See also Kleinhans M and Macdonald R, 'What is Critical Legal Pluralism?' (1997) 12 *Canadian Journal of Law and Society* 25 *passim*.

the description and analysis of legal and near legal orders. Further, pluralism has been interested in normative orders, such as traditions, that are very close to the lives of those they affect. With these various different types of 'living law' the concern has more often been how to protect them from disintegration under state law, or to revive them, if they have been suppressed by state law. It really has been a lesser concern of legal pluralism to consider whether the conditions of creation of the non-state law measure up to those of state law, although it has been recognized that some forms of non-state law are certainly not ideal. In most cases also, the non-state order has been less powerful than the state order, and it has therefore perhaps been less germane to consider whose interests are represented in its creation and administration.

However, with the observation that the global or transnational domain is plural, the focus changes. The non-state IOSCO principles, as we have seen, are conveyors of particular interests and views: those of Western state securities regulators and lawyers. They are very influential in the formation of the national laws of other IOSCO member states, and may also influence the meaning and application of norms in other non-state orders. It is therefore important that we understand how they are legitimated, what the institutional forms and criteria of that legitimation are,[107] and whether they may be found wanting. It is unlikely to be possible (or even desirable) to replicate the institutions of legitimation of nation states at the transnational level. Some functional equivalents, however, such as recognition of a greater diversity of interests and wider participation in IOSCO rule making, might be a start. In this way pluralism opens up the possibility of recognition of views about transnational securities regulation which are additional or even alternative to those of the developed economies which currently influence IOSCO.

---

[107] Macdonald, above n 60 at 78.

PART III:

GLOBALIZATION AND THE LAWS OF PEOPLE

Chapter 6

Relabelling the International Labour Problem: Globalization and Ideology

*Jill Murray**

William Twining has identified a number of challenges which globalization poses for legal theory. The 'black box' conceptualization of states and their legal systems as 'discrete, impervious entities that can be studied in isolation' is outmoded because of the growth in external forces shaping domestic law, and the concurrent revision of the principle of national sovereignty within international human rights regimes and regional legal orders. We find, he argues, 'a much more complex picture involving established, resurgent, developing, nascent, and potential forms of legal ordering'.[1]

These insights also serve to highlight the challenge for those writing about legal theory and globalization from the perspective of the discipline of labour law. This discipline has traversed a different trajectory to many other fields of law. Since 1919, something that is commonly called 'international labour law' has been created by a unique, permanent institution, the International Labour Organization (ILO). The ILO was created in response to a number of pressures, most of which had their roots in the transnational activities of both labour and capital. A nascent process of globalization was noted in 1919: a French delegate told the first International Labour Conference, 'labour markets of different countries are no longer, in our time, independent. A world system of economic life is being superimposed more and more on the national system'.[2] At the same time, the threat of the transnational spread of worker revolution from Russia to western European states following the First World War was

---

* This Chapter derives from a paper the author delivered at the Australian Society of Legal Philosophy Conference, held at the Australian National University, Canberra in June 2000. An earlier version of this argument was published in the *Australian Journal of Labour Law* in December 2001.

1 See, Twining W, 'Globalization and Legal Theory' (1996) 49 *Current Legal Problems*, 1, 7, and ch 2 in this collection.

2 ILO, International Labour Conference Record of Proceedings, 1919, Geneva, 34. For a full discussion of the creation of the ILO, see Murray J, *Transnational Labour Regulation: The ILO and EC Compared*, Kluwer Law International, The Hague, 2001, 16ff.

perceived as a real prospect. The ILO was created as an international rule-making body in which representatives of governments and representatives of workers and employers participated. The rule-making body, the International Labour Conference is made up of two representatives from each national government, and one each from the most representative organization of workers and employers.

Further, the ILO from the first did not rely on the traditional treaty-making processes of public international law. The first Director-General, Albert Thomas,[3] recognized that the success of its multilevel regulatory regime depended not simply on the responses of national governments, but on the transnational networking, lobbying and bargaining of interested parties. The representatives of labour and capital who attended the International Labour Conference in Geneva were charged with taking the international rules back to their local realm and ensuring their successful implementation by lobbying legislatures and the public at large. In 1920, a Liaison Branch within the ILO was created by Thomas. Its purpose was to have daily correspondence with ILO personnel in Paris, London, Rome, Berlin and Washington.[4] Thomas believed that the requirement in the ILO Constitution that states place Conventions before their relevant national authorities meant 'in the ultimate analysis (states) have to consult public opinion within their own territory'.[5] The ILO would 'make use of whatever forces and movements of opinion in favour of the reforms adopted by the Conference may reveal themselves'.[6]

That is, in the 'other than national' field of labour regulation, we find a long-standing international institution that was aware of the porous nature of the 'black box' of the state. Social forces would dictate changes in labour legislation in line with international norms, which were themselves created through a sophisticated, iterative process involving many actors. This pluralism was fundamentally Eurocentric. Although the ILO's view of the interconnectedness of state governance with economic and social forces was clothed in the language of universality, until the end of the Second World War, 'universal' was 'inevitably taken to a large extent to mean European'.[7]

---

3 Thomas is one of the most interesting theorists of international labour regulation. See, for example, his collection of essays, Thomas A, *International Social Policy*, International Labour Organisation, Geneva, 1948.

4 League of Nations, Report of the Director-General of the ILO to the International Labour Conference, 1921, Geneva at 15.

5 Ibid at 46.

6 Ibid at 47.

7 Yves-Ghebali V, *The ILO : A Case Study in the Evolution of a UN Specialised Agency*, Martinus Nijhoff, Dordrecht, 1989 at 14.

The principles of regulation evident in the ILO's structure and rule-making behaviour were derived from the model of labour regulation then emerging in European states and their colonies. This model itself deviated in important respects from the traditional view of law as a mechanism of command and control. Within western European countries (and many of their former colonies, including Australia) the national mode of labour regulation rarely took the form of sovereign command through legislation. As Otto Kahn-Freund observed of the United Kingdom, a system of collective *laissez-faire* existed, whereby state intervention was directed at levelling out the power imbalance between employers and employees (primarily by permitting the existence of collective labour organizations such as trade unions).[8] As Julius Stone noted, 'once a fair balance in bargaining power between labour and capital was reached ... the demands for intervention [through legislation] turned into demands for non-intervention'. Norms were created through '[t]he "free play of collective forces", [that] assumed a certain regulatory and administrative role ... the liberty to bargain [was invested] with a quasi-public power of regulation'.[9]

These two aspects of the field designated as labour law – the existence of a highly developed international rule-making body, and the fact that law played a shaping, rather than determinative, role in creating actual norms in the national sphere – meant that the discipline developed an early interest in the central issues now said to be raised by globalization. First, questions of the circulation of law, and its transplantability from one national setting to another have been considered in the context of the role of non-state actors and the systems in which they operate. Kahn-Freund noted in 1974 that differences in the 'habitat of industrial relations' may make cross-national transplanting difficult.[10] Second, the existence of the ILO has also generated a dedicated literature on 'what travels well', in Twining's phrase.[11] There is both a formal and *de facto* recognition of the contingent nature of the ILO's international rules. The ILO Constitution does not aim at achieving 'strict uniformity in conditions of labour', because of the 'differences of climate, habit and customs, of economic opportunity and

8 Davies P and Freedland M, *Kahn-Freund's Labour and the Law*, Stevens and Sons, London, 1983.

9 Stone J, *Social Dimensions of Law and Justice*, Maitland Publications, Sydney, 1966 at 414, 420.

10 Kahn-Freund O, 'On Uses and Misuses of Comparative Law' (1974) 37 *Modern Law Review* 1 at 25.

11 See, for example, the Reports of the ILO's Committee on Freedom of Association, available from www.ilo.org.

industrial tradition'.[12] The underlying goal of the ILO was expressed in the phrase 'social justice', which was not defined in the Constitution: 'social justice is thus looked upon as a movement, not something static'.[13] The ILO Conventions are not legally binding, and the ILO's key role is to create a space in which issues concerning labour and capital are raised, discussed, and at times resolved into principles and standards.[14] The primary principle protected by the ILO has been, since 1919, freedom of association and the right to collectively bargain: all nations which are members of the ILO are deemed to be bound by the conventions covering these matters, whether or not they have ratified them. Over the years, many alleged breaches of these principles have been considered by the ILO's supervisory bodies, leading to the confirmation of a myriad of different national systems as consistent with the international rules.[15]

Thus, although the discipline of labour law tends not to have a strong theoretical discourse (apart from the political theories about the relations between labour and capital, and the recent application of systems theory)[16] the discipline has nearly a century of experience with the kinds of pluralism of private ordering, and the evolving non-state relations which may shape transnational laws now being named in the literature on globalization.

The globalization literature has created a perturbance in the field of labour law. The view that globalization 'is first and foremost a vast project in political economy that is restructuring the global order in ways that maximize its compatability with the values and interests of multinational corporate enterprise ...' has been given expression in recent writings about the problems of global labour regulation.[17] One important issue raised by such claims is the relationship between the forces named as global, and the pre-existing institutions and processes which have, until now, been identified within the labour law discipline. This Chapter argues that the relabelling of forces in the globalization literature has important ideological ramifications for the traditional view of labour law, as defined in countries such as Australia. The identification of sites of production as within the

---

12 Thomas A, 'Introduction', *The International Labour Office*, Allen and Unwin, London, 1931 at 33.

13 Above n 4 at 96.

14 For a useful discussion of these processes, see Braithwaite J and Drahos P, *Global Business Regulation*, Cambridge University Press, Cambridge, 2000 at 237.

15 See, for example, the Reports of the ILO's Committee on Freedom of Association, which can be found at www.ilo.org.

16 See, for example, Teubner G (ed), *Global Law Without a State*, Aldershot, Dartmouth, 1997.

17 Sarat A and Scheingold S, *Cause Lawyering and the State in a Global Era*, Oxford University Press, Oxford, 2001 at 7.

regulatory control of multinational enterprises, it is argued, serves as a constitutive device to give life to claims of hollowing out of the state and the defencelessness of governments and other actors in the face of global economic forces.

This Chapter will proceed by describing one such proposal, the Ratcheting Labour Standards (RLS) thesis[18] of American academics Charles Sabel, Dara O'Rourke and Archon Fung.[19] This is a proposal for regulation using the multinational corporation as the primary actor in setting and implementing labour standards. Control over the decision-making of firms would be exercised by an informed consuming public and other non-governmental interest groups. The proposal is based on the perceived failure of 'command and control' regulation at the national level, a critique that is then applied to the problems of transnational regulation of the global production lines of Nike and similar producers. The ramifications of the RLS proposal are considered in the context of the ILO, which is taken as a marker of the traditional approach to labour regulation in an Australian context.

International Labour Regulation since the 1980s

The Special Nature of Transnational Rule Making

In order to understand the RLS proposal in the context of the ILO, it is necessary to set out in more detail what the ILO is and what it does. From a regulation perspective, the ILO can be seen as part of an institutional system designed to make transnational labour rules.[20] These rule are addressed to the ILO member states, which are obliged under the ILO Constitution to place them before the relevant national authority (for example, parliament) so that ratification can be considered. States are not obliged to ratify conventions and ratified rules do not have a mandatory character in the sense that the ILO can enforce compliance: the ILO

---

18 Fung A, O'Rourke D and Sabel C, 'Realizing Labour Standards' (2001) 26 *Boston Review* 1. References here are to page numbers in the electronic version, which can be found at <http://bostonreview.mit.edu.BR26.1/fung.htm>, on file with author, accessed 7 May 2001.

19 Charles Sabel is Professor of Law at Columbia University. Dara O'Rourke is Assistant Professor in the Department of Urban Studies and Planning at the Massachusetts Institute of Technology. Archon Fung is Assistant Professor at the John F Kennedy School of Government at Harvard University.

20 It also operates by providing direct technical assistance to member states. These processes are beyond the scope of this article, but are an important element of the ILO's regulatory function. See, for example, Cox RW, 'ILO: Limited Monarchy' in Cox RW (ed), *The Anatomy of Influence: Decision-Making in International Organisations*, Yale University Press, New Haven, 1973.

therefore does not have the classical power of the nation state to issue commands backed by sanctions. Further, the ILO Constitution requires that the international labour rules it makes must not interfere in any inappropriate way with national sovereignty over labour issues.[21] Most of the more than 180 ILO conventions include flexibility provisions which devolve actual determination of substantive labour standards to the level of ratifying national governments, or even to the social partners at national and workplace levels. This feature of ILO rule making was evident from its earliest times: the first ILO convention, the Hours of Work (Industry) Convention of 1919, required ratifying states to establish a cap on weekly hours (that is, ordinary hours plus overtime), but did not fix the level at which the cap should be set. This was left for determination in the national sphere. Another important example of the ILO's essentially subsidiary[22] or framing role can be found in the field of wage fixation. The ILO has never tried to create an international minimum wage. Rather, it has created rules that states may ratify which encourage the establishment of free collective bargaining, and state-sponsored wage fixing institutions to complement this bargaining where necessary.

While the ILO's role in determining final substantive outcomes at state level is subsidiary in this sense, it claims a more central role in relation to certain matters, including in relation to the key procedural principles that the ILO believes should shape these substantive outcomes. Here the ILO is commonly said to operate in the mode of identifying and defining fundamental human rights in the labour field, especially the key rights to freedom of association and to engage in free collective bargaining.[23] The ILO's human rights instruments seek, to the greatest degree possible given its essentially voluntarist system, to constrain states from breaching the

---

21 In addition to the voluntary nature of ratification, discussed below, the ILO Constitution states, 'In framing any Convention ... of general application the Conference shall have due regard to those countries in which climatic conditions, the imperfect development of industrial organization, or other circumstances make the industrial conditions substantially different and shall suggest any modifications, if any, which it considers may be required to meet the case of such countries'. Article 19(3).

22 The ILO operates on a principle of subsidiarity in the sense that this term is used in relation to the European Community. That is, the role of the international agency generally only comes into play where issues cannot be properly dealt with at lower levels down the regulatory chain – at the level of member state government, or even that of local governments or individual actors. See, for example, Bermann GA, 'Taking Subsidiarity Seriously: Federalism in the EC and the US' (1994) 94 *Columbia Law Review* 331.

23 Leary VA, 'The Paradox of Workers' Rights as Human Rights' in Compa LA and Diamond SF (eds), *Human Rights, Labour Rights and International Trade*, University of Pennsylvania Press, Philadelphia, 1996.

rights of their citizens in these fields. (In other respects, these rules differ from classical human rights regimes in that they are constitutive of collective, rather than individual rights. Importantly, the ILO interprets the right to association as including a right to strike, even though this is not specified in the texts of the relevant Conventions.)

In addition to seeking to shape member states' laws (either directly or indirectly through the educative and symbolic role of transnational rules)[24] many ILO rules are designed to generate *non-rule* outcomes at the national level, including the creation of national policies (for example, on discrimination in employment), to spend public funds to meet certain social goals (for example, in the payment of maternity leave) and to ensure that states cooperate together on issues of particular concern (such as the abolition of child labour). This is an important point when proposals to devolve ILO rule making to other economic actors, such as multinational corporations, are considered: such actors are unlikely to be willing or able to achieve the breadth of norm creation by *dominium* and *emperium* encouraged by the ILO.

Broadly speaking, the ILO conventions, if ratified and fully implemented, encourage national systems of industrial relations based on free collective bargaining, backed by flexible legislated substantive standards and wide-reaching government policies in areas such as poverty reduction, public education, social security, occupational health and safety, vocational training and so on. The ILO labour rules are best described as loosely constitutive of domestic action by state and other actors to achieve these goals.

The ILO is unique amongst supranational bodies in that its rule-making body comprises representatives of both governments and civil society from each member state.[25] In line with its commitment to pluralistic industrial relations, representatives of employers and unions send delegates to the rule-making institution, the International Labour Conference. In accordance with the principle of national sovereignty that also dominated the formation of the Organization, two government delegates from each state attend with one each from the social partners. Conventions are adopted by a two-thirds majority of a quorate meeting of the Conference. Other institutions, agencies, groups and individuals are often involved in the making of

---

[24] This indirect influence on rule making was identified by the first Director-General of the ILO, Thomas A, in 1924. ILO, *Report of the Director-General to the International Labour Conference*, ILO, Geneva, 1924 at 810.

[25] Braithwaite and Drahos, above n 14 at 254.

particular rules, although no one other than the tripartite delegates is permitted to vote.[26]

The ILO and Globalization

Controversy over the policies adopted by the ILO[27] in relation to its rule-making function is nothing new, but sharp differences of an ideological nature have become more apparent since the 1980s.[28] The winds of change that swept through many Western countries from that time were also felt within the ILO, leading to two trends. First, a transnational adaptation of the neo-liberal argument about labour regulation took hold in the ILO: international rules should be made which would aid the process of deregulation in the national sphere. This proposal for international deregulatory rules was first raised by the ILO Director-General himself in 1984, when he launched a wide-ranging attack on the standard setting activities of the ILO. In the current 'fluid and precarious setting, questions that deserve consideration ... are how to ensure observance of basic social guarantees in a period of recession, and *how far standard setting could contribute to adaption to change*'.[29] The Director-General argued that standard setting should be limited to 'essential principles', take a flexible form and proceed at a slower pace.[30] In his 1988 Report, he argued that 'existing ILO standards are being questioned as imposing too rigid a framework and as standing in the way of new practices ...'.[31] Similar criticisms of ILO rule making continue to be made to the present day, reflecting pressure on the organization to stop making rules, or to focus only on those which boost competitiveness or define a limited number of

---

26 Such groups, including the World Health Organization, the International Confederation of Free Trade Unions and the Commission of the European Communities are often granted the right to speak in certain sessions of the Conference.

27 To talk of a coherent ILO 'policy' is rather artificial, as the setting of rule-making agendas and the convoluted processes of creating conventions are the product of many different influences, some of which are invisible to those who are not direct participants. For a detailed consideration of these issues in the period up to the 1960s, see, Haas EB, *Beyond the Nation State: Functionalism and International Organisation*, Stanford University Press, Stanford, California, 1964.

28 A strong push for cessation of ILO rule making occurred immediately after the Second World War, when American participants took the lead in arguing that the ILO had made all the necessary rules, and should now focus on other regulatory methodologies, including direct assistance to member states in meeting their extant obligations: Haas, ibid at 235.

29 ILO, *International Labour Standards*, Report of the Director-General to the International Labour Conference, ILO, Geneva, 1984 at 8.

30 Ibid at 17.

31 ILO, *Human Rights – A Common Responsibility*, Report of the Director-General to the International Labour Conference, ILO, Geneva, 1988 at 46.

core rights. Cordova has argued that the ILO's tendency to make rules reflects institutional inertia, rather than need.[32] Most recently, Cooney has made a strong argument that the actual needs of the worst-off workers in the world are not being met by standards which reflect those which can only be attained in developed states.[33]

Thus, in the 1990s, the ILO produced rules designed to encourage developed states to flexibilize their labour markets. Several conventions, including the 1990 Convention on Night Work[34] and the 1994 Convention on Part-Time Work[35] have been characterized as furthering the interests of labour market deregulation, and the spread of non-standard work.[36] While these Conventions confirm the fact that ILO rule making continues a focus on the labour issues arising in the developed states of the world,[37] the actual rules made deviate from the commonly held view of the ILO as a benign institution devoted to improving workers' conditions.

The second trend in ILO rule making took a different, but arguably complementary, course. At the same time as pressure to promote flexibility was being given voice within the ILO, the Organization also began to hone its focus on the core of fundamental labour standards, as the Director-General proposed in the 1980s. This trend, although it too arose from a deregulatory impulse at the international level, was clearly designed to foster rule making and implementation across the whole span of ILO member states. The ILO was to support a minimum set of guarantees so that every worker could enjoy 'decent work', the new short-hand term for the ILO's mission in the twenty-first century.[38] This can be seen as a companion to a general policy of labour market deregulation, as the international regulatory role was focused on a narrow issue: the creation of a minimum floor of basic conditions and abstention from determining

---

32 Cordova E, 'Some Reflections on the Over-Production of International Labour Standards' (1993) 14 *Comparative Labor Law Journal* 138.

33 Cooney S, 'Testing Times for the ILO: Institutional Reform for the New International Political Economy' (1999) 20 *Comparative Labor Law and Policy Journal* 365.

34 Convention 171, Night Work, 1990.

35 Convention 175, Part-Time Work, 1994. It was argued in support of this Convention that it would 'increase the willingness of workers to be flexible'. International Labour Conference, Record of Proceedings, ILO, Geneva, 1994, 23.

36 Murray J, 'Social Justice for Women? The ILO Convention on Part-time Work' (1999) 15 *International Journal of Comparative Labour Law and Industrial Relations* 3.

37 Between 1919 and 1944, the concept of universal coverage of the ILO was 'inevitably taken to mean European', Yves-Ghebali V, *The ILO : A Case Study in the Evolution of a UN Specialised Agency*, Martinus Nijhoff, Dordrecht, 1989 at 14.

38 ILO, *Decent Work*, Report of the Director-General to the International Labour Conference, 1999.

substantive outcomes (except through the kinds of general encouragement of deregulation outlined above).

This refocussing of the ILO on the project of ensuring the widest possible application of core labour standards was also a response to a rise in concerns at the phenomenon of globalization which, it was feared, entailed 'the loss of autonomous regulatory powers by states'.[39] That is, the forces that were said to require the deregulation of national labour rules to promote economic competition and productivity were said at the international level to require additional regulatory action. It was argued that 'the ILO is even more essential in an age of globalised trade'.[40]

With this assertion of the loss of power of the individual nation state came a heightened interest in the role of multinational corporations, which seemed by implication to be operating freely on a transnational plane, seeking out low labour costs and influencing government social and economic policy at will. Within the ILO, and other institutions, a discourse emerged about the possibility of harnessing the power of multinational corporations to secure the application of ILO standards.[41] A (re)newed interest in ways in which transnational organizations such as the ILO and the Organization for Economic Cooperation and Development (OECD) could assist in the regulation of multinational enterprises was, once again, at the centre of debates.[42]

Proponents of increased binding labour regulation failed to create a 'social clause' policed by the World Trade Organization (WTO), but Ministers at the WTO 1996 meeting issued a declaration proclaiming their nations' commitments to the 'core' labour standards, and to the ILO as the international agency with responsibility for implementing them.[43] This was both a significant defeat for the actors seeking greater formal regulation in the globalized economy, and an important validation of the role of the ILO in relation to its core, minimum standards.

The ILO's response to globalization, and its attendant shift in ideology towards deregulation of national labour markets, was therefore to strengthen its regulatory role as a protector of the core labour standards – a

---

39 Cox RW, 'Perspectives on Globalization' in Mittelman JH (ed), *Globalization: Critical Reflections*, Lynne Rienner, Boulder, 1996 at 26.

40 Mehmet O et al, *Towards a Fair Global Labour Market*, Routledge, London, 1999 at 11.

41 Murray J, 'Labour Rights, Corporate Responsibilities: The Role of ILO Core Standards' in Jenkins R et al (eds), *Corporate Responsibility and Ethical Trade: Codes of Conduct in the Global Economy*, Earthscan, forthcoming 2002.

42 Murray J, 'Corporate Codes of Conduct and Labour Standards' in Kyloh R (ed), *Mastering the Challenge of Globalization: Towards a Trade Union Agenda*, ILO, Geneva, 1997 at 41.

43 OECD, *International Trade and Core Labour Standards*, Paris, 2000 at 10.

minimum core of conditions to apply to everyone, everywhere. The refocussing of its efforts on alleviating the worst abuses suffered by workers[44] has been received positively in some quarters. Cooney, for example, welcomed the most recent Convention on the Worst Forms of Child Labour as moving 'away from "aspirational" conventions towards fundamental rights'.[45] Juan Somavia, the current ILO Director-General, the first to be appointed from a country outside Western Europe and North America, has redesigned the ILO bureaucracy in order to achieve greater focus on the core labour standards, and progress is being made in embedding these standards in national and other international regulatory agendas.[46] This is not only being achieved by ILO rule making and supervision, but also through international technical assistance projects in countries struggling to meet these standards. For example, the International Programme for the Elimination of Child Labour, run by the ILO, has an annual budget of $US44,000,000.[47]

The 'Ratcheting Labour Standards' Proposal

'Ratcheting Labour Standards': A Proposal for International Regulatory Reform?

American academics Charles Sabel, Dara O'Rourke, and Archon Fung have developed a proposal for 'improving working conditions worldwide' that they label 'ratcheting labour standards'. Their proposal is based on the construction of an international labour problem based on the need to regulate multinational enterprises, and to avoid two polar regulatory extremes: the use of inefficient and inflexible fixed rules to constrain firms, and to avoid unmodified self-regulation by those firms.

The RLS proposal is clearly intended as some form of 'other than national' labour regulation. While a number of domestic regulatory initiatives in the US are examined by the authors, the primary focus of the RLS proposal is on multinational firms that produce goods in supply chains in the developing world for consumption in developed countries. Indeed, the authors argue that their proposal arises from the new opportunities for regulation created by 'the increasing decentralization of production into

44 See, for example, the 1998 Declaration on Fundamental Principles and Rights at Work.

45 Cooney, above n 33 at 379.

46 The OECD reports that 'since October 1995, the number of countries that have ratified all seven of the original fundamental conventions has more than doubled'. OECD, *International Trade*, above n 43 at 9. For details, see 'Review of Annual Reports under the Follow-Up to the Declaration on Fundamental Principles and Rights at Work', March 2001, ILO, Geneva, available from the ILO website www.ilo.org.

47 Ibid, accessed 10 October 2001

tiered networks of supply chains that span the globe'.[48] The authors refer to examples of firms targeted by the 'diffuse but insistent protest movement for *international* workers' rights'[49] including Nike, Adidas, Timberland, New Balance, Gap, Fila, Puma, Levi's, Disney, Mattel, Reebok and their factory production in countries including China, Taiwan, El Salvador, Vietnam, and Indonesia.[50] After discussing the activation of 'publicity-sensitive' trade bodies in environmental regulation within the US, the authors enquire, '[i]s there similar public concern for the welfare of [often distant] workers'? They answer this question in the affirmative, with reference to surveys of the ethical values of consumers in the US and western Europe.[51] They note that '*multinational* corporations take the polling data seriously ...'.[52] Workers who are to benefit from the RLS process are 'workers in developing countries', and the authors nominate 'protectionist effects that can come from uniform standards' as one of the regulatory evils they wish to avoid.[53]

Further, the authors seek to ground their proposal by differentiating RLS from 'conventional regulation'.[54] They argue that RLS represents a third way between inappropriate state regulation and unsupervised voluntary self-regulation by firms: '(RLS) charts a course beyond conventional top-down regulation based on uniform standards on one hand, and reliance on voluntary initiatives taken by corporations in response to social protest on the other'.[55] The authors oppose the use of rules that impose 'uniform' standards on firms,[56] 'fixed, minimum standards in workplace conditions',[57] and the use of sanctions that 'punish firms for failing to meet established standards'.[58] They draw inspiration from 'new

---

48 Fung et al, above n 18 at 3.

49 Ibid at 19, emphasis added.

50 All these multinational companies produce brand-specific clothing, footwear, sporting goods and/or toys for major markets in the developed world.

51 Fung et al, above n 18 at 8.

52 Ibid, emphasis added.

53 Ibid at 15-16. The authors' focus in the first instance is on the task of regulating multinational corporations on this 'other than national' plane. The authors do note that the RLS concepts could also apply to systems of domestic labour relation, although this aspect of the proposal appears to be secondary to the initial task of regulatory multinational businesses in respect of their operations in the developing world: 'states could transform their own regulatory systems from fixed-rule to ratcheting by requiring *domestic* firms to score high on RLS measures or face sanctions'. Ibid at 20.

54 Ibid at 16.

55 Ibid at 2.

56 Ibid at 3.

57 Ibid at 13.

58 Ibid.

ways to regulate' that are emerging in the fields of environmental and labour monitoring in the US.[59]

In fact, these two features of the RLS thesis – its international scope and its underlying justification based on a critique of command and control regulation – represent an uneasy intermingling of national and transnational concerns. The tension between these two aspects of the proposals provides us with a means of exploring the ideological ramifications of this renaming of traditional labour law issues in the new language of globalization.

RLS: Institutional Structure and Standard Setting

The RLS proposal is based on a belief that market competition can be used to ensure that firms compete on the basis of their labour standards, leading to a 'ratcheting up' of standards 'as quickly as economic and technological conditions permit'.[60] RLS seeks to promulgate four principles: transparency, competition, continuous improvement, and sanctions. The principle of *transparency* would be deployed to create 'a world in which consumers, workers, activists and the public at large have the information they need to accurately and confidently identify initiatives to improve labour standards, gauge the results of these efforts, and compare the successes of firms, localities and even nations against one another'.[61]

The principle of *competition* is to apply in a number of senses. Greater transparency would ensure that firms competed on the basis of their labour standards. In this way, 'the norms of acceptable social performance, or labour standards, could emerge from evolving practices. As firms improve, the standards should become more demanding'.[62] Competition is also to be the means by which standards would be created in the monitoring of firms, and the means by which some of the formal RLS institutions themselves would emerge.

The principle of *continuous improvement* expresses the RLS project's interest in raising labour standards over time. This principle 'grows out of the principle competitive comparison. Social and market pressures would push firms, perhaps working with public agencies, NGOs, or unions – to constantly develop new methods of improving occupational health and safety, labour management practices, and the like'.[63]

The final principle in the RLS system is the pressure of *sanctions*. The authors note that much of the RLS success would emerge from voluntary

59 Ibid at 5.
60 Ibid at 13.
61 Ibid at 11.
62 Ibid at 13.
63 Ibid at 12.

actions, but 'more forceful regulatory institutions backed by punishments, however, are necessary to extend and deepen the promising dynamics behind these trends'.[64] The authors argue that it is necessary to avoid the traditional sanctions of conventional regulation, which seek to punish firms for 'failing to meet minimum performance criteria'.[65] No concrete proposals for new kinds of sanctioning regimes are made, but the authors state that RLS would act to 'dislodge' information using 'public power' to 'trigger more nuanced and ultimately powerful incentives to improve social performance'.[66]

The RLS authors are opposed to the use of 'fixed rules', as we have seen: 'Unlike conventional regulation, [the RLS] corrigible yet enforceable standards would be the product – not the starting point – of a process that was centrally focused on producing widely accessible and accurate knowledge of actual practices and deploying that knowledge to improve practices over time'.[67] RLS therefore does not have a normative component in the sense that it does not intend to foster some kind of centralized determination or advocacy of labour rules with universal application. The RLS philosophical and practical rejection of fixed rules has one exception. The authors state that they wish to ensure that workers play their role in 'conduct[ing] social audits and workplace monitoring'.[68] They go on to argue that 'freedom of association is an *essential implication* of RLS. Unions could therefore also use RLS to press governments and corporations to respect the freedoms that workers require to collectively understand and improve their workplaces'.[69]

The RLS proposal envisages the establishment of new regulatory institutions, although in keeping with the authors' aversion to centralized control, these too are to emerge gradually as the forces of free competition and greater public transparency work to create the best form of agency in the circumstances. The first step in RLS is that multinational firms determine a code of conduct that elaborates 'their labour standards',[70] and where necessary give assistance in meeting the standards.[71] The RLS schema then proposes that the firms select *monitors*, who would be responsible for investigating whether or not a firm had properly applied the terms of its code of conduct. Firms would be required to supply monitors

---

64 Ibid at 13.
65 Ibid.
66 Ibid.
67 Ibid at 16.
68 Ibid at 20.
69 Ibid at 21, emphasis added.
70 Ibid at 2.
71 Ibid at 14.

with details of wages, workforce profiles, environmental and labour management systems. Firms would also be subject to another process of '*independent audits* from [sic] NGOs, governmental bodies, or even unions to prevent collusion and assure veracity of reported data'.[72]

The 'social performance' of firms would then be ranked by the monitors, and these rankings passed to a second agency, a *council* or '*super umpire*'. The council 'perhaps emerges from one of the current non-governmental social certification organizations or from a collaboration between intergovernmental organisations'.[73] The council would 'assure the comparability of the information on key dimensions and disseminate much of it publicly'.[74] The authors also state that the council would 'set minimum performance and procedural standards for firms'.[75] These standards presumably relate to procedures for complying with RLS, rather than establish any substantive labour rules, as the authors make clear their opposition to the establishment of centralized, 'top-down' decision making. The council would also be responsible for ensuring competition between the monitors themselves to foster a race-to-the-top in this field.

The information generated would be used to 'ratchet up' standards through the processes of competition, based on the principle of continuous improvement discussed above. Poorly performing companies would be 'shamed', and 'increased veracity' would be demanded from poor monitors. A general *public debate* about 'global labour conditions' would follow, informed by knowledge of the best labour conditions achieved by the best-performing companies under RLS. 'Pushed by this public debate, officials at local, national or international levels could use information generated by RLS to formulate minimum substantive labour standards based on actual performance and procedural standards for improvement'.[76] It is not clear what form RLS proposes these minimum substantive standards would take, although presumably they would not be in the form of uniform, enforceable, fixed rules, as these are the reason for instituting RLS in the first place.

The authors give consideration as to how RLS could be kick-started. They note, 'transnational organisations such as the ILO, the United Nations, or the World Bank could begin to build RLS (given that) all three claim to be moved by sincere concern for the impact of globalization on

72 Ibid.

73 Ibid.

74 Ibid. The authors do not specify what categories of information would not be made public.

75 Ibid at 17.

76 Ibid at 15.

labour, the environment, women and native peoples'.[77] A detailed case is made out for the *World Bank* undertaking this foundation role, and playing the preliminary role of '*precursor or sponsor to the super monitor*, or umpire-governance [sic] body'.[78]

The 'Command and Control' Critique

As noted above, the RLS authors are highly critical of 'command and control' regulation, which they describe as *governance of firms by the state* through fixed, uniform rules backed by inflexible sanctions. In other words, the authors are referring to a mode of regulation that is domestic in nature. This section considers whether or not this argument can be meaningfully translated to the international level, and what the ramifications of doing so might be.

The first difficulty with such a translation is that the RLS critique of command and control regulation is in fact embedded, for its logical force, within a set of assumptions about the national sphere. This is clear from the use made by the RLS authors of various American examples of regulatory innovation. Thus, for example, the authors describe how new regulatory processes have been used to ensure that the relevant state laws have been complied with in the textile industry's large informal sector in the US, thus achieving improved wage and hours regulation.[79] In the environmental field, the authors refer to various novel regulatory processes of 'outreach and capacity building', which have achieved 'environmental compliance' with existing laws.[80] In an example of such regulation, firms were asked to contribute to a publicly accessible database that recorded the amount of some 650 chemicals released into the atmosphere by participating firms each year.[81]

In each of these examples, the regulatory innovation does not extend to the firms themselves deciding what the standard should be, the starting point for the processes of RLS. What would the ratcheting-up process described in these American examples look like if the state had *not* specified wage and hours standards in labour law, or had not set the standards for environmental compliance, or specified on which chemicals firms had to provide a public report? It is true that the RLS proposal does

---

77 Ibid at 17. This is a startling understatement of the role accorded to the ILO by its constitution, and by the Ministers of the WTO Member States in 1996, discussed above, see n 43.

78 Fung et al, above n 18. The authors note that 'space permitting, a case for the ILO's cooperation could also be made'.

79 Ibid at 6.

80 Ibid at 7.

81 Ibid.

not stop with the corporate self-determination of standards, optimistically predicting upward pressure through public campaigns and consumer purchasing power. But surely these processes, even if they worked at all, might be flawed by patchy outcomes, lack of technical information, and the disenfranchising from a public role in shaping social standards of those unwilling or unable to purchase particular products. These are the very problems that provide support for the role of the democratic state in governing certain social issues.

This view of the continuing role for the state is supported by Sabel in his work (with Dorf) on the 'democratic experimentalism' project, which appears to provide the philosophical inspiration for the RLS proposal.[82] The 'democratic experimentalism' project emerges from concerns about the essentially unknowable and ungovernable nature of society, combined with an optimistic belief in direct, communitarian participation in the testing and implementing of provisional solutions. Like the earlier 'pragmatist' philosophy, 'democratic experimentalists' believe that standards should emerge through lived experience, rather than top-down command. (This is clearly echoed in the RLS proposal that 'the norms of acceptable social performance, or labour standards, could emerge from evolving practice'.)[83]

Dorf and Sabel argue of the American domestic regulatory system:

> national affairs are too complex, diverse and volatile to be governed by the lapidary expressions of the public will – laws of Congress, administrative rules, judicial judgements, that indicate precisely how to dispose of most of the cases to which they will eventually be applied ... Again and again, general principles that command respect in the abstract are devalued through contradictory application. In these circumstances, whatever government does ... contributes to its undoing.[84]

Dorf and Sabel seek to develop new, localized forms of participative decision making, but this is to occur within the traditional architecture of the liberal state. They argue, for example, that under their proposed new order, US Courts 'would [continue] to ensure that sub-national experiments fall within the authorising legislation and respect the rights of citizens'.[85]

The true analogy between transnational labour regulation and the kinds of regulatory innovation proclaimed by the RLS authors would require one of two things: either a transnational regulatory authority would frame some equivalent 'authorising legislation' and name and protect rights, or it would

---

82 I am grateful to Sean Cooney for bringing this to my attention.

83 Fung et al, above n 18 at 13.

84 Dorf MC and Sabel CF, 'A Constitution of Democratic Experimentalism' (1998) 98 *Columbia Law Review* 267 at 270.

85 Ibid at 274.

be an integral part of RLS that the nations participating in the RLS project would be called on to do so in their domestic spheres. In relation to the first possibility, it is clear that RLS does not envisage any such role for its proposed institutions. On the contrary, the authors stress the fact that standards would emerge over time through the operation of the four principles of transparency, competition, continuous improvement and sanctions, not from any determination by structures of international governance. There is no recognition or support within the RLS proposal for international agencies designed to identify and protect rights. Nor does RLS make explicit a case for such regulation within the domestic sphere. Each of these issues is considered in more detail below.

The Assumption of a Transnational Regulatory Void

The RLS thesis does not contain a detailed analysis of the failings (or otherwise) of the existing institutions and processes of international labour regulation, other than the central criticism of the inappropriate application of fixed rules in the 'command and control' critique (discussed further below) and the criticism implied in the description of abhorrent labour conditions RLS is intended to relieve. (A detailed analysis of the ILO in RLS terms would be interesting, because many of the flexibilities sought by RLS have been identified in the ILO. Braithwaite and Drahos, for example, argue that, 'From its inception, the ILO's tripartite collaboration in all areas of labour standards has involved the commitment of all three social partners to continuous improvement…'.)[86] Indeed, RLS scarcely mentions the ILO at all,[87] and is completely silent as to the roles and responsibilities of other agencies such as the OECD (which has an important instrument dealing with multinational enterprises), the European Community,[88] and NAFTA. Whatever the reasons behind these omissions, by and large the RLS thesis proceeds on the basis that the transnational sphere is unregulated and that the RLS proposal should be rolled out into this void.

What meaning can we ascribe to the fact that RLS appears to assume a regulatory void at the transnational level? There are two fundamentally different possibilities. The first is that the RLS authors intend their system to be supplemental to these international and regional schemas. Under this

86 Braithwaite and Drahos, above n 14 at 247.

87 For example, in discussing the role the ILO or World Bank may take as precursors to the super monitor, the authors ask '… if the ILO is a promising partner, why are NGOs so prominent in new movements that the ILO, given its mandate and history, should be leading?' Fung et al, above n 18 at 17.

88 The EC is not only a significant regulator of labour within its member states, but has also integrated labour matters into some of its significant trade agreements, including those with African and Caribbean countries.

view, RLS could act as an additional delivery system, bolstering regional and global initiatives by linking together powerful economic actors (reputation conscious multinational corporations and consumer/special interest lobbies in America and western Europe).[89] The second possibility is that the authors intend RLS to be implemented to the exclusion of existing transnational systems, or are indifferent as to whether or not this implication is drawn from their work. On this view, RLS is an alternative to the ILO, not a complementary program to be run alongside it.

It is not possible to say which of these alternatives is intended by the authors. However, important aspects of the RLS proposal are fundamentally at odds with the basic operating premises of the ILO, suggesting that the first option is simply impossible. (RLS opposes the centralized fixing of labour standards, and the ILO regards itself as a universal body committed to just this task. This focus has increased in recent years, as discussed above. How could firms in the RLS project 'deliver' for the ILO if they would not commit to supporting the application of these standards in the countries in which they operated?) Given the current state of debates about labour regulation at the international level, the fact that the second meaning is available is important.

The RLS assumption of a transnational regulatory void coincides with an ideological position that seeks to make this assumption a reality. Resistance to international regulation, especially binding rules, has been a feature of the attitude of the employer negotiators within the ILO and the OECD since these institutions were created. That is, resistance to international regulation is located amongst representatives of the same multinational corporations that are at the heart of the RLS proposal. There is a danger that the RLS proposal could be used in the ongoing and intensifying battle over the future of these extant institutions by implying that the ILO and the OECD can be consigned to history, and new structures built around 'self-regulation' by multinational firms.[90]

The history of the ILO, the European Community, NAFTA, APEC and the OECD shows that building institutions at the 'other than national' level

---

89 There are many examples of efforts to harness transnational corporate and consumer power to further the spread of recognized labour standards in developing states. See, for example, the United Nation's Global Compact <www.globalcompact.org>, the United Kingdom's Ethical Trading Initiative (<www.eti.org.uk>), the European Code of Conduct in the footwear sector (<http://europa.eu.int/comm/employment_social/soc-dial/news/charterfootwear_en.htm>), and the recent Banana Industry agreement signed in Costa Rica (<www.iuf.org/iuf/editorials/banana01-00.htm>). All of these systems seek to ensure the firms and their suppliers respect the core ILO standards.

90 The extent to which RLS differs from simple self-regulation is discussed in the following part of this article.

which might have a hand in improving the lot of workers or empowering their representatives is always going to be a matter of great contestation amongst parties with different social, political and economic interests and, crucially, power. Workers' interests have only been institutionalized through a history of struggle against the force of ideologies that favour free competition and the dilution of workers' collective power where it exists. The contemporary political climate is highly inimical to institutional innovation of a kind which would further workers' interests,[91] suggesting that those who wish to further the conditions of workers with their (that is, the workers') institutional involvement should not weaken the hard-won transnational structures we already have.

As mentioned above, the ILO is the only international institution whose central rule-making body includes representatives of civil society, as well as states. Contrary to the claims of the RLS authors that the voices of workers in the developing world are rarely heard in the context of labour standards debates, worker representatives from the developing countries mentioned in the RLS proposal attend the International Labour Conference, and formally put their views in the rule-making fora. (One may question whether or not this process really does represent a genuine 'voice' for the 'sweatshop' workers targeted in RLS, but this is an issue that deserves to be addressed in its own right.) Of course, recognizing the fact that current institutions were hard won is not the same thing as mindlessly opposing improvements to their structures. Many now argue that parties other than representatives of labour and capital should also be included in the processes of international labour regulation within the ILO.[92] An appropriate response to these demands would be to examine the current structure of the ILO, rather than to start from a position based on the absence or irrelevance of the ILO to the issues addressed by the RLS proposal.

In any event, what is the validity of the criticism that the ILO has instituted inflexible fixed rules that constrain multinational firms? The ILO cannot be said to operate through the kind of modality criticized in the RLS thesis. As noted earlier, the ILO itself does not 'command and control' firms. We also noted that it does not 'command and control' states, for the

---

91 The most recent failure to strengthen international regulation of labour was the failure of the social clause proposal. See, Leary VA, 'Workers' Rights and International Trade: the Social Clause' in Bhagwati J and Hudec RE (eds), *Fair Trade and Harmonisation*, Vol II, MIT Press, Cambridge, Massachusetts, 1996.

92 The OECD has recently moved to involve representatives of Non-Governmental Organizations in its consultative fora. See Murray J, 'A New Phase in the Regulation of Multinational Enterprises: The Role of the OECD' (2001) 30 *Industrial Law Journal* 255.

simple reason that states in the ILO schema are not obliged to ratify any of the labour Conventions, and obligations arising from ratification are not enforced through binding powers. On the other hand, it could be argued in support of the RLS thesis that the command and control critique is directed at the role institutions such as the ILO play in shaping the way that nation states command and control firms, for example, by requiring that member states enforce 'fixed', 'uniform', and/or 'minimum' standards on firms. We can examine these claims in the context of an example given in an earlier version of the RLS thesis. Here, the authors provide a vivid picture of the failings of 'command and control' regulation: 'simple prohibitions, if enforced, can push children out of abusive factory work into outright prostitution'.[93]

The key provision of the general ILO Convention on child labour[94] states that '[e]ach Member [State] for which this Convention is in force undertakes to pursue a *national policy* designed to ensure the effective abolition of child labour and to *raise progressively* the minimum age for admission to employment or work to a level consistent with the fullest physical and mental development of young persons'.[95] The Convention refers to a calibrated set of standards which ratifying states may adopt depending on a range of factors. It refers to minimum employment ages of 13, 14, 15, 16, and 18, as well as to several less-specific regulatory markers such as 'the age of completion of compulsory schooling'. The Convention outlines a range of circumstances in which no minimum standards need apply. In fact, the minimum requirement enshrined in the ILO Convention on child labour is that ratifying states become familiar with the nature of child labour in their jurisdiction, and reach decisions on how to apply the open-textured framework proposed by the ILO. The Convention cannot be categorized as the kind of 'conventional top-down regulation based on uniform standards'[96] which RLS opposes.[97]

Of course, as discussed above, some ILO rules do take on the appearance of commands to states (that is, within the ILO schema, strict

93 Sabel C, O'Rourke D and Fung A, 'Open Labor Standards: Towards a System of Rolling Rule Regulation of Labor Practices', Discussion Paper presented at the Annual Meeting of the World Bank, Seminar on Labor Standards, September 29, 1999, 2. The authors state that this version of their work 'has been prepared as a discussion draft' at 1 fn 1.

94 Convention 138, Convention concerning Minimum Age for Admission to Employment, 1973.

95 Convention 138, Article 1, emphasis added.

96 Fung et al, above n 18 at 2.

97 It should be noted, too, that ILO standards are minima, so that any state wishing to pursue higher standards may do so without damaging any commitments they may have made to ILO Conventions.

demands are placed on the future behaviour of ratifying states), particularly those that take the form of the enunciation of fundamental human rights. These Conventions have as an international regulatory goal the restraint of the inappropriate exercise of power by a nation state over its citizens. As a direct result of concerns about globalization, the ILO has emphasised its role as guardian of a core of such standards, including its centrepiece core standards, the ILO Conventions on freedom of association and the right to collectively bargain.[98] And, of course, freedom of association (but not the associated right to collectively bargain) is the one 'fixed' principle that the RLS authors regard as 'implicit' in their system. If fixed rules and uniform standards, and the regulatory agencies charged with their attainment and protection, are rejected or ignored, how is freedom of association to be defined and attained in the brave new world of RLS?

The Assumption of the Domestic Regulatory Void in Developing States

The RLS authors also appear to proceed from the basis that there is a regulatory void in the domestic jurisdictions of the states in which manufacturing for the multinational corporations is occurring. In the following quotation from an earlier version of the RLS paper, the authors appear to acknowledge the existence of governments in the developed world only:

> The most effective regulatory bodies belong to national governments, but the subjects they seek to regulate are by definition international, sprawling across the globe. At most, these national authorities can enforce labour standards by rejecting goods that they identify as having been produced under sub-standard conditions ...[99]

This statement can only make sense if we assume that host states like China, Taiwan, El Salvador, Vietnam and Indonesia do not have national governments with effective regulatory bodies. The RLS authors conceptualize the state as the Western developed nation, the importer of goods made by 'others' in the supply chains of the multinational enterprises.

It was argued above that a robust conception of the state would be necessary if RLS were to operate under conditions equivalent to those assumed to exist in the examples of American regulatory reform discussed

---

[98] Convention 87, Freedom of Association and Protection of the Right to Organise Convention, 1948; Convention 98, Right to Organise and Collective Bargaining Convention, 1949.

[99] Sabel C, O'Rourke D and Fung A, 'Ratcheting Labor Standards: Regulation for Continuous Improvement in the Global Workplace', May 2000 at 11, available at www.law.columbia.edu/sabel/papers.htm.

by the authors. Such a conception is not evident from the RLS schema as it is presently stated. Standards are to be set and monitored through the auspices of multinational corporations under the supervision of private monitors and the 'governance council'. The entire public pressure brought to bear may exist thousands of miles away from the local setting in which the goods are produced. The RLS authors do not articulate a role within their proposal for the domestic laws and regulatory policies of the developing countries to interact with the multinational corporation centred approach advocated.

In terms of the history of transnational labour regulation, this fact in itself marks a stark break with past regulatory policy. Where international agencies have sought to deal with multinational corporations, as in the case of the OECD's Guidelines on Multinational Enterprises, the primary concern from the 1970s onwards has been the need to control the power of corporations vis-à-vis these states, and the central principle enshrined in this and other instruments was the fundamental requirement that multinational corporations abide by the laws of the states in which they operate. RLS is silent on the possibility that the standards adopted by multinational corporations, and indeed the standards acceptable to developed world consumers and activists, may be lower than or different from those of the country in which the companies choose to base their production. Within the long-standing discourse on the regulation of transnational corporations, this silence represents a serious omission and fits comfortably with an ideological position that supports freedom for multinational companies in their dealings with state regulatory regimes.[100]

---

[100] In his monumental study of the ILO, Haas concluded that in general the International Organisation of Employers 'opposed most (ILO) Conventions and Recommendations and tried to limit the role of the ILO': Haas, above n 27, 204. The present author's own research shows that western European employer representatives (except those from communist or fascist states) opposed every labour standard on working time made by the ILO after 1919. This involved bargaining down the content of the rules, seeking limitations to their scope, and then voting against the final version. Murray J, *Transnational Labour Regulation: The ILO and EC Compared*, Kluwer Law International, The Hague, 2001 at 52. Representatives of business in international fora have opposed binding regulation through these institutions, and within them, sought to limit the scope and effect of the non-binding rules created. When the International Labour Conference was considering its most recent Convention on maternity protection, employers' representatives argued that a simple statement that workers should be entitled to some maternity leave should replace any detailed international rule. The employer representative told the Conference, 'We recognise that each member State is sovereign, and that accordingly it must set its domestic legislation depending on the view of its constituents – the people in the country who live there – as to what must take priority, particularly in terms of extending rights and benefits'. Quoted in Murray J, 'The International Regulation of Maternity: Still Waiting for the Reconciliation of Work

As with the apparent assumption of the transnational void discussed above, the absence of recognition of a role for domestic governments and regulation in the RLS schema is important. We are living through an age in which it is both claimed and celebrated that globalization 'is a superior power; its momentum is a superior power to any other, even that of the State …'.[101] Within the burgeoning literature on globalization, the alleged vacuum left by the negation of state power is claimed by some to be filled by multinational corporations: globalization has been described as 'a vast project in political economy that is restructuring the global order in ways that maximize its compatability with values and interests of multinational corporate enterprise …'.[102] Teubner, for example, identifies codes of conduct of multinational firms as a 'proto-law' which 'has no legislation, no political constitution and no politically ordered hierarchy of norms which could keep the paradox of self-regulation latent'.[103] Alongside this kind of description of change has come the normative view that multinational corporate self-regulation is the 'default' setting in times of globalization, only to be questioned in special circumstances.[104]

It is important to remember that every factory producing goods in a global production chain is located within the national boundaries of a particular country. Recent trends in multinational enterprise structure suggest that this element of locality is becoming more significant.[105] When the high-profile companies mentioned in the RLS proposal proclaim their 'factory-less' production,[106] they mean that there are no factories in the developed consumer societies, leading some academics of the developed world now to claim that 'the industrial working class is almost ceasing to

---

and Family Life' (2001) 17 *International Journal of Comparative Labour Law and Industrial Relations* 25, 42. This 'visceral opposition' of international business to regulation has also been evident in negotiations within the OECD. Murray J, 'A New Phase in the Regulation of Multinational Enterprises: the Role of the OECD' (2001) 30 *Industrial Law Journal* 255 at 260 and 261 (fn 32).

101 Hutton W and Giddens A, 'Preface', in Hutton W and Giddens A (eds), *On the Edge: Living with Global Capitalism*, Jonathan Cape, London at viii.

102 Sarat A and Scheingold S, 'Introduction', in Sarat A and Scheingold S (eds), *Cause Lawyering and the State in a Global Era*, Oxford University Press, Oxford, 2001 at 5.

103 Teubner G, 'Foreword', in Teubner G (ed), *Global Law Without a State*, Aldershot, Dartmouth, 1997 at xiii.

104 Mehmet et al, n 40 at 19.

105 Birkinshaw J, 'Multinational Corporate Strategy and Organisation' in Hood N and Young S (eds), *The Globalization of Multinational Enterprise Activity and Economic Development*, Macmillan, London, 2000 at 67.

106 United Nations Commission on Trade and Development, 'Transnational Corporations, Employment and the Workplace', *World Investment Report*, Geneva, 1994.

exist'.[107] On the contrary, many thousands, perhaps millions, of workers are making the goods produced through globalization, and the factories in which they work have a local, as well as a transnational, identity. The Nike factory in Vietnam is a Vietnamese factory, as well as a link in a global chain. As Twining points out, 'the global does not exclude the local, but rather they interact in very complex, sometimes contradictory, ways'.[108]

Whereas the ILO is engaged in a regulatory conversation with states,[109] the RLS names the domestic problem as a transnational issue for the multinational corporation and its supply chain. The RLS proposals does not start from the point of enquiring what role the Vietnamese government should take in securing the 'international labour standards' of the Nike workers ('international' in the RLS schema by virtue of the fact that the workers are producing for an American-owned company, but from the perspective of a Vietnamese worker, domestic). There is a respectable argument that there are good practical reasons for not beginning at this point, given the endemic failure of many national regimes in the Asia Pacific effectively to uphold their own labour codes. Indeed, the fact that legislated domestic labour standards can be avoided, possibly with the tacit or active support of government agencies, appears to be one reason why multinational corporations select these countries in which to base their production.[110]

But what is the consequence of taking this national failure to regulate for granted, and assigning the regulatory function to the multinational corporation in the absence of a commitment to further the domestic standards in the host countries? The RLS authors are committed to the principles of participation and empowerment of actors in civil society, yet the structures and processes they propose may turn out to be another version of top-down rule imposition of a neo-colonial kind. The authors state, 'RLS enables society to sort out the abhorrent from the acceptable', but there is a possibility that this 'society' may consist of wealthy consumers of good produced in developing host states, rather than the 'society' in which those goods are made.

Transnational consumer movements are a significant social force. It is possible that practical changes for the better can be achieved through such processes, as the RLS authors make clear in their discussion of the successful operation of some corporate codes of conduct in multinational

---

107 'Giddens A and Hutton W in Conversation', in Hutton W and Giddens A (eds), above n 101 at 111.

108 Twining W, 'Globalization and Legal Theory' (1996) 49 *Current Legal Problems* 1 at 3.

109 The phrase 'regulatory conversation' is Julia Black's. See, Black J, *Rules and Regulators*, Oxford University Press, New York, 1996.

110 See Mehmet et al, above n 40 at 15-16, 48 9.

firms. It is important to recognize the principle that every person has a legitimate moral interest in the inhumane treatment of workers anywhere in the world. Indeed, it could be argued that the international human rights schema places moral duties on individual citizens and consumers to act as best they can to alleviate abuses elsewhere in the world. The key seems to be to ensure that this interest is appropriately meshed with requirements of autonomy and democracy wherever possible.

As it stands, the RLS proposal does not avoid the argument made by some developing states against ILO standards, that such standards represent the illegitimate imposition of rules derived from Western values onto states with different traditions and interests. Rather, the RLS proposal offers regulatory power to the hands of corporate actors traditionally regarded as holding disproportionate power over developing states and their workers, and places the controls of this system not in the hands of domestic government or local governance structures, but in the processes of public debate and consumerism in another country.

New Ideology for Old

The RLS proposal scarcely acknowledges the ILO and explicitly rejects the efficacy and legitimacy of centrally determined standards. This can be read as an ideological position in its own right, given the bitter debates over the ILO's role and the hard-won concession on the ILO's future role wrung from the WTO Ministers in 1996. The RLS attack on 'fixed rules', although misplaced in terms of the character of most ILO rules, apparently extends to any centrally determined rule, including those designed to protect fundamental human rights. There is an important conjunction between the RLS proposal and the neo-liberal philosophy opposed to state regulation of labour matters.

The RLS proposal derives from a particular construction of the labour 'problem' in an age of globalization. This construction and the response offered bear some similarity to a much earlier regulatory philosophy of labour regulation. The abhorrent circumstances that are the motivating force for the RLS system are:

> widespread abuses of labor including child labor, punishingly long days, harsh discipline, hazardous working conditions, sexual predation, and suppression of freedom to associate ... Insofar as these abuses come to light, they provoke moral outrage the world over – not least among those schooled since Adam Smith to see raw power used for economic gain as a threat to market order and freedom generally.[111]

[111] Sabel C, O'Rourke D, Fung A, 'Open Labor Standards: Towards a System of Rolling Rule Regulation of Labor Practices' above n 93 at 1.

Although the RLS authors make it clear that they are opposed to fixed rules applying strict standards to firms, their proposal has much in common with the British Protective Model that formed the Factory Acts in nineteenth and twentieth century Britain.[112] Here, the problem for regulation was conceptualized as being the need to restrain capitalist firms from exploiting completely helpless workers, particularly women and children. Like the British Protective Model, the RLS proposal appears to regard the beneficiaries of its system as 'passive recipients' of paternalistic protection.[113] That is, the key is to ensure intervention to remove the most vile conditions from those perceived as incapable of defending themselves against naked economic power.

The similarities between RLS and the British Protective Model are also evident in the RLS proposal's focus on what has been called the '"factory" vision'[114] of labour regulation. This approach both limits the scope of workers about whom RLS professes an interest, and serves to limit the kinds of regulatory answers the system is designed to foster. Thus it appears that forms of work beyond the purview of the multinational corporation that makes an identifiable physical product sold to people in the developed world are apparently not encompassed by RLS. Workers in the black economy, sex workers, service-sector workers and many others do not seem to be imagined in the RLS schema. The casting of the problem in terms of 'sweated labour' suggests a narrowly defined set of answers based around the removal of sweated conditions, an approach which is blind to broader regulatory traditions typically associated with the role of the state (such as 'law and policy designed to educate and train a workforce, the planning of industry development and locations, and other related labour market issues')[115] and with the ILO itself in terms of its regulatory conversations with states.

Finally, the RLS proposal carries important ideological implications because it focuses on the regulation of the firm, not the regulation of work. In the labour law traditions that shaped the history of the ILO, work is at least partly the regulatory business of the worker, and her or his representatives. Indeed, one of the cornerstone provisions of the ILO's constitutional framework is the following principle: 'labour is not a

---

112 Ramm T, 'Laissez-faire and State Protection of Workers' in Hepple BA (ed), *The Making of Labour Law in Europe*, Mansell, London, 1986 at 76.

113 Murray J, *Transnational Labour Regulation*, above n 100 at 15.

114 Mitchell R, 'Introduction: A New Scope and a New Task for Labour Law?' in Mitchell R (ed), *Redefining Labour Law: New Perspectives on the Future of Teaching and Research*, Centre for Employment and Labour Relations Law, Melbourne, 1995 at xii.

115 Ibid.

commodity'.[116] Adherence to this principle means not only that workers are not to be subject to the unalloyed power of their employer in the determination of the terms and worth of their work, but that they are also expected to be involved in the processes of establishing these conditions. Industrial democracy, collective labour relations, and the dignity and autonomy of workers' decision-making over their work derive from this central principle. RLS, in starting with the regulatory subject of the firm and its satellite suppliers, wipes the slate clean of these earlier conceptions of labour law, and even avoids the new language of the 'third way' concerning the need to 'promote mechanisms at work that facilitate cooperative work relations on the ground ... to achieve efficient and more competitive production'.[117] The equivocation of the RLS authors over the principle of freedom of association (and their pointed silence on the associated principle of right to bargain collectively) suggests a suspicion of trade union involvement, and a preference for other groups from civil society to engage in dialogue with firms as they set 'their' (that is, the firms') standards.

The essentially unitarist view of the firm in the RLS proposal means that the power imbalance between employer and employee, the central motivating feature of traditional labour law, is tacitly approved. The problems that then arise are twofold. Will the RLS institutions and the public(s) involved in setting standards be willing and able to act in ways which limit the power of multinational firms vis-à-vis their workers, in those workers' interests? Second, in the RLS system, what becomes of the choices for those workers, and indeed, the concept of harnessing worker innovation to ensure more equitable and efficient working practices? In any particular workplace, labour costs and worker productivity will interact in subtle ways, and there will often be options in the way in which change develops. For example, a factory owner may be able to afford a small wage increase, or for the same cost to the business, provide better meals in the staff canteen. Why should someone who buys sports shoes in another country 'determine' this issue, rather than the people whose pay and food it is? The ILO says that workers should be involved in these choices, while RLS proposes the more passive role for workers of 'monitoring [the firm's code of conduct] and understanding their workplace'.

---

[116] See, for example, the Declaration of Philadelphia (1944), www.ilo.org.

[117] Collins H, 'Is There a Third Way in Labour Law?', in Giddens A (ed), *The Global Third Way Debate*, Polity Press, Maldon, at 304.

Conclusion

In international labour law, the questions raised by Twining‘s research – including the extent to which concepts generated at surpranational levels can be, or should be, applied in diverse national settings – have been subject to scrutiny for nearly a century. The old answers, as seen in the institutional structures and rules of the ILO, were based on an assumption of integrity of the nation state, and the efficacy of free collective bargaining between representatives of labour and capital to achieve optimal results. This did not entail a naïve faith in centralized, monolithic rule making: on the contrary, international labour rules are remarkable for their plurality of meaning in diverse national contexts. The important point was that, to use Julia Black's phrase, the regulatory conversation of international labour law was between the ILO and its member states, which were asked to undertake a range of rule making, expenditure and policy actions in order to comply with the international standards. At the core of the system was the belief that 'labour is not a commodity', and that workers themselves should be involved in setting labour standards at international, national and local levels.

The recent literature on globalization, taken in combination with the rise in neo-liberal economic theory, contains the basis for a fundamental challenge to this older discourse. The globalization literature tends to focus on the multinational corporation, and, as in the case study considered here, welcomes the global production chain as an opportunity for re-regulation. But this focus tends to displace the local character of work and work rules, a problem that becomes serious when both the transnational and national realms were claimed to be void of extant regulation. At issue here is the active participation of workers in the determination of their own conditions at work, and the role of citizens and their governments in making social and economic laws in the face of the power of multinational corporations.

The main task of labour law (as defined within the Western dominated field) was to ensure that workers met employers with equal power: after that, free collective bargaining was to be the vehicle by which regulatory solutions were created. For those too weak to join forces and bargain, legislated solutions were to be the answer. The identification of a labour problem residing within the sole regulatory scope of multinational corporations has given rise to offers of self-regulation, the new 'proto-law' identified by Teubner. This Chapter has argued that this amounts to a retelling of the longstanding story of international labour regulation. The ideological ramification of this retelling is that it involves a significant shift in the power relationships between workers and their employers and between multinational corporations and nation states hosting their activities.

Chapter 7

Globalization and Citizenship and Nationality

Kim Rubenstein[*]

William Twining writes of his preference for the use of the word 'cosmopolitan' over the terms 'global' and 'international'. A 'cosmopolite' is a 'citizen of the world' he reminds us, as the dictionary defines the term as one who regards or treats the whole world as his [sic] country; one who has no national attachments and prejudices'.[1] The concept of citizenship is central to this chapter and the 'real-life problem'[2] of the legal status of people in their domestic and international environs requires some jurisprudential rethinking due to the impact and reality of globalization.

How well are the legal concepts of citizenship and nationality travelling in a globalized world? This section addresses the effects of globalization on people's status and membership within their own territory, and beyond it. Citizenship is a legal, political, and social construct that has domestic and international consequences. I argue that citizenship, in its traditional meaning of participation in and membership of the nation state, will be fundamentally altered by globalization and will not continue to travel in the same manner that it has been. The familiar domestic and international consequences of citizenship, such as political voting rights, legal rights including the right to leave and enter a country, and social welfare rights, will be fundamentally affected by the changes in people's connection to the nation state. This means that it cannot be recognized as a generalizable legal notion, to the extent that it may have been in the past.[3] Moreover, as people identify and become members of more than one community, we will witness an acceptance of multi-citizenship/membership within the nation

---

* This chapter draws on and further develops the central arguments of two separate pieces previously published. See Rubenstein K, 'Citizenship in a Borderless World' in Anghie A and Sturgess G, *Legal Visions of the 21st Century: Essays in Honour of Judge Christopher Weeramantry*, Kluwer Law International, The Hague, 1998; and Rubenstein K and Adler D, 'International Citizenship: The Future of Nationality in a Globalized World' (2000) 7 *Indiana Journal of Global Legal Studies* 519.

1 Chapter 2 of this volume at 13.

2 Ibid at 18.

3 It is of course questionable whether the notion of citizen has ever really been generalizable in a normative sense. See below n 24 ff. The legal category of citizen, however, can be identified as the formal status of a person within a sovereign state.

state and within the international order. The rise of the world citizen and the changes that have occurred in the nation state mean that citizenship and nationality will be revised concepts in the twenty-first century. If they are able to adapt to these changed frameworks, then citizenship and nationally may continue to travel well.

Since ancient Athens,[4] theories of citizenship have rested on the idea of an autonomous polity. Common membership of a political entity forms the basis of most discussions of citizenship from Aristotle onwards. Whether by Aristotle himself or in the writings of Bodin, Hobbes, Rousseau or Marshall, citizenship is conceived of in terms of political institutions which are free to act according to the will of (as per Aristotle),[5] in the interests of (as per Rousseau) ,[6] or at least with authority over (as per Bodin or Hobbes)[7] their citizenry. Since the Enlightenment, national sovereignty has been the theoretical basis of this freedom, and its subject, the modern state.

In its classical form,[8] the principle of sovereignty describes a world in which supreme power is exercised within a particular territorial unit.[9] Sovereignty is universal, and accordingly the whole world is divided into these units. Socially and territorially, cohesive states are capable of making rational decisions reflecting a national interest. These states, then, are seen as the primary actors in the international arena, engaging with each other on the basis of formal equality.[10] While the system operates under the assumption of (legal/moral) equality there are and have always been great power differentials between individual states. In light of this and other criticisms sovereignty is more an ideal; a paradigm for the analysis and regulation of international relations than a strictly descriptive category.[11] Nevertheless, reflecting the dominant paradigm of international relations

---

4 For a concise historical account of the origins of the different concepts of citizenship see Klumeyer D, *Between Consent and Descent: Conceptions of Democratic Citizenship*, Carnegie Endowment for International Peace, Washington, DC, 1996.

5 Aristotle, 'Politics', [c 334 BCE] in Clark P (ed), *Texts on Citizenship*, Pluto Press, London, 1994, 43ff.

6 Rousseau J-J, [1762] *The Social Contract*, Reclam, Stuttgart, 1977.

7 Boudin, J, [1576] 'Six Books of the Commonwealth' in Clark, above n 5 at 86ff; Hobbes T, [1642] 'De Cive' in ibid at 89.

8 As espoused by the realist school of international relations. For an overview of this school see Gill S and Law D, *The Global Political Economy: Perspectives, Problems and Policies*, Harvester and Wheatsheaf, New York, 1988 at 25ff.

9 Camilleri J and Falk J, *The End of Sovereignty? The Politics of a Shrinking and Fragmenting World*, Edward Elgar, Aldershot, 1992 at 3.

10 Giddens A, *The Consequences of Modernity*, Stanford University Press, Stanford, 1990 at 65.

11 For a feminist critique of the notion of sovereignty, see Knop K, 'Re/statements: Feminism and State Sovereignty in International Law' (1993) 3 *Transnational Law and Contemporary Problems* 293.

over the past three centuries, the principle of sovereignty has had a strong normative effect. Sovereignty has greatly influenced the way we perceive our relationships with our national communities and their interactions with each other. It has also fundamentally informed the legal principles of citizenship and nationality.

This section begins by defining citizenship, nationality, and, globalization. It then concentrates on some tensions endemic to citizenship and nationality particularly in a globalized world. Finally it suggests some visions of citizenship and nationality for the future.

Citizenship and Nationality

The terms citizenship and nationality are different in a technical legal sense. While essentially the same concept, they reflect two different legal frameworks. Both terms identify the legal status of an individual in light of his or her state membership. But the term citizenship is confined mostly to domestic legal forums, and the term nationality to the international law forum. As Weis states, '[c]onceptually and linguistically, the terms ... emphasize two different aspects of the same notion ... "Nationality" stresses the international, "citizenship" the national, municipal aspect'.[12] To this extent, they are generalizable concepts.

While citizenship describes the technical legal relationship between the individual and the polity, it is more than a merely descriptive category. It is a normative project whereby 'social membership becomes increasingly comprehensive and open ended'.[13] At the beginning of the twenty-first century, however, there is considerable debate about the continued viability and future directions of this project. Citizenship represents cohesion in a world increasingly characterized by fragmentation. As such, citizenship is drawn upon both in critique of contemporary individualism and (in some altered form) as a possible counterpoint to it. This stands in contrast to an earlier, confident, even triumphalist discourse of citizenship as emancipation.

Though often talked of as a singular concept, the term 'citizenship' is used to describe a number of discrete but related phenomena surrounding the relationship between the individual and the polity.[14] In this section I am concentrating upon citizenship in two senses. The first is citizenship as a

---

12 Weis P, *Nationality and Statelessness in International Law*, Stevens, London, 1956 at 5.

13 Turner B, *Citizenship and Capitalism*, Unwin Hyman, London, 1985 at 134.

14 See Rubenstein K, 'Citizenship in Australia, Unscrambling its Meaning' (1995) 20 *Melbourne University Law Review* 503 and Bosniak L, 'Citizenship Denationalized' (2000) 7 *Indiana Journal of Global Legal Studies* 447 at 456.

legal status:[15] the question as to whom the state recognizes as a citizen and so the formal basis for the rights and responsibilities of the individual in the state. The second is a broader view of citizenship as the collection of rights, duties and opportunities for participation which define the extent of socio-political membership[16] within a community. It is broader than legal status because it looks beyond it to the material circumstances of life within the polity, notably questions of social membership and substantive equality.[17]

The legal rank of 'citizen' in democratic societies is often intended to represent the progressive project of a broader conception of membership of the community. This is rarely achieved,[18] however, as formal equality rarely embodies the need for substantial equality in social terms. Feminist and critical scholarship particularly, has highlighted the failure of gender and race-neutral conceptions such as citizenship to take account for the differences of individuals within communities.[19] In Australia, for instance, legal status has not always accorded full and equal membership rights as the position of Aboriginal people attests. While formal legal citizens they were denied the most basic rights of citizenship, such as voting[20] and travel.[21] Even today, some 30 years after achieving formal equality in terms of voting and travel rights, the social, cultural and economic position of

15 Roberto Alejandro refers to this as 'Citizenship as universality and as a legal construction' in Alejandro R, *Hermeneutics, Citizenship, and the Public Sphere*, State University of New York Press, New York, 1993 at 14.

16 Alejandro, ibid, refers to this as citizenship as communality and participation at 21.

17 A third view of citizenship which will not be of direct concern in this paper is citizenship as 'desirable – activity'. That is, looking at what we want citizens to be like; the 'civic virtues' concept of citizenship. See Kymlicka W and Norman W, 'Return of the Citizen: A Survey of Recent Work on Citizenship Theory' (1994) 104 *Ethics* 352; Alejandro also refers to other models, such as citizenship as amelioration of class conflicts, Alejandro, above n 16 at 26; citizenship as self sufficiency at 28; and finally, his thesis, of citizenship as a hermeneutic endeavour at 33 ff.

18 Bosniak refers to this in *Citizenship Denationalized*, above n 14 at 464, when she discussed Charles Black and Kenneth Karst's legal work on citizenship representing 'full and equal membership'.

19 See Young IM, *Justice and the Politics of Difference*, Princeton University Press, Princeton; and Thornton M, 'Historicising Citizenship: Remembering Broken Promises' (1996) 20 *Melbourne University Law Review* 1072.

20 The right to vote exists in Federal and State jurisdictions. In 1902 when the federal universal franchise was introduced, it denied the vote for Aboriginal people who were not already voting in their own states. It was not until 1962 that the federal electoral system universally allowed Aboriginal people the vote.

21 For a fuller account of Australia's historical treatment of Aboriginal people, women and migrants see Jordens A-M, *Redefining Australians: Immigration, Citizenship and National Identity*, Hale and Iremonger, Sydney, 1995; and Galligan B and Chesterman J, *Citizenship Without Rights*, Cambridge University Press, Cambridge, 1997.

Aboriginal people falls short of other Australian citizens. This undermines the nature of their membership of the community and our understanding of substantive citizenship. It gives rise to the notion of second-class citizens that Bosniak discusses in the context of 'Citizenship as Rights'.[22]

Citizenship as neither gender, class, nor race neutral, but affected by different groups' positions within nation states has been evident throughout the ages, and continues to be so. History, however, also relates a progression whereby our understanding of equality and membership has been challenged and expanded over time.[23] There is, then, an inherent tension in the development of citizenship. The citizenship project is about the expansion of equality among citizens. But as equality is based upon membership, citizenship status forms the basis of an exclusive politics and identity. At once anathema to the fulfillment of the citizenship project, they have also been essential to it as the sense of solidarity required for the development of modern citizenship is provided by the nation state.[24]

Globalization tears further at the tension within citizenship between membership and equality. Globalization emphasizes different identities of membership as the norm, according less reason to utilize a singular notion of citizenship, or a single legal status linking directly to the nation state, as a central concept in domestic and international law. Instead of identifying our rights and responsibilities by virtue of legal citizenship our political, legal and social rights and obligations could be determined through a myriad of alternative, non-nation state frameworks.[25] In this context, then, citizenship is only generalizable in establishing citizenship as a status upon which legal rights and responsibilities are often linked. These include political rights of voting and representation in democratic systems, legal rights of mobility and travel, and social rights such as welfare. Often, in the broader, non-legal sense of membership of community, we include expressions of membership or citizenship that are not only provided to formal citizens such as paying taxation and other social rights and duties,[26] and issues concerning one's self identification – the identity of citizenship.

---

22 See Bosniak, above n 14 at 463.

23 A most influential account of this process is found in Marshall's collection: Marshall TH, *Citizenship and Social Class*, Cambridge University Press, Cambridge, 1950.

24 Anna Yeatman discusses this tension in international law and human rights contexts in Yeatman A, 'Who is the Subject of Human Rights?' in Meredyth D and Minson J (eds), *Citizenship and Cultural Policy: Statecraft, Markets and Community*, Sage, London, 2001.

25 For an excellent discussion of this in a domestic context see Legomsky S, 'Why Citizenship' (1994) 35 *Virginia Journal of International Law* 279.

26 For a discussion of social citizenship in the US context see Demleitner NV, 'The Fallacy of Social "Citizenship", or The Threat of Exclusion' (1997) 12 *Georgetown Immigration*

The definition of citizenship in a domestic sense is linked to nationality and international law. International law affirms that it is for each state to determine who are its nationals.[27] Domestic laws about who is and who is not a citizen vary significantly, and laws relating to citizenship in each of the different states are also different.[28] As a result, many people hold more than one nationality by fulfilling the formal requirements for citizenship in more than one domestic legal framework.

Nationality is important in international law in a variety of contexts, including:[29]

- Entitlement to diplomatic protection.
- State responsibility to another state for failing in its duty to prevent certain wrongful acts committed by one of its nationals extra-territorially.
- State receipt of its own nationals. Paragraph 4 of article 12 of the International Covenant on Civil and Political Rights of 1966 provides 'No-one shall be arbitrarily deprived of the right to enter his own country'.
- Nationality is said to import allegiance, and one of the principal incidents of allegiance is the duty to perform military service for the state to which allegiance is owed.
- A state has a general right, in the absence of a specific treaty binding it to do so, to refuse to extradite its own nationals to another state requesting surrender.
- Enemy status in time of war may be determined by the nationality of the person concerned.
- States may frequently exercise criminal or other jurisdiction on the basis of nationality.

As the preliminary report on *Women's Equality and Nationality in International Law* explains, 'nationality secures rights for the individual by linking her to the state ... By forging a link between individual and state, nationality makes one state's interference with the national of another a

---

Law Journal 35 and Linda Bosniak's earlier work: Bosniak L, 'Exclusion and Membership: The Dual Identity of the Undocumented Worker under United States Law' [1988] *Wisconsin Law Review* 955 and 'Membership, Equality and the Difference that Alienage Makes' [1994] *New York University Law Review* 1047.

27 Article 1, 1930 Hague Convention on Certain Questions Relating to the Conflict of Nationality Laws (in force 1937) hereinafter referred to as the 'Hague Convention'.

28 This means the discussion on citizenship within the domestic sphere will be limited in this chapter to discussions of a general nature, rather than specific consequences for a range of different legislative regimes.

29 This listing has been conveniently compiled in Shearer IA, *Starke's International Law*, 11th ed, Butterworths, London, 1994 at 309.

violation of the other state's sovereignty'.[30] There are also treaties and conventions that impact on nationality.[31] Some of these issues of dual nationality, and nationality in case law will be examined further. For the moment, though, nationality is a central dynamic of international law.

Globalization

Just as citizenship describes a number of discrete but related phenomena surrounding the relationship between individual and polity, so too is globalization a term of multidimensional import.[32] I, like Twining, use the term broadly to 'refer to those trends, processes and interactions which are making the world more interdependent in many complex ways, in respect of communications, cultures, language, and politics, not just the alleged development of a single world economy'.[33] So by globalization I am essentially referring to the continued effect of the internationalization of the world framework. I am not discussing a world without nation states, rather nation states fundamentally altered by the growth and interconnection of relationships between nation states and individuals around the world. This is not to say that the nation state is obsolete or that globalization is an entirely new phenomenon.[34] The rapidity of the assault upon the nation state by the quickening turns of globalization is new, however, and states

---

30 Committee on Feminism and International Law, *Women's Equality and Nationality in International Law*, Preliminary Report, Taipei, May 1998 at 6.

31 These are quite extensive, but those specifically dealing with nationality include: 1906 Convention on the Status of Naturalized Citizens (Rio de Janeiro); 1930 Hague Convention on Certain Questions relating to the Conflict of Nationality Laws; Protocol relating to Military Obligations in Certain Cases of Double Nationality; Special Protocol relating to Statelessness; 1933 Montevideo Convention on Nationality and Montevideo Convention on Nationality of Women; 1954 Convention relating to the Status of Stateless Persons; Convention on Nationality between the members of the Arab League; 1957 Convention on the Nationality of Married Women; 1963 European Convention on Reduction of Cases of Multiple Nationality and Military Obligations in Cases of Multiple Nationality; 1973 Convention for the Reduction of the Number of Cases of Statelessness; 1977 Protocol to the European Convention on Reduction of Cases of Multiple Nationality and Military Obligations in Cases of Multiple Nationality and Additional Protocol to the European Convention on Reduction of Cases of Multiple Nationality and Military Obligations in Cases of Multiple Nationality as cited in Bar-Yaacov N, *Dual Nationality*, Stevens, London, 1961 and Weis P, *Nationality and Statelessness in International Law*, 2nd ed, Hyperion, Westport, Connecticut, 1979. See also 1997 European Convention on Nationality.

32 Adelle Blackett argues in Blackett A, 'Globalization and its Ambiguities: Implications for Law School Curricula Reform' (1998) 37 *Columbia Journal of Transnational Law* 57, that the differences in the employment of the term may be as important as the similarities, at 60.

33 Above n 1 at 13.

34 See David Goldman chapter 3 in this collection.

have sought for a range of economic and social directions to steady their statecraft. Not surprisingly, the policy choices made by modern states have shifted with the gale-force pressure of the international political economy. Sovereignty has necessarily been altered without being abolished. States hold their place as key planks in the world system (though they are no longer the only important actors),[35] but globalization has transformed and will continue to revise the extent to which the ship of state is sovereign.

So too have regional economies and markets altered the ideal of sovereignty by promoting free movement of goods and labour across nation state borders. The General Agreement on Trade and Tariffs, the North American Free Trade Agreement, the European Union and the Asia Pacific Economic Cooperation are examples of the trend. Isolationist views of single states about any matter, wilt under the pressure of the new frameworks. As Kennedy argues, 'globalization threatens to undermine the assumed integrity of the nation state as the central organizing unit of domestic and external affairs'.[36]

Related to trade, yet also distinct, is the development of global institutions with authority beyond single governments. These include organizations established to manage the machinery of transnational activities.[37] Financial markets are one example where the massive ebb and flow of international capital is beyond the control of nation states however constituted. A contrasting example is the World Trade Organization, evidencing again global institutional development. Furthermore, procedures to resolve disputes between countries, if we take the World Trade Organization as a case in point are more legalistic, and, therefore more binding over the participants, the nation states.[38] Thus global regimes and institutions regulate matters beyond the control of any single government; national sovereignty is inevitably undermined as a consequence.

Supranational institutions like the United Nations General Assembly and Security Council, the International Court of Justice and the European Court of Justice, to name but a few, are additions to this picture. These

35 In fact, Paul Kennedy argues that even if the autonomy and functions of the state have been eroded by transnational trends, no adequate substitute has emerged to replace it as the key unit in responding to global change. See Kennedy P, *Preparing for the 21st Century*, Fontana, London, 1994 at 134 and Hirst P and Thompson G, 'Globalization and the Future of the Nation State' (1995) 24 *Economy and Society* 408.

36 Kennedy, ibid at 53.

37 David Held discusses this as the disjuncture of international organizations in Held D, 'Democracy, the Nation State and the Global System' (1991) 20 *Economy and Society* 138 at 152.

38 See Rubenstein K and Schultz J, 'Bringing Law and Order to International Trade: Administrative Law Principles and the GATT/WTO' (1996) 12 *St John's Journal of Legal Commentary* 271.

bodies are responsible to a world where borders and national laws are less relevant and 'universal principles'[39] are called upon to determine disputes within the international community. The whole development of international law and, more particularly, of a human rights framework provides for global accountability of a new order. For the human rights framework deals with citizens within nation states, and undermines older notions of sovereignty articulated in international law whereby matters within a country were solely for its own determination. The human rights framework highlights that the state can no longer be protected from scrutiny in how it treats individuals within its territory.[40] The human rights aspect of globalization is further developed below.

In addition to these developments, there is growing recognition that many issues of policy for individual states are not the sole concern of the nation state but of the global order. This recognition dates back to the beginning of the nation state; postal reciprocity, international travel, and communication, were and will continue to be affected by this reality. Environmental and nuclear problems represent pressing current concerns. Single nation state action will not be sufficient to deal with global disorder. The 'interconnectedness of global changes [is] now affecting our whole planet'.[41]

Many writers talk about this phenomenon as an expression of a global civil society.[42] Adding to the picture the work of non-governmental

---

39 There is a valuable debate over the terminology of universal human rights. See Murumba SK, 'Cross-Cultural Dimensions of Human Rights' in Anghie A and Sturgess G, *Legal Visions of the 21st Century: Essays in Honour of Judge Christopher Weeramantry*, Kluwer Law International, The Hague, 1998, Cerna C, 'Universality of Human Rights and Cultural Diversity: Implementation of Human Rights in Different Socio-Cultural Contexts' (1994) 16 *Human Rights Quarterly* 740; An-Na'im A, 'What Do We Mean by Universal?' (1994) 4/5 *Index on Censorship* 120; and Kim N, 'Towards a Feminist Theory of Human Rights: Straddling the Fence Between Western Imperialism and Uncritical Absolutism' (1993) 25 *Columbia Human Rights Law Review* 49.

40 See Hernandez-Truyol BE, 'Reconciling Rights in Collision: An International Human Rights Strategy' in Perea JF, *Immigrants Out*, New York University Press, New York, 1997 and 'Natives, Newcomers and Nativism: A Human Rights Model for the Twenty-first Century' (1993) 23 *Fordham Urban Law Journal* 1075, which argue that legislative proposals such as the Californian Proposition 187 are contrary to the international human rights framework and as such could be fought against and potentially invalidated.

41 Kennedy, above n 35 at 114.

42 There is also much concern about the ramifications for democracy in such a context. For a discussion of some of those issues see Cochran M, 'Democracy, Global Governance and Public Spheres in International Relations' Paper presented for APSA Annual Meeting 1998, Boston, Massachusetts, on file with author.

organizations and other non-state-based organizations are expressions of politics beyond the nation state, as identified by Paul Wapner in his work on environmental activism on the world civic stage.[43]

Finally, the continued growth and reliance on information technology has made knowledge accessible well beyond borders. Electronic mail, the World Wide Web, the Internet in its other guises, corporate intranets and other forms of data flow, all promote discussion and knowledge. International collaboration on research and other projects is thereby facilitated. Libraries across the world are broken open at the beck of individuals tapping away at their desks. Thus we have moved well beyond the dissemination of knowledge through television networks and wire services that already contributed to our knowledge of issues and events outside domestic borders.

This dissemination of knowledge has meant that the concept of globalization includes the 'the compression of the world and ... the intensification of the consciousness of the world as a whole'.[44] People are directly affected by these changes to be sure, but there is also a keen consciousness of changes swirling about us but perhaps yet to prick our own skin. As Professor Jonathan Friedman argues, the essence of globalization 'resides in the consciousness of the global, that is consciousness by individuals of the global situation, specifically that the world is an arena in which we all participate'.[45]

The Impact of Globalization on Citizenship and Nationality

Having established the meanings of the key terms and shown that the terms themselves are not easily generalizable, this section now addresses how well citizenship and nationality are travelling in a globalized world.

Citizenship as a Political/Legal Concept

Nation states have the responsibility for defining the status of citizen within their own territory. International law allows each nation state to determine who it regards as citizens[46] because the classification is of the essence of

---

43 Wapner P, 'Politics Beyond the State: Environmental Activism and World Civic Politics' (1995) 47 *World Politics* 311.

44 Robertson R, *Globalization*: *Social Theory and Global Culture*, Sage, London, 1992, quoted by Friedman J in *Cultural Identity and Global Process*, Sage, London, 1994 at 196. Note, however, the persuasive comments of Kennedy, that while the global economy is becoming more integrated and richer overall, the wealth is uneven. Above n 35 at 49.

45 Friedman, ibid at 196.

46 See Shearer, above n 29, mentioning the *Nottebohm Case* (Second Phases) ICJ Reports 1955 at 4. *Nottebohm* is discussed further in this chapter below at n 72.

sovereignty. Citizenship provides the means for exclusion and entitles the nation to determine its composition.[47] Liberal theorists attempt to provide a broader view of citizenship. The status of 'citizen' as opposed to 'subject' infuses the individual's relationship with the state with principles of equality – the state represents the will of the people and all individuals are to be treated on equal terms with each other.[48]

However, there are core responsibilities and rights that are often solely of the citizen. Those rights and responsibilities include: political participation in the state through voting and representation, responsibilities towards, and protection through, the legal system, responsibilities to defend the nation in times of war, rights associated with residence in the country itself, and mobility within the country. Noticeably, each of these core rights are situated in the public domain and have excluded women who are often responsible in the private, family domain in a way that precludes them from equal participation in the public domain. It has also excluded disadvantaged groups who often do not have the social and economic basis upon which to participate in this domain. Each of these core responsibilities and rights will continue to be affected by the process of globalization. I highlight a few of them here.[49]

Political Participation

Voting and representation reflect political power and governance. Citizens have the right to, and, in some instances, are obliged[50] to vote for a person

---

47 Catherine Dauvergne discusses the theoretical consequences of this in Dauvergne C, 'Confronting Chaos: Migration Law Responds to Images of Disorder' (1999) 5 *Res Publica* 23 and 'Citizenship, Migration Laws and Women: Gendering Permanent Residency Statistics' (2000) 24 *Melbourne University Law Review* 280, in which she argues that migration law is more important than citizenship law for the question of who can become an Australian citizen. I am not discussing migration issues in this chapter due to the adequacy and attention received by it in Dauvergne's chapter 8 in this volume, but it is another example of the consequences of citizenship that is affected by globalization. Interestingly, as Dauvergne illustrates, it impacts differently on different groups, highlighting the inequitable consequences of globalization on people.

48 See Jayasuriya L, 'Citizens' in Nile R (ed), *Australian Civilization*, Oxford University Press, Melbourne, 1994 at 94 and Craig P, 'Public Law, Sovereignty and Citizenship' in Blackburn R (ed), *Rights of Citizenship*, Mansell, London, 1993 at 307. Note, however, that even in the liberal-democratic systems, this measure for inclusion is not absolute. Examples above illustrate that formal equality may not translate into substantial equality. Moreover, control is still maintained over non-citizens for the purpose of exclusion.

49 A more elaborate explanation can be found in Rubenstein K, 'Citizenship in a Borderless World' above n *.

50 Australia is one example where voting in the federal and state elections is mandatory, and failure by a person on the electoral roll to do so is punishable by a monetary fine.

to represent them in the democratic system of government. Underlying this political right and responsibility is the belief that those elected persons will have control over the process of governing; they represent the will of the people, and make laws to govern the society on the community's behalf. 'Sovereign nation states claimed as their distinctive feature the right to determine how any activity within their territory was governed'.[51] Citizenship, therefore, involves the ability to influence, and be part of, that governance; to influence the political outcomes of the state. But the process of 'governance' has changed substantially in light of globalization.

Governance now exists beyond the realm of the state, through a 'wide variety of public and private, state and non-state, national and international, institutions and practices'.[52] People who are not citizens of a particular territory can, nevertheless, influence its governance. These people include non-citizens in multinational companies who influence the economic decisions made by states, and individuals participating in international non-governmental organizations who have lobbied successfully in many countries.[53] The non-government organizations such as Greenpeace, Amnesty International, the world's religious bodies, and other international organizations have the capacity to lobby domestic governments when a policy issue that interests them is on the agenda. These organizations have developed extensive networks that have shaped and influenced a significant amount of the United Nation's work and they have created a framework for an international civil society.[54] The activity of the United Nations impacts on domestic governance, as do the regional arrangements between governments. Each of these examples illustrates the capacity of non nation state players to influence the governance of a range of nation states. This may not be formal representation in the governmental system of the state, but it is a significant substantive governance. As a consequence, individual citizens within the state have less responsibility and power and political

---

51 Hirst and Thompson, above n 35 at 422.

52 Ibid at 422.

53 The growth of non-governmental organizations is terrific. Kenneth Gergen refers to the 20,000 transnational organizations that have emerged since 1950 devoted to social change. Gergen KJ, *The Saturated Self: Dilemmas of Identity in Contemporary Life*, Basic Books, New York, 1991 at 255.

54 See Otto D, 'Nongovernmental Organizations in the United Nations System: The Emerging Role of International Civil Society' (1996) 18 *Human Rights Quarterly* 107; Posner M and Whittome C, 'The Status of Human Rights NGOs' (1994) 25 *Columbia Human Rights Law Review* 269; Cohen CP, 'The Role of NGOs in the Drafting of the Convention on the Rights of the Child' (1990) 12 *Human Rights Quarterly* 138; and Weiss TG and Gordenker L (eds), *NGOs, The UN and Global Governance*, Lynne Reinner, Boulder, 1996.

control in their own nation state. The value of citizenship for political governance has been drastically reduced in the nation state.

There are many who are concerned about these changes, fearing that individuals have less and less control over their own lives and that existing inequalities will be further entrenched.[55] However, these changes have the potential to be used positively in the twenty-first century. Rather than being concerned that citizenship is less meaningful in the nation state context, it can be refigured to entitling the same individuals to political participation both within the nation state and beyond the nation state. This could enhance an individual's political power in a more global context.[56] For instance, feminist groups around the world may be able to coordinate and deliberate on collective responses to global issues, as could other groups within various nation states.

To some extent the concept of the citizen beyond one nation state is already in existence within the European Union. This idea has been described as 'transborder participatory democracy',[57] both at grass-root levels through the development of non-governmental organizations that have developed transnational links and coalitions, and through business and corporate frameworks. In this political context the state will have even less responsibility for governance, and the people themselves will have a more direct input into world politics.[58]

The people who are concerned that this move will lessen the value of democratic citizenship,[59] that is, direct involvement of citizens in their own domestic political context, need to be answered. Their argument is that

---

55 Otto D, 'Challenging the "New World Order": International Law, Global Democracy and the Possibilities for Women' (1993) 3 *Transnational Law and Contemporary Law* 371.

56 This also gives rise to consideration of voting rights being granted to all residents in nation states, rather than keeping it the preserve of citizens. In New Zealand, the Electoral Act 1993 entitles permanent residents to be registered as electors. (Section 74). Both citizens and permanent residents must have continuously resided in New Zealand for six months. (Section 74(b)).

57 This is a term used in Ichiyo M, 'For an Alliance of Hope', in Brecher J et al (eds), *Global Visions: Beyond the New World Order*, Black Rose Books, Montreal, 1993 at 155.

58 Daniele Archibugi discusses this as cosmopolitan democracy, involving political representation for people beyond their borders and independently from their governments. See Archibugi D, 'From the United Nations to Cosmopolitan Democracy' in Archibugi D and Held D (eds), *Cosmopolitan Democracy*, Polity Press, Cambridge, Massachusetts, 1995 at 134-5.

59 I thank all the participants in the Law Schools of the University of Victoria, British Columbia, Canada; Haifa University and Bar-Ilan University in Israel, and the government employees in Ottawa at the citizenship branch of the Canadian government, for raising these concerns during my presentation of some of the material in this chapter.

rather than enhancing the valuable participatory democratic principles of allowing individuals to have control over their own lives, this notion of citizenship in a global context widens the gap between power and people. In order to alleviate those concerns, there needs to be a conscious and active commitment to linking citizenship in the twenty-first century global context with substantive political participation, for all groups within society.[60] This philosophy can be directed to the global context as much as the domestic context. The fact that different groups have varying levels of power is often more transparent in the global context than in the domestic realm. In recognising that participation definitely will not be focused solely on the nation state, attention can be directed to highlighting the power differentials in the global context. Once this is recognized, practical means for securing different groups within the world community a place in world decision-making can be developed. This may mean advocating, for instance, that multinational corporations guarantee that there is representation within their decision-making structures for those affected by their decisions; that is democratizing the international business system as much as the political system. Similarly it may mean advocating that non-governmental organizations be given voting rights in the United Nations. These suggestions develop Iris Marion Young's view of radical democratic pluralism[61] which demands social equality (an aim of democratic governance) by acknowledging and affirming group difference, and, fostering participation for all groups within society. This must be extended into the global context, and if successful it will enable citizenship to travel in the twenty-first century as a more meaningful representation of political participation.

Legal Structures and Frameworks

All residents within a territory are subject to the laws of the territory, and to that extent the status of citizenship is not relevant to obeying the law. However, the laws themselves may differentiate the treatment of citizens from non-citizens. In some countries, jury service is an example of legal responsibility flowing solely from citizenship of the nation state. This service declares one's membership of the community by allowing a citizen to judge and adjudicate upon residents' legal rights and responsibilities. In this instance, while all residents are subject to the law, only citizens represent the community by playing an official adjudicatory role in the trial of residents.

---

60 I have been influenced by Iris Marion Young's views of radical democratic pluralism. See Young above n 6 at ch 6.

61 Ibid.

However, just as globalization continues to affect the political frameworks of nation states, the legal frameworks of countries are changing and will be significantly different in the twenty-first century. This development is not new; it has been growing since the end of the Second World War with the 'vast increase in power and reach of the judiciary in the international community'.[62] In Australia this is expressed through the increased use of treaties as a basis for national legislation, the use of international legal norms by the judiciary in the development of the common law and the interpretation of statutes, and the international scrutiny of human rights.[63] The national legal order to which citizens and non-citizens are subject is inextricably linked to the international legal order. Citizenship is no longer legitimately the major foundation upon which rights are restricted and determined, even within the nation state.[64]

This point is emphasised by Yasemin Soysal.[65] By analysing the incorporation of guest workers in Europe, she 'reveals a shift in the major organizing principle of membership in contemporary polities; the logic of personhood supersedes the logic of national citizenship'.[66] She further argues that 'this trend is informed by a dialectical tension between national citizenship and universal human rights'.[67]

Universal human rights have been the basis for international legal developments that impact on all nation states to differing degrees. With the optimism that such a view involves we must be mindful of the criticisms of Soysal's work, offered by scholars such as Stephen Castles. He points out that 'UN and International Labour Organization conventions and the like are often not ratified, and above all are ignored by the countries where abuses are worst'.[68] With these reservations in mind we can still

---

62 See Sturgess G and Chubb P, *Judging the World: Law and Politics in the World's Leading Courts*, Butterworths, Sydney, 1988 at ch 4.

63 See Mathew P, 'International Law and the Protection of Human Rights in Australia: Recent Trends' (1995) 17 *Sydney Law Review* 177.

64 Many country's constitutions are interesting in the way that rights are not necessarily distinguished between citizens and non-citizens and often extend to all persons within the territory, rather than only citizens.

65 Soysal YN, *Limits of Citizenship: Migrants and Postnational Membership in Europe*, University of Chicago Press, Chicago, 1994.

66 Ibid at 164.

67 Ibid.

68 Castles S, 'Globalisation and the Ambiguities of National Citizenship', paper delivered to the conference 'Blurred Boundaries: Living with Cultural Diversity', University of Melbourne 3-5 July 1996 at 14. See also, Castles S, 'The Future of Australian Citizenship in a Globalizing World' in Rubenstein K (ed), *Individual, Community, Nation: 50 Years of Australian Citizenship*, Australian Scholarly Publishing, Melbourne, 2000 at 119 and Castles S and Davidson A, *Citizenship and Migration: Globalization and the Politics of Belonging*, Macmillan, Basingstoke, 2000.

acknowledge that legal structures within nation states are continually re-examined by the global order.

Therefore, the desire to distinguish between citizens and non-citizens in domestic legal systems in the twenty-first century will be open to greater scrutiny. This will fundamentally alter the legal status of citizenship, and further illustrate that the legal frameworks of the nation states will not be determined solely by their citizens, but by principles developed by an overarching jurisdiction with citizens from the world over playing a role.

Nationality

What does globalization mean for the legal term nationality? This part of the chapter looks at nationality in law and analyses how globalization is affecting its functionality as a legal and social tool. Is it as useful a legal concept if its operational framework is subject to significant change? And, if the nation state is so wrought by a changing global environment, what is the impact on our legal understanding of nationality?

Two important points are crucial to the development of my argument. The historical development in international law of nationality is from more rigid to more flexible forms; and second, this development has occurred in response to the changing structure of the international political economy.[69] Nationality therefore can continue its development to better reflect the current political framework within which it operates, a framework where the dominance of the nation state has reduced in its function. Therefore, I argue that the principles against dual or multiple nationality are no longer valid in the current framework and that multiple citizenships are in fact the norm and will be embraced in the future.

The importance of nationality arises variously in international law linked to the centrality of states to the international law machinery. If the state's value decreases in international governance,[70] then so too will the value of nationality. Looking specifically at the development of international law principles within the current system there are tensions that need addressing for it to continue to travel well in the twenty-first century. This section looks at some of those principles through decisions of the International Court of Justice, The European Human Rights Court, the United Nation's Compensation Commission, the Iran-US Claims Tribunal and the Human Rights Committee under the International Covenant on

69 A more substantiated basis for this statement is made in Rubenstein and Adler, above n *.

70 See Kennedy D, 'New Approaches to Comparative Law, Comparativism and International Governance' 1997 *Utah Law Review* 545 at fn 4, which reviews notions of governance.

Civil and Political Rights. The emergence of this later Committee in itself reflects changes that are altering the nature of nationality in a globalized world.

International Case Law

This review of international case law on nationality discloses two broad categories of cases: (1) standing cases and (2) human rights cases. The standing cases require international arbitration because they involve a conflict between two states over the nationality of an individual. These are labelled standing cases as the question at issue is whether a particular state has standing to represent an individual in an action vis-à-vis another state. The principle of state sovereignty underlies these cases and can be expressed as follows; what a state does to one of its own nationals is not a matter for international law whereas what a state does to a national of another state can be the subject of international law if the state to which the individual belongs takes issue on behalf of the citizen.[71] This principle itself is open to question within a globalized world.

The Standing Cases

The leading case on the question of nationality for the purpose of diplomatic protection is *Nottebohm*.[72] It concerned a German national who lived and conducted business in Guatemala for most of his adult life. Shortly after the outbreak of war in 1939, Nottebohm made moves to acquire Liechtenstein nationality and was granted it in October of that year. After the grant, Nottebohm stayed in Liechtenstein for some seven weeks before returning to Guatemala, this time on Liechtenstein papers. Despite having acquired Liechtenstein nationality, Nottebohm was declared an enemy alien in Guatemala and was deported and his property confiscated. In response, Liechtenstein sought to seize the court asserting an alleged breach of international law in relation to its national, Nottebohm.

At hearing, the preliminary question was whether Nottebohm's Liechtenstein nationality was effective at international law vis-à-vis Guatemala. In finding that it was not, the Court held that 'nationality is a legal bond having as its basis a social fact of attachment, a genuine connection of existence, interests and sentiments, together with the existence of reciprocal rights and duties'.[73] While municipal law regarding citizenship is binding within a state, it need only be recognized in the international arena when 'the legal bond of nationality accord(s) with the

---

71 Weis (1956) above n 12 at 35.

72 Judgment of 6 April 1955, *International Court of Justice Reports* 1955 at 4.

73 Ibid at 23.

individual's genuine connection with the state which assumes the defence of its citizens by means of protection against other states'. [74]

The preference for social connections over legal formalities could be read to allow the recognition at international law of a number of effective nationalities. This, however, does not appear to be the intent of the Court in *Nottebohm*. The International Court of Justice's concept of effective nationality is grounded in the concept of allegiance and a reluctance to recognize nationality without allegiance. Thus, the majority judges state that naturalization involves '[the] breaking of a bond of allegiance and [the] establishment of a new bond of allegiance'.[75] Similarly, the possibility of effective dual nationality is far from countenanced in the statement 'the juridical expression of the fact that the individual upon whom it is conferred ... is in fact *more closely connected with the population of the State conferring nationality than with that of any other State*'.[76]

Based on notions of national allegiance, this test has difficulty recognising multiple nationality for the purposes of public international law. Its justification is the apparent inequity of allowing one individual diplomatic protection against their own state under cover of a second nationality where that action would not be available to fellow citizens with a single nationality. As a result, multiple nationality is the exception rather than the rule. Historically, this was indeed the case. In a world where links to more than one nation are increasingly common, however, an alternative to so restricting the cause of action is to expand it, allowing states to intervene on behalf of anyone who has a significant link to that country be it by birth, blood, or later association. Another alternative is to allow individuals and other non-state entities greater access to international justice. While both of these suggestions undermine the principle making international law mute on the way a state treats its own nationals, this expression of unfettered sovereignty has already lost much of its weight through the development of international human rights law in the second half of the twentieth century.

Cases decided since *Nottebohm* evidence some movement in this direction.

---

[74] Ibid.

[75] Ibid at 24.

[76] Ibid at 23, emphasis added by author.

Iran – US Claims Tribunal[77]

One of the functions of the Iran – US Claims Tribunal was to determine claims under the *Claims Settlement Declaration of the Democratic and Popular Republic of Algeria.*[78]

Article II of the Declaration states the Tribunal was established 'for the purpose of deciding claims of nationals of the US against Iran and claims of nationals of Iran against the US'.[79] In its deliberations the Tribunal considered the claims of some applicants who were both Iranian citizens under Iranian law and US citizens under US law.

The Tribunal found it had 'jurisdiction over claims against Iran by dual Iran–US nationals when the dominant and effective nationality of the claimant during the relevant period ... was that of the US'.[80] In so finding, the Tribunal rejected an argument based on the Hague Convention and older customary law that diplomatic protection is excluded in the case of dual nationality.[81] Its reasons were twofold:

- as individuals had standing before the tribunal, the questions arising do not replicate those involving the right of states to represent individuals at public international law;[82] and
- even in regard to cases such as *Nottebohm* involving diplomatic protection in the stricter sense, the law has developed from the codification in The Hague Convention (Art 4) that 'A State may not afford diplomatic protection to one of its nationals against a State whose nationality such a person also possesses'.[83]

Thus, the current law allows claims of dual nationals where their dominant and effective nationality is not that of the respondent state. This ratio is based on the *Nottebohm* principle that nationality is a juridical translation of social fact.[84]

Two further comments in the majority judgment advance this argument:

---

77 Iran–US Claims Tribunal: Decision in Case No. A/18 Concerning the Question of Jurisdiction over Claims of Persons with Dual Nationality [April 6, 1984] reprinted in 23 *International Legal Materials* 489 (1984).

78 19 January 1981, 20 *International Legal Materials* 230 (1981).

79 Ibid.

80 Iran–US Claims Tribunal: Decision in Case No A/18 Concerning the Question of Jurisdiction over Claims of Persons with Dual Nationality [April 6, 1984] at p 25 of the decision or 23 *International Legal Materials* 489 (1984) at 501.

81 Ibid at 22 or 23 *International Legal Materials* 489 (1984) at 500.

82 Ibid at 18 or 23 *International Legal Materials* 489 (1984) at 498.

83 Ibid at 17 or 23 *International Legal Materials* 489 (1984) at 497.

84 Ibid at 22 or 23 *International Legal Materials* 489 (1984) at 500.

- the Tribunal's statement that the move toward the recognition of effective over formal nationality is consistent with 'the contemporaneous development of international law to accord legal protections to individuals, even against the State of which they are nationals';[85] and
- the final sentence of the judgment stating that in cases where 'the tribunal finds jurisdiction based upon a dominant and effective nationality ... the other nationality may remain relevant to the merits of the claim'.[86]

Though the decision maintains the notion that an individual must have a dominant and effective nationality, the two quotes in the preceding paragraph indicate a broadening of the *Nottebohm* notion of one nationality based on allegiance.

This position is developed in the concurring opinions of Members Holzman, Aldrich, and Mosk[87] who would all allow claims by all nationals of the US and Iran regardless of whether they held dual nationality.

UN Compensation Commission – Claims against Iraq[88]

A more radical position comes from the UN Compensation Commission when assessing individual claims against Iraq following the Iraqi invasion of Kuwait in 1990. While not a court it did have a quasi judicial function. Its chief purpose was to process claims against Iraq arising from the invasion and occupation of Kuwait and to make payments from the Compensation Fund.

When confronted with Iraqi dual nationals making claims against the Fund, it dealt with the question in an administrative fashion. The Commission developed a strategy for determining claims in an expedited manner. The application of the dominant and effective nationality test was incompatible with the speedy administration of the Fund.[89] As a result there were no inquiries made into the factual attachments and connections of dual national applicants. Instead a test of *bona fides* was applied. Thus Iraqi dual nationals were entitled to have their application considered so long as they were not seen to have acquired their second nationality mainly or solely for the purpose of claiming compensation.[90] As there were no claims from Iraqi dual nationals who had applied for a second nationality after

85 Ibid at 24 or 23 *International Legal Materials* 489 (1984) at 501.
86 Ibid at 26 or 23 *International Legal Materials* 489 (1984) at 502.
87 The concurring opinion of Holtzmann and Aldrich and Mosk appears at 23 *International Legal Materials* (1984) at 503ff.
88 109 *International Law Reports* (1996) 2.
89 Ibid, Category 'A' Claims (Sixth Installment) at 107.
90 Ibid.

establishment of the eligibility criteria for compensation, the Commission did not deny any claims from dual nationals on the basis of the acquisition of a second nationality *mala fides*.[91]

Each of these standing cases show a move away from traditional approaches to dual nationality. Unlike *Nottebohm* where allegiance was the central factor in nationality determination, effective nationality is considered more in the fuller sense of social fact. This is highlighted further in the human rights cases.

Human Rights Cases

Whereas the standing cases present nationality as a preliminary issue, the human rights cases consider the rights of citizenship/nationality in a substantive sense. They are justiciable because of international instruments that stand with state sovereignty at the basis of international law. By and large, the cases evolve where human rights law is called upon to imbue an individual with certain rights of membership though citizenship is formally lacking, for example where they have the right to reside in a certain country. There are also other human rights cases where human rights law is called upon by individuals seeking to escape undesirable consequences of unwanted nationality.[92] Finally, there are other international law cases not centred upon human rights as such where nationality issues raised in *Nottebohm* arise. One example, for instance, concerns fishing rights.[93] This section concentrates on human rights cases where an individual seeks the protection of principles associated with nationality, when nationality is lacking.

Beljoudi v France[94]

In 1950 Mr Beljoudi was born in France to Algerian parents. He lived in France from birth and was unacquainted with either the Islamic religion or Arabic, the language of Algeria. He went to school in France and in 1970

---

91 Ibid.

92 To raise just a few, see *Chantal Van den Brock v Commission of the European Communities* (Case 37/74) [1975] *European Community Reports* 235, where nationality was imposed by law on a female official upon her marriage and was disregarded by the Court in determining a right to an expatriation allowance; *Evelyn Devred, nee Kenny-Levick v Commission of the European Communities* (Case 257/78) [1979] *European Community Reports* 3767, also dealing with expatriation allowance and holding that the concept of 'nationality' should be interpreted so as to avoid any unwarranted difference in treatment between male and female officials.

93 For example, *Re British Fishing Boats*: *EC Commission (Spain Intervening) v Ireland* [1993] 1 Common Market Law Reports 273 regarding the nationality of vessels. In this article we do not go into great detail in the area of maritime law.

94 14 *European Human Rights Reports* (1992) 801.

he married a French woman. Nevertheless, Mr Beljoudi did not attain French citizenship because he did not comply with the relevant statutory procedure for converting his 'special civil status' to full citizenship.

On the basis of a history of criminal convictions resulting in a number of terms of imprisonment, the relevant Minister issued a deportation order. The case cited is the decision of the European Court of Human Rights with regard to Mr Beljoudi's deportation.

While not decided on grounds of nationality,[95] the logic of effective nationality underwrites the majority opinion and the concurring judgments in their finding that the decision to deport Mr Beljoudi, if implemented, would be in breach of Article 8 of the European Convention on Human Rights.[96]

Article 8 of the Convention provides:

- Everyone has the right to respect for his private and family life, his home and his correspondence.
- There shall be no interference by a public authority with the exercise of this right except as is in accordance with the law and is necessary in a democratic society in the interests of national security, public safety or the economic well-being of the country, for the prevention of disorder or crime, for the protection of health or morals, or for the protection of the rights and freedoms of others.

In interpreting this section, the majority explains that the expulsion of a person from the country in which his immediate family resides will give rise to a contravention of 'the right to respect for family life afforded by Article 8' if it is not justified when weighed up against what may be regarded as necessary and thus allowable pursuant to Article 8(2).[97] In order for an action to be within the bounds of the Convention 'the interference [must] correspond(s) to a pressing social need and, in particular, [one] that it is proportionate to the legitimate aim pursued'.[98]

Though citizenship is not the issue, the Court's discussion of the level of the interference caused by deporting the applicant engages the discourse of effective nationality. In the end, the applicant's deportation is so severely disruptive of his private and family life for the very reason that his social and familial networks are so thoroughly entrenched in the French state. The applicant has the fullest effective nationality in the *Nottebohm*

---

95 It is noted by the majority that the Convention does not in principle prohibit the Contracting States from regulating the entry and length of stay of aliens. Ibid at 820.

96 Council of Europe, The European Convention on Human Rights, Rome, 4 November 1950.

97 Above n 94 at 820ff.

98 Ibid at 822.

sense where nationality is expressed as 'having as its basis a social fact of attachment, a genuine connection of existence, interests and sentiments together with the existence of reciprocal rights and duties'.[99] In such situations, the majority found, deportation is justifiably proportionate only in 'exceptional circumstances'.[100] Though the applicant was convicted of various crimes and made eligible for deportation under the relevant statute, the disruption to the applicant's family life made deportation unjustified from a public policy point of view.

The logical extension of the effective nationality principle is explored in the concurring opinion of Judge Martens. If effective nationality represents a shift from nationality based on formal admission to a state to nationality acknowledged on the social facts of an individual's participation in the life of a community, it is arguable that any distinction between the formal citizens and fully effective citizens is artificial. Or as Martens puts it in his analysis of Mr Beljoudi's case, 'In my opinion, mere nationality does not constitute an objective and reasonable justification for the existence of a difference as regards the admissibility of expelling someone from what, in both cases, may be called his own country'.[101]

Here we see a fluid approach to the place of nationality in international law.

Charles Edward Stewart v Canada[102]

The Human Rights Committee under the International Covenant on Civil and Political Rights is an example of globalization as argued in this piece. It is a decision-making body in an international law context that determines disputes brought to it from individuals in countries who have signed the Optional Protocol of the International Covenant on Civil and Political Rights. While the Committee lacks determinative powers, and so does not destroy notions of sovereignty, its political might and existence weakens the nation state's total control over human rights matters within its jurisdiction. In this case the applicant was a British citizen born in 1960 who then lived in Ontario, Canada with his family from the age of seven. Though he considered himself to be a Canadian citizen for most of his life he was never naturalized and as such never achieved that status.

Between 1978 and 1991 he was convicted of some 42 criminal offenses, the last of which triggered a move by the Canadian Government

99 *Nottebohm*, above n 72 at 23.
100 Above note 94 at 823.
101 Ibid at 841.
102 CCPR/C/58D/538/1993 16 December 1996, Human Rights Committee, UNICCPR, 1 November 1996.

to deport him to the UK in accordance with Canadian immigration law. As a result he complained of violations of various articles of the International Covenant on Civil and Political Rights.

The determinative article was Article 12(4). Article 12(4) of the Covenant provides: 'No one shall be arbitrarily deprived of the right to enter his own country'. Thus, the Committee considered two questions of mixed law and fact: (a) was Canada the author's own country; and if so (b) was the author being arbitrarily deprived of his right to enter Canada.

The Committee answered both these in the negative. It held the words 'own country' used in Article 12(4) of the Covenant are broader than the concept 'country of his nationality' and applied to individuals who, while not nationals in a formal sense, are also not 'aliens' within the meaning of Article 13.[103] In coming to this view they were influenced by Article 13 of the Covenant which speaks of 'an alien lawfully in the territory of a State party' when discussing the rights of state parties to expel these persons.

The Committee then commented that it is less clear:

> ... who in addition to nationals, is protected by the provisions of Article 12(4). Since the concept 'his own country' is not limited to nationality in the formal sense, that is, nationality acquired on birth or by conferral, it embraces, at the very least, an individual who, because of his special ties or claims in relation to any given country cannot there be considered to be a mere alien. [104]

In considering the category of person described in the preceding paragraph, the Committee saw it as including '... nationals of a country who have been stripped of their nationality in violation of international law and individuals whose country of nationality has been incorporated into or transferred to another national entity whose nationality is being denied them'.[105]

As Canada placed no unreasonable impediments on the applicant from acquiring formal nationality, the Committee held Canada was not the applicant's 'own country' for the purposes of Article 12(4). The Committee was not prepared to find that the words 'his own country' extended to individuals who had either chosen not to acquire the nationality of their home country or who commit criminal acts which prevent them from doing so.

This reasoning is based on a 'rights and obligations' view of citizenship. In the opinion of the Committee:

> Countries like Canada, which enable immigrants to become nationals after a reasonable period of residence, have a right to expect that such immigrants will

---

[103] Ibid at para 12.3.

[104] Ibid at para 12.4.

[105] Ibid.

> in due course acquire all the rights and assume all the obligations that nationality entails. Individuals who do not take advantage of this opportunity and thus escape the obligations nationality imposes can be deemed to have opted to remain aliens in Canada. They have the right to do so, but must bear the consequences.[106]

A dissenting opinion by Elizabeth Evatt and Cecilia Medina Ouroga and supported by a further four members of the Committee offers a more liberal interpretation. Evatt and Ouroga criticize the majority for failing to recognize the protection offered by Article 12(4) exists, '... because it is deemed unacceptable to deprive any person of close contact with his family or his friends or (...) the web of relationships that form his or her social environment'.[107]

Considering the applicant's family ties and his long-standing residence and desire to remain in Canada, the dissenters found Canada was his own country and he was entitled to protection from deportation. In a separate dissenting opinion P Bhagwati took the argument a step further by allowing that an individual may have more than one country as his 'own' within the meaning of Article 12(4).[108]

The decision dilutes nationality as a legal tool for resolving international law dilemmas involving a person's connection to the nation state. The dissenters are in fact more consistent in interpreting nationality as a progressive project, concerned with the broader indicia determining a person's attachment to a community, and identifying that person as a member.

Both the standing cases and the human rights cases display tensions in the functionality of the formal status of nationality in international law. In order to travel well and be an effective tool for the resolution of international matters it needs to be refashioned in the future.

Citizenship and Nationality in the Future

In looking at the definitions of citizenship and nationality and globalization this section highlights that the link between the individual and the nation state is less relevant to people in both a domestic sense and an international sense when considering the consequences of citizenship for international law. While it will not be redundant, its centrality to the laws of people will be diminished. Moreover, in international law, this section argues that one significant consequence is the altering of the legal principles of

[106] Ibid at para 12.8.
[107] Ibid at para 5 of dissenting opinion of Evatt and Ouroga.
[108] Ibid.

nationality.[109] In concrete terms, I predict a future that includes the following:

- An increasing willingness in international treaty law to acknowledge and encourage dual and multiple nationality.
- A dilution of the centrality of allegiance and the consequences of nationality in domestic and international case law.
- A movement away from the centrality of the state in international law.

All the conventions against multiple nationality are premised upon resolution of conflict and the difficulties arising from multiple nationality. Due to the developments described in this chapter as globalization, multiple nationality should become the norm in international law. This trend can already be seen in the 1997 European Convention on Nationality[110] that includes a chapter on 'Multiple Nationality' and allows the retention of multiple nationality in certain circumstances.[111] This does not necessarily reflect the demise of the nation state, but rather citizenship multinationalized. In this situation, notions of effective nationality will become even more important in the resolution of conflicts. Thus, effective nationality takes into account a much broader notion of citizenship. It is not concerned with the formal legal status of an individual, nor solely concerned with allegiance, but issues of social fact, identity and justice in a given situation.

The concept of effective nationality facilitates a theoretical (if not yet a practical) entry point for the acknowledgment of layered and or fragmented nationality appropriate to the circumstances of our participation in a given national, supranational, regional or even non-territorial communities. Surely, such a diversity of participation will produce conundrums in terms of conflicts and priorities of interest. But in a theoretical framework that privileges a fluidity of networks over a static allegiance, our legal concept of citizenship and nationality must have the flexibility to accommodate the struggle for membership and participation in the polity which has defined

---

[109] I have suggested some consequences in the domestic context for citizenship in 'Citizenship in a Borderless World' in Anghie A and Sturgess G, above n *. Gary Sturgess has also suggested some practical consequences in 'Citizen, Customer, Community: Changing Attitudes to Political Membership' in Rubenstein, above n 68.

[110] Strasbourg 6.XI.1997 [European Treaty Series No 166], 37 *International Legal Materials* 44 The Convention has institutionalized and recognized as a fact of international life the concept of multiple nationality. See also Pitrowicz R, 'One Nation or Two? New Developments in Citizenship Law' (1999) 72 *Australian Law Journal* 673.

[111] Strasbourg 6.XI.1997 [European Treaty Series No 166], 37 *International Legal Materials* 44, Chapter V Articles 14-17.

the citizenship project since the development of civil rights in eighteenth century Britain.

In tracing the development of principles of nationality in international law this chapter has highlighted the centrality of allegiance in *Nottebohm*. The case law since has broadened the concept of effective nationality, concentrating less on sole nationality and allowing consideration of other matters. This broadening of approach to issues of nationality will no doubt continue. While not totally denationalizing nationality, as there is still some interest in the relationship between the individual and the state, formal links to the state are but one factor under consideration. The theoretical notions of effective nationality are concerned with a person's connections, in fact – their social, political, psychological connections. Accepting this, one would think current restrictions confining causes of action in international law to state nationals should be lifted to allow states to intervene on behalf of anyone who has a significant link to that country be it by birth, blood, or later association.

Another alternative is to allow individuals and other non-state entities greater access to international justice. To do so denationalizes citizenship still further in certain circumstances. Identities previously unseen by international law are suddenly recognized through their attachment to non-state players. For instance, membership of a non-government organization or a religious body could be recognized in international law as granting standing. The acceptance of this will open the face of citizenship to incorporate multi-faceted connections well beyond the nation state. While both these suggestions undermine the principle that international law says nothing about the way a state treats its own nationals, this expression of unfettered sovereignty has already lost much of its weight through the development of international human rights law in the second half of the twentieth century.

Where does this leave the principles outlined in the definitions of nationality, such as the entitlement to diplomatic protection and a state's general right in the absence of a treaty to refuse to extradite its own nationals to another state requesting surrender? My argument about multiple nationalities extends to all of these principles. Effective nationality should be the stronger consideration rather than formal nationality. It is not based simply on allegiance as in *Nottebohm*, but on the social, psychological and cultural facts relevant to the situation.

All of these changes represent the continued growth of citizenship as a flexible concept. In doing this it flows into the international arena through nationality. As international law becomes more flexible in its use of nationality so too it becomes part of citizenship's progressive project. This is where it has the ability to travel well. While this may lead to less certainty in the resolution of disputes between nations, it will lead to more appropriate just outcomes in individual cases. It places nationality more in line with a rights-based, individualized focus for international law, rather than a sovereignty-based one. It will enable Twining's 'cosmopolite' to become more common. This is where the progressive citizenship project meets nationality, melding, strengthening and integrating them as one and the same tool for building justice.

Chapter 8

Illegal Migration and Sovereignty

Catherine Dauvergne

Talk of illegal migration is almost as prevalent as talk of globalization. Accounts of stowaways dying in lorries at Dover,[1] of people making the 'suicide run' up Interstate-95 over the US-Mexican border,[2] of a string of less-than-seaworthy vessels attempting to reach Australian shores,[3] and of what happens to these people before, during and after their various arrivals appear in media around the world weekly if not daily. American cabinet nominees are now routinely disqualified because of having employed an illegal migrant and the concept of 'people trafficking' has entered common parlance. The increased presence of these events may be an indicator that illegal migration is increasing, or that our concern about it is, or that our ability to detect it is. Whichever reason is most applicable to a given group of people in a particular place and time, there are linkages between globalization and illegal migration. In my view, these links can be grouped in two categories. First, the two are related because illegal migration feeds on the advances in communication and transportation technologies that are part of the globalization phenomenon. Second, the linkage is heightened because the challenges which globalization poses to sovereignty and the nation state provoke a response which is inscribed in the texts of our migration laws, policies and discourses.

The notion of illegal migration is amorphous. While it literally could encompass all those who somehow violate the migration laws of the state they are currently in, the label associates itself in our minds only with certain types of migration law infringers. 'Illegals' are people who have arrived in a prosperous state by illegal and often dangerous means; who are

---

1 Mann S, 'Gasping for Freedom', *Sydney Morning Herald*, June 24 2000 at 29; Mann S, 'The Hideout of Hope that Became a Tomb', *Sydney Morning Herald*, June 21 2000 at 1.

2 Martin PL, 'Economic Integration and Migration: The Case of NAFTA' (1998) 3 *University of California Los Angeles Journal of International and Foreign Affairs* 419; 'Going North: Immigrants in the US' *The Guardian*, 26 August 2000, Dow Jones Interactive Document No. GRDN0023800545.

3 The most well known of these is the boat rescued by the *Tampa* in August 2001. For one account see 'Tampa Crisis Won't be a Slur on Australia, claims Howard' (03/09/2001) *The West Australian* (on line version); For two other examples of these recounts see Taylor K, 'More than 250 boat people feared drowned', *The Age*, April 14 2000; Way D,. 'Illegals switch from air to sea', *The Age*, May 16 2000.

poor and come from a state which is itself poor; and who seek to improve their economic circumstances by participating in the hidden sectors of a prosperous economy where they will presumably be better off than they previously were as legal participants in a struggling economy. Illegals are rarely, if ever, envisaged as backpacking students who overstay their visas, as 'working holidayers' who exceed their employable hours, or as prosperous business people who evade residency requirements or fail to declare the full extent of their cash flows. The label 'illegal' is laden with stereotypes about race, nationality, education and skill, and it has a firm place in the class hierarchy.

My argument in this Chapter is that migration laws, especially those aspects that define and seek to control illegal migration, are one useful indicator for assessing the impact and character of globalization. Migration laws are a vital site for constructing responses to the some of the central questions at the core of theoretical accounts of globalization. I set out this argument in three stages. First, I survey trends in globalization theory and identify the questions which underlie the tensions at the heart of this still emerging body of theory. Second, I detail the argument that migration laws provide an ideal testing site for the propositions of globalization theory both because of how migration is positioned within globalization theory and because of how migration law is situated within nation states. Finally, I examine the relationship between illegal migration and sovereignty, arguing that considering illegal migration in particular provides a way of assessing the changing – and indeed the unchanging – nature of national sovereignty.

The Central Questions of Globalization Theory

In an ironic mirroring of the phenomenon it describes, the term globalization has grown out of control. There is no longer much to be gained in pinning down a definition for this shape shifter. Rather, it makes sense to use it with full consciousness of its fluidity, its inevitable incorporation by reference of layers of meaning from the popular to the erudite. When precision is required, we must look elsewhere, as William Twining demonstrates by choosing 'cosmopolitan' over 'globalized'.[4] Among the meanings that have accreted to globalization, a common theme is economic. Thus globalization is often understood as being about the interconnectedness of world markets, the hegemony of the American dollar, the worldwide predominance of transnational corporations, and the Macdonalds on Tiannamen Square. All of these economic phenomena and more are symptoms or signifiers of globalization. Another key aspect of

---

4 See Chapter 2.

globalization, which facilitates the economic, is technological: from email and real-time chatrooms, to live around the world television broadcasts and the breaking wave of the new wireless era. These too are symbols and symptoms of globalization, literally shrinking the globe by making all corners of it simultaneously imaginable and accessible.

Most accounts of globalization go further than the economic or the technological, but these two elements are the ever present backdrop to whatever follows. While some theorists assert that globalization is predominantly economic and that its non-economic effects therefore are to be interpreted as a secondary offshoot,[5] those who hold this view are being outnumbered by others who find the most compelling aspects of globalization to be related to how people experience the world, their place in it, and their relationships with others. In Giddens' analysis, although everyone lives a local life, phenomenal worlds for the most part are truly global.[6] Gill links the economic and the psychological elements, asserting that globalization, '... in its present mythic and ideological representations, ... serves to reify a global economic system dominated by large institutional investors and transnational firms'.[7] For Held and McGrew, the key to globalization is in '... the multiplicity of linkages and interconnections between the states and societies which make up the modern world system'.[8] What each of these perspectives has in common is an emphasis on a reordering of the social. Whether this is cast in terms of phenomenal worlds, or mythic and ideological representations of the global or in societal interconnections, the focus is on something beyond a mechanically conceived economic and technological shift.

This is significant for law and legal theory because law, like globalization, is positioned as an element of social ordering. That is, law occupies the same conceptual terrain as many accounts of globalization. The challenge globalization poses for law is not simply to keep pace with technological and economic developments,[9] but moreover to keep pace with the social reconceptualization which globalization brings. Each of

---

5 See for example, Ohmae K, *End of the Nation State: The Rise of Regional Economies*, 1995, Harper Collins, London, 1995; Reich RB, *The Work of Nations: Preparing Ourselves for 21st Century Capitalism*, Simon and Schuster, London, 1983.

6 Giddens A, *The Consequences of Modernity*, Stanford University Press, Stanford, 1990.

7 Gill S, 'Globalization, Market Civilization and Disciplinary Neo-liberalism' (1995) 24 *Millennium* 3.

8 Held D and McGrew A, 'Globalization and the Liberal-Democratic State' in Sakamoto Y (ed), *Global Transformation: Challenges to the State System*, United Nations University Press, Tokyo and New York, 1994.

9 This in itself is a formidable challenge for the law, one which is discussed in the work of Dimity Kingsford Smith and Sundhya Pahuja, Chapters 4 and 5.

these challenges engages jurisprudence as the conceptual part of the discipline of law, in Julius Stone's words the 'lawyer's extraversion'. The challenge is first to map the present from which future directions can be plotted, and second to describe the place of law in the shifting social order. Law mediates and shapes the 'linkages and interconnections' to which Held and McGrew refer. It is interwoven with the 'mythic and ideological representations' Gill addresses. It is because globalization is not merely an economic and technological event, because it operates on diverse discursive planes, and because its contours are amorphous, that it is of vital concern to law and legal theory.

Given that diverse scholarship on globalization means the term has slipped beyond precise definition, one useful way to survey globalization theory is to identify the central questions it raises. In their comprehensive volume which tracks approaches to and effects of globalization, Held, McGrew, Goldblatt and Perraton identify three schools of thought about globalization: sceptics, transformationalists, and hyperglobalizers.[10] They argue that categorizing scholars into these camps interestingly does not reflect traditional ideological positions, but rather approaches to globalization itself.[11] In other words, diverse scholars answer the central questions of globalization differently and in ways that do not conform to theoretical positions independent of globalization. It is these central questions that I will outline here to ground my argument that migration law provides one useful site in which to formulate answers to, or at least practical perspectives on, some of them.

One predominant question in the globalization debate is whether globalization threatens the capacity or the existence of the nation state. The centrality of this question is partially due to the vigour with which opposing sides of the argument have been put. Those asserting that globalization has rendered the nation state redundant have put their case in the strongest possible terms. Ohmae states that '... in terms of real flows of economic activity, nation states have already lost their role as meaningful units of

---

10 Held D, McGrew A, Goldblatt D and Perraton J, *Global Transformations: Politics, Economics and Culture*, Polity Press, Cambridge, 1999 at 2-8.

11 Ibid at 2. To oversimplify greatly their categorization; the hyperglobalizers assert that the nation state has already been superseded and that all is now subject to the discipline of the market, which is to be understood in global terms and as responding to global imperatives. The sceptics disagree with the hyperglobalizers on almost all points, and emphasise that current economic trends are not historically unprecedented and should be understood in an historical context. Transformationalists argue that globalization is a profound power transformation, bringing unprecedented change to states and societies on social, economic and governance levels.

participation in the global economy of today's borderless world'.[12] Reich similarly argues that nation states are now no more than local authorities of the global economic system.[13] The counter-arguments are equally assertive. Linda Weiss argues that in the future, '... nation states will matter more rather than less ...'.[14] In her assessment, globalists have both overstated and overgeneralized state powerlessness, particularly because they have not taken account of state variety and adaptability. Weiss argues that the enhanced importance of nation states will in fact advance the development of the world economy. In between these polarized positions, others assert a range of options. Hirst and Thompson argue that the state remains a crucial institution, even though some aspects of its governance capacity have been weakened.[15] Ruggie asserts that states are 'anything but irrelevant',[16] in opening his argument that notions of territoriality are shifting, and with them the settled position of the nation state. Held and McGrew claim that the state has some continued importance, but that current theory does not adequately situate it within the global system.[17] The debate over the relative health of the nation state is sometimes cast in terms of sovereignty. Sovereignty is thus viewed as the distinguishing characteristic of the nation state and its erosion is seen as a measure of impaired state capacity. The question being asked is essentially similar whether the key term is state capacity or sovereignty.

A second vital question in globalization theory is whether globalization is essential to economic growth. There is an assumed relationship between globalization and free trade, and between free trade and market efficiency. There is increasing tension between support among the governments of prosperous nations for a variety of initiatives which foster free trade (from strengthening regional trading alliances to supporting the World Trade Organization) and resistence from non-governmental actors arguing that free trade will damage conditions of local lives. The protests which are now named the Battle of Seattle, and which were reflected on a smaller scale at recent multilateral trade meetings in Vancouver,[18] Melbourne,[19] Quebec

---

12 Ohmae K, *End of the Nation State*, Harper Collins, London, 1995 at 11.

13 Reich R, *The Work of Nations: Preparing Ourselves for 21st Century Capitalism*, Vintage Books, New York, 1992.

14 Weiss L, *The Myth of the Powerless State: Governing the Economy in a Global Era*, Polity Press, Cambridge, 1998 at 195.

15 Hirst P and Thompson G, *Globalization in Question*, Polity Press, Cambridge, 1996.

16 Ruggie J, 'Territoriality and Beyond: Problematizing Modernity in International Relations' (1993) 47 *International Organization* 139 at 142.

17 Held D and McGrew A, above n 8 at 57.

18 These events are analyzed in the collection, Wesley Pue W (ed), *Pepper in Our Eyes: The APEC Affair*, University of British Columbia Press, Vancouver, 2000.

19 Clark A, 'S11 Can Celebrate at Least One Win' *The Age*, September 16 2000 at 27.

City[20] and Genoa are symptomatic of the increasing importance of this tension. A somewhat different take on this issue is to regard it as a debate over whether economic growth is a value to be pursued. To the extent that the debate takes that form, it shifts ground somewhat and operates on the assumption that globalization *does* promote economic growth, but that economic growth is not to be presumed as a common good. As globalization theory advances the debate becomes more nuanced. Hurrell and Woods make an important contribution in this area by arguing that globalization exacerbates existing inequalities between states and therefore contributes differentially to both economic growth and state capacity.[21]

A third issue that circulates through the literature on globalization theory is whether globalization is a liberal phenomenon or a 'transmission belt' for liberal values. For Young, globalization and liberalism are inextricably intertwined. He asserts that '... from the beginning, it [liberalism] has always been about globalization'[22] and argues that since the end of the Cold War the universalizing aspects of the liberal project have become more prominent. The question of liberal values has economic resonance, but reaches beyond that. The global spread of ideas such as Western human rights norms, with their strong liberal pedigree, are also an aspect of this question, as is the counter-cry of cultural imperialism. Often the two are tied, as in discussions of tied aid or linking trade status with human rights 'performance'. This aspect of the theory is of particular importance to the law, where the universalization of legal norms can often be equated with the spread of legal norms from hegemonic states to others.[23]

A final preoccupation of globalization theory is the question of whether the phenomenon is indeed something new, or just an intensification of developments that can be traced for a century or more. Held and his co-authors have taken this issue as a crucial starting point for their extensive empirical work in *Global Transformations*.[24] To an extent the issue is a false one, as the mere prevalence of the term provides

20 MacKinnon M, 'Breaking the Barriers The Summit of the Organization of the Americas Summit, April 20-22, 2001 Outside' *The Globe and Mail*, April 23 2001 at A10; Travers J, 'This was no sequel to Battle of Seattle' *The Toronto Star*, April 23 2001 at A1.

21 Hurrell A and Woods N, 'Globalization and Inequality' (1995) 24 *Millennium* 447.

22 Young T, '"A Project to be Realized": Global Liberalism and Contemporary Africa' (1995) 24 *Millennium* 527 at 527.

23 An interesting discussion of this issue is presented in Wiener J, *Globalization and the Harmonization of Law*, Pinter, London and New York, 1999. See especially the concluding chapter entitled, 'Re-establishing Protective Jurisprudence in the Era of Globalization – Empire of Law?'.

24 Above n 10.

justification for taking it seriously and considering it analytically. To the degree that it may not be 'completely new', its passage into the banality of everyday parlance assuredly is. What this alerts us to, however, is a wariness against assuming that all facets of globalization are unprecedented, and a need to investigate what has triggered the increased commonplace usage of the term.

The four questions of the prevalence of the nation state, the place of economic growth, the role of liberal values and the debate about 'newness' provide an oversimplified map of the burgeoning body of globalization theory. These questions overlap and intertwine. Most theorists who assert that the capacity of the nation state is affected by globalization, for example, rely in their argument on assertions about economic growth and the place of liberalism. These themes are rarely presented in isolation, and are being pushed in new and increasingly sophisticated directions. The value of grouping them in this way is to present a view of the theoretical area, and a substitute for a static definition of globalization. This is useful for considering how migration law can be used as a testing ground for the propositions of globalization theory.

Migration Law as a Test of Globalization

One of the hardest globalization myths to assess is whether it is true that more people are on the move now than at any other time in history. Held and his co-authors tackle this question in comprehensive detail, assessing human migration patterns over history on the basis of their extensity, intensity, velocity, and impact on host and home states and societies.[25] Their conclusion is tentative, stating that if present trends continue the contemporary pattern of migration '... may supersede its predecessors in terms of intensity as well as extensity'.[26] If any aspect of the 'more people on the move' idea holds true, it is probably that international travel has increased greatly. Nonetheless, the proportion of the world's population that travels across borders may not have changed significantly if we consider the recent exponential growth of the world's population and that

---

25 Ibid, Chapter 6, 'People on the Move'.

26 Ibid at 312. In full they state: 'In the end, it is a close call. The transatlantic surge of 1880-1920 was certainly more intense than the early colonial emigrations, the slave trade, or the Asian migrations of the nineteenth century. It was probably more intense than the global flows of the postwar-era – but only just. The comparison between nineteenth century Asian migrations and contemporary ones is more clear cut. The former were greater. However, intra-Asian migratory flows are only just beginning to mount as differential rates of economic development generate the preconditions for large movements of labour. If these migrations continue to expand, and American migrations continue – and there is no sign of them abating – then the contemporary pattern of migration may supersede its predecessors in terms of intensity as well as extensity'.

most people in the most densely populated parts of the earth do not participate either in the backpacking or sun seeking rituals.

The mobility of people, or in the economists' terms 'labour', is never assumed to be as great as that of capital within the globalized economy. While money and ideas circumvent the globe, people remain in place. The removal of most passport controls within the European Union is so far an isolated example, which covers a relatively small geographic area. Increased options to move within Europe are not yet challenging national or cultural identity groupings. The most pressing migration issue in European public discourse at the outset of the twenty-first century is the question of illegal migration, the one area where increased potential mobility within Europe makes little difference. There is no evidence that the removal of passport controls has triggered widespread permanent migration between European nations.[27] The North American Free Trade Agreement loosens some migration controls, but primarily for business people.[28] Neither the Asia Pacific Economic Cooperation group nor the narrower Association of South East Asian Nations sets out any migration provisions in their constituting agreements, although the former has recently developed a fast track travel pass program.[29] In sum, even these regional groupings have not fundamentally altered migration: they have made movement easier for those who would have been able to obtain permission, and an incentive, to move anyway under the earlier regimes. Even Hirst and Thompson's pilloried 'ideal type' global economy does not operate primarily by actual labour mobility from country to country but 'by mobile capital selecting locations with the best deal in terms of labour costs

[27] See annual net migration rates reported at <www.europa.eu.int/comm/eurostat/Public/datashop/print-product/EN?catalogue=Eurostat&product=3-po020in-EN&mode=download>.

[28] See *NAFTA*: *Key Provisions*, at <www.mac.doc.gov/nafta/3001.htm>, which notes that the key beneficiaries of the NAFTA's easing of entry for business persons are after-sales service providers, sales representatives/agents/buyers/market researchers and financial service personnel, professionals, and company executives and managerial personnel. See also Martin, above n 2.

[29] This program is aimed at facilitating speed and efficiency in short-term business travel within APEC member countries. As of the end of 2001 eleven member states (Australia, Chile, Hong Kong, Korea, China, Philippines, Malaysia, New Zealand, Thailand, Peru and Brunei Darussalam) were participating in the scheme, which has allowed governments and customs personnel to share a large amount of information with each other before arrivals. Once a businessperson is issued with the APEC Business Travel Card they are able to travel visa-free to participating countries, as well as enjoy the benefits of accelerated customs processing on arrival. For a brief overview of the scheme under APEC's Mobility of Business People Working Group, see <www.apecsec.org.sg/committee/mobility_upd.html>.

and supply'.[30] Hirst and Thompson argue that one persistent bastion of strength for the nation state is its control over the mobility of its population: 'People are less mobile than money, goods or ideas: in a sense they remain "nationalized", dependent on passports, visas and residency and labour qualifications'.[31]

Each of the factors they list is a product of migration law. When we, as lawyers, search to test their thesis we are led to migration law texts and the means that states deploy to enforce them. Thus one reason why migration law is a vital site for assessing effects of globalization is because migration law's features occupy a place in accounts of globalization which are produced by those who hold no interest in either the law or this branch of it. In Sundhya Pahuja's terms, migration law plays a role in the globalization script.[32] Assumptions about migration, and the laws which control it, are embedded in the stock stories of globalization at all levels of the discursive spectrum from popular to political to theoretical. The reason for this, in turn, leads us to the other features of migration law which suit it to this analysis: its importance for the liberal state, the absence of international law in the area, and its symmetry with sovereignty.

Migration law is constitutive of liberal communities,[33] both as 'nations' and as 'states'. Migration laws establish the border of the community, determining who will be members and who will be outsiders. This is important to the community as a state, for a state has defined borders and a population.[34] If one requirement of a state is that there be a population, there must be a means of identifying – of labeling – that population.[35]

---

30 Above n 15 at 12.

31 Ibid at 171.

32 Pahuja S, '"Normalizing" Pathologies of Difference: The Discursive Functions of International Monetary Fund Conditionality' (1998) *International Intersections: Law's Changing Territories*, Proceedings of a Conference held at Green College, University of British Columbia, compiled by University of British Columbia Faculty of Law, Vancouver, 181.

33 This is also true of nation states which are not presently governed by liberal regimes, however, because the nation state paradigm is a product of liberalism and because the nations which are most active in defining illegal migration and the most attractive to illegal migrants are liberal states, it is appropriate to put primary focus on liberal states in this argument.

34 This is reflected in the international legal definition of a state set out in the *Montevideo Convention on Rights and Duties of States 1933* (a permanent population, defined territory, government and the capacity to enter into relations with other States).

35 The role of citizenship and other membership laws in the consolidation and capillarization of state power is the subject of John Torpey's argument in Torpey J, *The Invention of the Passport: Surveillance, Citizenship and the State*, Cambridge University Press, Cambridge, 2000. From a jurisprudential perspective, his argument is enriched by a discussion of the relationship between citizenship laws and migration laws. See

Citizenship law provides one set of population labels, but it is migration law which prescribes the rights of citizens in regard to crossing the border. It is also migration law which establishes who will be eligible to become citizens and who will be eligible for other forms of membership in the community. In addition to controlling permanent membership of the community, migration law is the law of the border. It encodes border enforcement or lack of enforcement, both projecting and determining how rigorously that state will attempt to control population flows.

In terms of the more emotive concept 'nation', migration law is equally vital. A nation is imagined, or conceptualized, as a community of a certain number of like-minded people, sharing similar values, beliefs, traditions and mythologies.[36] Migration law is important in providing a location where images of the nation are depicted and national mythology is nurtured. Migration laws reveal who the nation will accept as members, setting out a code of those whom we envision to be 'like us' and those whom we believe are too different, dangerous, or difficult to fit within our traditions and beliefs. For nations with formal immigration programs, or that count themselves as nations of immigration, the simple existence of migration law forms part of the mythology of the nation. In the New World nations of immigration, migration laws and policies have provided both the 'who' of the nation and the 'what' of the state's population.

Liberal theory, the paradigm within which nation states came to divide and dominate the world's political landscape, by and large makes the assumption that the borders to the community are, or at least can morally be, closed.[37] Michael Walzer, the dominant theorist to have taken up the issue of the border of the liberal community in detail, argues that the question of membership is of a prior order than those of justice or equality, and that accordingly membership is the primary good which a community

---

Dauvergne C, 'Citizenship, Migration Laws and Women: Gendering Permanent Residency Statistics' (2000) 24 *Melbourne University Law Review* 280.

36 This account draws on understandings of nation presented by Benedict Anderson in Anderson B, *Imagined Communities: Reflections on the Origin and Spread of Nationalism*, rev ed, Verso, London and New York, 1991; and Hobsbawn E, *Nations and Nationalism since 1780: Programme, Myth, Reality*, 2nd ed, Cambridge University Press, Cambridge, 1992. It also corresponds with important elements of Anthony Smith's more ethnically based account of nations. See Smith A, *The Ethnic Origins of Nations*, Blackwell, Oxford and New York, 1986; and *National Identity* Penguin, London and New York, 1989.

37 I make this argument in detail in Dauvergne C, 'Beyond Justice: The Consequences of Liberalism for Immigration Law' (1997) *Canadian Journal of Law and Jurisprudence* 323; and Dauvergne C, 'Amorality and Humanitarianism in Immigration Law' (1999) 37 *Osgoode Hall Law Journal* 597.

bestows.[38] In order for the community to operate against an assumption of closed borders, there must be a way of closing them, of identifying who has a right to cross them, and of providing for enforcement of their closure. While ultimately the coercive power of the state provides these things, it is the rule of law which legitimates them and makes them part of the liberal state. Again, as in considering the factors which Hirst and Thompson identified as crucial to the nationalization of people, the answers here are, from the jurist's point of view, provided by migration laws.

The role of migration law in giving form to a key assumption of the liberal community points in the direction of the two other features which make it an ideal site for assessing globalization's dilemmas. The first of these is that in questions of migration and citizenship, there is almost no international law. International law leaves it to individual states to determine who may enter their territory – through migration law – and who may become full members – through citizenship law.[39] The three potential qualifications to this rule do not dislodge it. I have argued above that the emergence of regional trading alliances is not necessarily hinged to movements of people, and would add that the establishment of European Union law is firstly not international law[40] and secondly does not represent a commitment to easing migration restrictions in a more general sense.[41]

---

38 Walzer M, *Spheres of Justice: A Defense of Pluralism and Equality*, Basic Books, New York, 1983, see especially Chapter Two: Membership. Having argued this point, Walzer moves on to his central argument about justice, leaving the question of membership behind. Thus his argument is similar to other liberals such as Rawls (for whom the community is one which one enters at birth and leaves at death; 'Justice as Fairness: Political not Metaphysical' (1985) 14 *Philosophy and Public Affairs* 223 at 233) or Dworkin (for whom communities of principle must settle questions of equality and justice among members; Dworkin R, *Law's Empire*, Harvard University Press, Cambridge, Massachusetts, 1986 at 208) for whom justice is to be understood within the border rather than across it.

39 *Nottebohm Case (Lichtenstein v Guatemala) (Second Phase)* ICJ Rep 1955 4. There were some discussions in the early years of the twentieth century suggesting that international standards be developed in the areas of citizenship and migration. The idea was raised in international fora and explicitly rejected, largely because of the question of racial exclusion, see Brawley S, *The White Peril: Foreign Relations and Asian Immigration to Australasia and North America 1919-1978*, University of New South Wales Press, Sydney, 1995.

40 Note however the importance of a jurisprudence for a global era of mapping the layers of legal order which are neither international nor domestic, but nonetheless legal (Twining, Chapter 2). In the case of European Community law I believe it is important to understand that it is the law of one region, with a particular geography and history, and not the inevitable future direction of global developments.

41 Talk of Fortress Europe enjoyed a popular resurgence following the UN Human Rights Commissioner's warning regarding European treatment of asylum seekers; 'UN Commissioner warns against "Fortress Europe" laws' *Australian* 8 February 2001 at 8.

The second potential qualification to this rule is that there is an increasing prevalence of provisions for dual citizenships and changing citizenships over a person's lifetime.[42] While this makes citizenship less restrictive than previously, it does not alter its role as the legal signifier of full membership. I return to this point, and a discussion of Kim Rubenstein's argument, in the final section of this chapter, as I believe it forms part of a response to one of globalization's puzzles.

The third potential qualification to the statement that individual nation states exercise full control over their membership, is the role of international refugee law. The *Refugee Convention*[43] however, does not function as a constraint upon a nation state's abilities to control membership or entry. Rather, those who are determined to be refugees must not be returned to states where they are likely to face certain types of persecution. It is precisely because of individual nation states' control over their own borders and memberships that the *Refugee Convention* is sometimes read as providing the refugee a right to remain in a country where the refugee is not a member.[44] Because a state cannot expel a refugee into empty, un-nationalized, space[45] and because states are only required to admit their own members, when individuals are likely to face persecution at home international refugee law provides them with a temporary and contingent 'right to remain' in a country of asylum.[46] Refugee law does not provide a right to enter another state, and thus individuals who wish to claim refugee protection have a strong incentive to use extra-legal means to enter other countries.[47]

The absence of international law in this area means that in questions of migration outside Europe, legal order at the level of the nation state overshadows all else. This is worthy of attention because it is increasingly

---

42 This is discussed in detail by Kim Rubenstein in Chapter 7.

43 The 1951 Convention Relating to the Status of Refugees 189 *United Nations Treaty Series* 150, as amended by the 1967 Protocol Relating to the Status of Refugees 606 *United Nations Treaty Series* 267.

44 Provided, of course, that that country is a party in good faith to the *Convention*. As of May 2002, 143 countries are.

45 Short of taking them out and leaving them on the literal and legal high seas.

46 This is set out in Article 33 of the *Convention*, known as the 'non-refoulement' provision. I discuss the failure of the non-refoulement provision to function as a 'right' in Dauvergne C, 'The Dilemma of Rights for Refugees' (2000) 23 *University of New South Wales Law Journal* 56.

47 A great number of the refugees who are successfully resettled in third countries arrive in those countries after having been assessed and determined to meet refugee criteria while in overseas camps. It is important to recognise that 'illegal entrants' are not the only people who resettle as refugees. The numeric balance between those brought from other countries and those who arrive by illegal means varies greatly among states that receive refugees and this variation is accounted for largely by geography.

atypical of law in the contemporary era, and because it contributes to the final feature of migration law rendering it an ideal globalization test site: the strong association of migration law and sovereignty. In some legal accounts of sovereignty, the state's ability to control access to membership is the 'essence of sovereignty'.[48] In states that follow the English common law tradition, control over questions of immigration was originally part of the royal prerogative.[49] In the contemporary era, this has evolved into a strong tradition of deference on the part of the courts to executive decision making in questions of immigration,[50] and to leaving key aspects of immigration law in the hands of the executive rather than turning them over to democratic law making processes.[51] All of these factors contribute a close conceptual association between control over the definition of membership and physical crossings of the border and state sovereignty. To adapt Joseph Carens' image, borders are meaningful because they are ultimately defended by the coercive power of the state.[52] This image of sovereignty parallels Weberian definitions of the state. This is why the question of illegal migration is so important to a consideration of sovereignty and globalization, because the persistence of illegal migration affects the state at precisely this point – the ultimate definition of sovereign power – the border itself is breached. No nation today can hermetically seal its borders. In an ironic challenge to traditional state sovereignty, the uncontested hegemon of the contemporary world hosts perhaps the largest illegal population in the world.[53]

---

48 Rubenstein K, 'Citizenship in a Borderless World' in Anghie A and Sturgess G (eds), *Legal Visions of the 21st Century*, Kluwer Law International, The Hague, 1998, 183 at 189.

49 Cronin K, 'A Culture of Control: An Overview of Immigration Policy-Making' in Jupp J and Kabala M (eds), *The Politics of Australian Immigration*, Australian Government Publishing Service, Canberra, 1993.

50 See Stephen Legomsky's seminal study comparing the immigration law traditions of the United States and Britain and finding strong similarities on this point, Legomsky S, *Immigration and the Judiciary: Law and Politics in Britain and America*, Clarendon Press, Oxford, 1987.

51 For example, the all important 'quotas' which determine how many migrants in which categories will actually be admitted are determined directly by the executive in the United States, Canada, and Australia. Similarly, deportation decisions, which are the aspects of migration law involving the highest levels of state coercion, are generally left to the executive as well.

52 Carens J, 'Aliens and Citizens: The Case for Open Borders' (1987) 49 *The Review of Politics* 251, which opens with the statement: 'Borders have guards and guards have guns'.

53 Illegal immigrants made up 1.9 per cent of the US population in 1996, Department of Justice, Immigration and Naturalization Service, *Illegal Alien Resident Population*, <http://www.ins.usdoj.gov/graphics/aboutins/statistics/illegalalien/index.htm>. The esti-

National Sovereignty and Illegal Migration

Migration laws are a vital test case for globalization and provisions attacking illegal migration are the most important aspects of the test because of the threat illegal migration poses to the geopolitical state and to the nation-as-community. Over the past five years, as concerns about globalization and its implications have intensified, many prosperous nations have introduced stronger legal provisions to limit movements of people outside the law. In the United States the *Illegal Immigration Reform and Immigrant Responsibility Act* of 1996 tightened exclusions from social welfare benefits and increased employer sanctions as purported means of cracking down on the illegal labour force.[54] In addition, enforcement mechanisms were enhanced with additional dollars devoted to efforts at controlling illegal crossings of the US-Mexican border.[55] The British government has moved illegal migrants into regular jails rather than migration detention.[56] The European Union is exploring a variety of means for tightening controls on all unauthorized migration.[57] In Canada, the government's long awaited new immigration legislation set out a newly named crime of 'people smuggling' and provisions requiring that inability to prove one's identity must be the basis of an adverse evidentiary inference.[58] In Australia, which has had a mandatory detention regime for illegal arrivals since 1989,[59] the law was altered in late 1999 to create two tiers of refugee protection in order to reduce entitlements for those who arrive illegally[60] and beginning in 2001 the navy was deployed to prevent boats carrying intending asylum seekers from reaching Australian shores.

This worldwide tightening of sanctions against illegal movements of people can be read as a response to globalization on two levels. On one level, it is a state based and largely uncoordinated reply to the ability of those who profit from moving people around the globe outside the law to

mated size of the illegal population in the United States is somewhere between four and six million people, although of course the number is not precise.

54 *Illegal Immigration Reform and Immigrant Responsibility Act* 1996 (Pub.L. 104-208, Div. C, 110 Stat. 3009-546).

55 Kitfield J, 'Crossing the Line' *Government Executive Magazine* 7/1/97 found at <www.govevec.com/features/0797s5.html>, at 5-6; Palafox J, 'Militarizing the Border' (1996) 56 *Covert Action Quarterly* found at www.caq.com/CAQ56border.html.

56 I Burrell, 'Prisons Inspector Attacks Jailing of Asylum Seekers' *The Independent*, 22 January, 2001, http://www.independent.co.uk/story.jsp?story=51361.

57 Nacheman A, 'EU moves to tighten immigration, asylum, human trafficking' *Agence France Press*, 11 February 2001, accessed at Dow Jones Interactive.

58 *Immigration and Refugee Protection Act* S.C. 2001, c. 27.

59 *Migration Act 1958* (Cth), Division 6.

60 New visa class 785.

use the technologies of globalization to their advantage.[61] At another, which builds necessarily on the first, it is an assertion of sovereignty against a threat that goes to the core of sovereign power. As control over the population, its movements and its membership is held up as evidence that the nation state remains relevant, powerful and sovereign, strong assertions of power against people who threaten this control are vital. 'Cracking down' on illegal migration provides a rhetorical demonstration that the nation retains this power. It serves to demonstrate that it can both know and name those who enter illegally. The latter capacity is often stronger: the state has an unchallenged capacity to name those who transgress its laws as 'illegal'. Given the absence of international law provisions in the area, the distinction between those within the law and those outside it is controlled by the state. Even refugees can be labelled 'illegal' on entry as the web of domestic and international provisions which provide for their eventual protection usually require them to transgress the law in order to attain that protection. As to the former capacity, states have long been aware that they often do not know the number of people inside their borders who have overstayed their legal entitlement or entered without one. In some cases this lack of knowledge is acute, as is the case in the United States where estimates of the size of the illegal population range from four to six million.[62] In a smaller number of cases, such as Australia, which has long had a universal visa requirement and has no land borders, the magnitude of the problem is less. There the size of the illegal population is theoretically 'knowable' even if the effort required to obtain this knowledge is not always made.

The capacity to use the label 'illegal' reinforces the nation's power even when the border is breached. Migration laws provide for a hierarchy of membership within the nation, and it has long been recognized that membership extends beyond citizenship to several, lesser, categories.[63] Brubaker and others have argued that many in these 'other' categories have earned by virtue of their presence within the nation, at least some moral

[61] While many illegal migrants travel in cargo holds and decrepit vessels in conditions associated with the nineteenth century rather than the twenty-first, there is increasing evidence that the 'business' of people smuggling is lucrative, highly organized, and relies on sophisticated communication technologies and the ability to have news about developments all over the world simultaneously. See 'People-smuggling trade booming' in *The Grand Rapids Press* Associated Press, 16 April, 1999, accessed at Dow Jones Interactive; Roberts G, 'Holes in the Net' *Sydney Morning Herald* 13 April, 1999, accessed at Dow Jones Interactive; Williams D, '20,000 per migrant and a journey of six months' *Daily Mail* 20 June, 2000, accessed at Dow Jones Interactive.

[62] See above note 42.

[63] The categories 'below' citizen bear labels such as: permanent resident, temporary resident, guest worker, international student, visitor.

rights of membership.[64] The effect of the label 'illegal' is to create a category that has no place on the hierarchy; a group physically within the nation but nonetheless excluded, no matter how long its members remain. The label illegal names these outsiders as transgressors – those who have broken 'our laws'. This provides a moral ballast against arguments that their presence, economic contribution, and general adherence to societal norms – including laws – mean they deserve legal recognition and rights of political participation. The power to name the other as bad in this way enforces both the nation's sovereign authority and its vision of its own 'goodness'.

The recent tightening by many states of provisions aimed at illegal migration therefore responds to both internal and external understandings of sovereignty: internal, in that they operate as controls imposed on those within their borders, external in that they operate in the international realm as a reinforcement of the border itself. This new spate of controls can be read as a reinforcement of sovereignty as traditionally understood. Hirst and Thompson trace the modern notion of sovereignty from the Treaty of Westphalia to consider the challenges to a traditional view of sovereignty which are presented by nationalism and democracy. In their view, the challenge to sovereignty presented by globalization is greater than any other, but the concept is resilient nonetheless. As war between nuclear states has become an impossibility, '... states in the advanced world no longer have war as a central support for their claims to sovereignty'.[65] Similarly, the exclusive control of states over their own territories has lessened, reducing their capacity for cultural control and homogenization.[66] In their view, however, these changes are countered by the nation state's continuing control over its borders and the movement of people across them. This is the primary support that sustains the more-or-less traditional notion of sovereignty they discuss.

The growing prevalence of illegal migration fits into this analysis awkwardly. To the extent that it is actually on the increase, illegal migration suggests that these globalization sceptics will be disproved. It is a sign that states are no longer in control of their borders and their populations. On the other hand, if the increased prevalence of illegal migration reflects a global level 'moral panic' or an increase in rhetoric, the current crack down by all prosperous nations can then be understood as a reassertion of a traditional sovereignty. Furthermore, the sovereignty that is

---

64 Brubaker WR, 'Introduction' in Brubaker WR (ed), *Immigration and the Politics of Citizenship in Europe and North America*, University Press of America, Lanham, 1989.

65 Above n 15 at 180.

66 Ibid.

threatened by illegal migration is primarily external sovereignty, the power to reinforce the border against outsiders. The power to name part of its population as illegal, to use the law to exclude part of its permanent population from entitlements of membership reinforces an internal projection of sovereignty.

Many theorists of globalization argue that while the concept of sovereignty remains meaningful, its nature has changed. Ruggie's carefully nuanced thesis contributes a solid grounding to this argument.[67] In what he frames as a modest attempt to find a means of expressing the vital questions about transformations within the international sphere, he argues the nation state system of reciprocal sovereignty is an historically unique product of modernity's movement towards exclusive territoriality. He traces this movement and argues that there is now evidence to suggest we are moving, unevenly, towards some postmodern reconceptualization of space. Ruggie argues that developments such as the growing integration of the European Union, transnational microeconomic links, the transformative potential of global ecology and emerging fragments of international security communities each provide evidence of 'multiperspectival institutional forms'.[68] The importance of these shifts lies in how we imagine our collective existence, how we identify ourselves.[69] Each of these shifts represents some challenge to 'national' identity. Increasingly stringent responses to illegal migration provide a counter to the examples Ruggie suggests. The notion that migration *can* be illegal reinforces directly the type of exclusive territoriality that Ruggie traces to modernity. The enforcement within the nation of stringent boundaries between illegal and legitimate communities underscores the 'us' and 'them' divide, which is at the heart of national identity.

Like Ruggie, Jayasuriya's analysis of sovereignty begins with the concept of territoriality. Arguing that sovereignty is a complex concept that is transformed rather than diminished by globalizing trends, he asserts that the concept of sovereignty itself remains important, but that it must be reconceptualized by severing the link between sovereignty and territoriality.[70] Jayasuriya's work is important in this context because of its explicit attention to the law. (One part of his argument is that the system of international law relies on a theory of sovereignty.) The transformed

---

67 Above n 16.

68 Ibid at 174.

69 Ibid.

70 Jayasuriya K, 'Globalization, Law and the Transformation of Sovereignty: The Emergence of Global Regulatory Governance' (1999) 6 *Indiana Journal of Global Legal Studies* 425. This prescriptive element of Jayasuriya's work, as well as his focus on the law, distinguishes his analysis from Ruggie's.

sovereignty, that Jayasuriya both describes and prescribes, contributes to the weakening of the nation state because '... emerging forms of "complex sovereignty" break down the internal structural coherence of the State, replacing it with often autonomous regulatory agencies whose purpose is to mediate between the international or the local and the nation'.[71]

The two examples that Jayasuriya draws from to support his argument are global financial arrangements and the 'interlocking politics' of the European Union.[72] The example of illegal migration, including responses to it within the European Union, provides a counter to Jayasuriya's examples. Responses to illegal migration are articulated at a nation state level.[73] This is true even within the European Union, where different states have taken up somewhat differing approaches despite the cooperation which is necessitated by the abolition of many passport controls within the European Union. To the extent that European approaches to illegal migration are coordinated, the effect is to replicate the border to the nation at the border of the Union. While sovereignty within the Union may be developing in the complex and de-territorialized way that Jayasuriya suggests, at the border the concept is seen to operate in the same way it has in traditional nation states: sovereignty embodies an absolute power to exclude non-members. As far as global financial arrangements are concerned, the comparison with illegal migration points out a stark contrast. While illegal migration is globally organized and highly lucrative, orders of governance at levels between the national and the international are simply not emerging to confront it. One explanation of this may be simply a time lag. Nonetheless, given that the communications and technology that fuel global transactions also support globalized networks of illegal migration, this answer alone is not compelling.

In questions of people and borders, a traditional territorialized version of sovereignty has a resilience that is almost astonishing given the prevalence of cogent arguments for its demise. Even if people cross borders illegally, this does not transform sovereignty; it merely points up one potential weakness in it. To the extent that a case for transformed sovereignty can be made out, illegal migration demonstrates a shift principally in internal measures of sovereignty. By this I mean that the

---

71 Ibid at 437.

72 This is Jayasuriya's term, ibid at 443.

73 The recent establishment of an international protocol against human trafficking (Protocol to Prevent, Suppress and Punish Trafficking in Persons, Especially Women and Children, Supplementing the United Nations Convention Against Organized Crime 2000) addresses one small part of the illegal migration issue. As one of its central foci is on tools for law enforcement and border control, it reinforces a traditional view of state sovereignty relying on both coercion and territorial boundedness.

power of a state to label part of its population as illegal and thereby exclude it in spite of its territorial inclusion does move beyond territoriality in this one aspect. The potential transformation of sovereignty is therefore not in articulating a sovereign order between the national and the international but rather in moving the concept of internal sovereignty from one linked primarily with territory to one linked primarily with territory and membership in renewed combination.

Another approach to sovereignty in theoretical accounts of globalization is that which asserts that we have already moved beyond sovereignty. Some primarily economic based accounts of globalization take this view:[74] however for my purposes it is more compelling to examine the shape this argument takes when articulated within the tradition of legal theory. Where Jayasuriya's argument is primarily about the need to de-link sovereignty and territory, MacCormick's parallel argument is that law and sovereignty are already de-linked.[75] For this reason, sovereignty and the state are therefore also de-linked, and we have already moved, in the words of his title, 'beyond the sovereign state'. Arguing from the proposition that a sovereign state is both a Janus-faced concept which belongs partially to politics and partially to law, MacCormick demonstrates how theorists within the jurisprudential canon position their views of sovereignty as either predominantly legal (as Dicey) or predominantly political (as Austin). To support his conclusion that sovereignty is not a requirement for law, MacCormick asserts a definition of state that embraces territory but removes law.[76] A focus on the sovereignty of states' privileges state law inappropriately, ignoring other legal orders at all levels, not just those between the national and the international. Like Jayasuriya, MacCormick uses the European Union as a principal example, but he concludes that sovereignty is not being transformed but instead being lost, although to mutual benefit. In his conclusion, the way forward politically is to let go of the idea that sovereignty is a legal necessity or inevitability; to construct imaginatively '... a world in which our normative existence and our practical life are anchored in, or related to, a variety of institutional

---

[74] Two examples are Ohmae, above n 12 and Reich above n 13.

[75] MacCormick N, 'Beyond the Sovereign State' (1993) 56 *Modern Law Review* 1.

[76] He states at ibid 13: 'We should retain from Kelsen the idea of territoriality and effectiveness of order, but drop the juridical elements from his definition. Let us then consider the state as a political order, a territorially organized political community, where in that community political power is effectively exercised over a given territory with respect to the economic resources available in it, and to the use of force in interpersonal relations within that community. When these conditions hold good for a given territory, then in that territory there is a state and those who exercise the power are agencies of the state'.

systems, each of which has validity or operation in relation to some range of concerns, none of which is absolute over all others ...'.[77]

Presumably in the world MacCormick urges us to imagine, illegal migration and attempts to control it, would be anchored in some institutional system, but not the sovereign state. The European Union example provides one alternative here, although this example is already weak in the case of illegal migration. The enduring place of territory in MacCormick's analysis suggests that exclusion from territory would remain important, even if it came to be anchored in an institutional system distinct from the state. This reordering approaches the hard end of MacCormick's imaginative challenge. From a practical point of view, the increasingly rigid responses to illegal migration around the world suggest that states do not view the disappearance of sovereignty as mutually beneficial. To the extent that sovereignty as it is traditionally understood may be under some threat, control over borders and populations is being set up as a proverbial last stand. This could be expressed in MacCormick's terms by arguing that sovereignty remains politically important despite being legally dispensable. One is, however, left with an uncomfortable sense of skirting the issue. If states cling to the trappings of a legally void sovereignty for political purposes, they must use legal tools, and legal discourses like that of 'il'legal migration to do so.

Looking at this phenomenon then brings us full circle, to a reiteration of the importance of migration laws for the bounding of communities and a persistence of at least some core elements of a traditionally understood sovereignty. Tighter provisions against illegal migration are also inevitably tied to the ugliest side of the coercive power of the state. Ultimately, removing those who do not wish to go from one's territory involves a range of coercive measures which starts with detention and can include forced movement, drugged sedation, binding and gagging.[78] Whether or not sovereignty is required to theoretically ground the authority of the law, law is implicated in grounding the authority of the state in these matters. We would not have it otherwise.

---

77 Ibid at 17.

78 In the Australian case of *Re Minister for Immigration and Multicultural Affairs; Ex parte SE* (1998) 158 ALR 735, the High Court held that coercive measures which a private security firm proposed to use in assisting British Airways with the removal of a deportee were not the responsibility of the state because the Department of Immigration, which had objected to the plan because it included coercive measures, was not directly involved.

Conclusions

The relationship between illegal migration and sovereignty leads back to the central questions posed in theoretical accounts of globalization and provides one set of responses to them. In large measure the phenomenon of illegal migration and the increasingly stringent legal responses to it reinforce a traditional view of sovereignty: sovereignty understood in terms of exclusive jurisdiction over territory. Conceptually, the notion that migration can be illegal – outside the law – represents this view of exclusive territoriality. In practical terms, increasingly stringent responses to illegal migration at the level of the nation state are an indicator of states seeking to reinforce this traditional sovereignty. The authority of the nation state to assert external sovereignty through border control is unaltered.

In terms of internal sovereignty, the evidence is more challenging. The effect of 'cracking down' on illegal migration from a domestic point of view sends a message that the state is strong externally. More interestingly, however, it asserts a clear division between members and non-members by designating some whom are territorially included as transgressors. This has the effect of shoring up a picture of sovereignty – in the form of a clear distinction between 'us' and 'them' – even when the border has been breached. In defining some people as 'illegals', migration law plays its established role in constituting the community. The effect of recognizing but not expelling illegal communities does potentially transform internal sovereignty. It initiates a shift from sovereignty being territorially defined to sovereignty being defined in terms of membership. In other words, the state's capacity to control the population within its borders is altered somewhat by signifying that some of that population is 'illegal' – both outside, and beyond the reach of, the law. Illegal populations are largely beyond the reach of the law but live nonetheless in its shadow because breaches of domestic provisions such as criminal or welfare net laws bring increasing vulnerability to expulsion.

The sum of the relationship between migration law and sovereignty suggests that in this area at least, globalization has not significantly eroded state capacity. The importance of the nation state in terms of authorizing border crossing and membership remains vital. Tightening of controls against illegal migration reinforces rather than transforms sovereignty and the politics of illegal migration provide a platform for the reinforcement of the identity of the nation state.

Illegal migration is also a useful site for some analysis of other themes in globalization theory. In terms of whether economic growth depends upon globalization and the free trading associated with it, illegal migration suggests two insights. One is that while the mobility of labour has never been considered part of the free trade agenda in any serious way, individuals are nonetheless motivated to move to better economic circumstances. Many who are now considered to be illegal migrants, or who simply have no option to migrate, moved in great numbers in support of economic growth in earlier centuries. The present focus on illegal migration suggests that the nature of economic growth at the beginning of the twenty-first century is significantly different than it was at the start of the twentieth century because population movement is not a key element. The second insight of illegal migration at this juncture is that the technologies of globalization make disparities in economic growth more apparent around the world. The reality of a better life elsewhere has become easier to imagine than at any other point in time. This also probably plays a role in increasing at least the incentives to migrate – legally or otherwise.

Underlying both of these observations is the reality of the unequal effects of globalization. While the case of illegal migration tells us little about globalization as a transmission belt for liberal values, it does demonstrate a challenge to some liberal assumptions about globalization. Not only are states differentially affected by globalization, as Hurrell and Woods demonstrate, but this analysis extends to individuals as well. For those who are well educated and well off, globalization increases their opportunities for mobility. This holds true to some extent even for those whose home nations are not prospering, because the highly trained professionals are internationally sought out as migrants regardless of their nationality. The contrast is pointed up sharply when my analysis of illegal migration is contrasted with Kim Rubenstein's analysis of citizenship.[79] In Rubenstein's analysis, globalization is ushering in an era of increasing inclusion and increasing opportunities for belonging. When considering illegal migration, however, the analysis is quite the opposite. The difference can be explained in liberal terms. When what we are investigating is inclusion, we find globalization brings increasing opportunities for inclusion. When what we are investigating is exclusion, however, we also find an increase. These cross-cutting trends correspond with homogenizing and universalizing elements of the liberal project. The impulse towards inclusion depends for its success on an equal impulse towards exclusion. Migration law is important in this analysis because of its function in policing the lines between 'us' – increasingly broadly defined – and 'them', even when they have breached our borders.

Finally, a consideration of the role of law in delimiting the illegal migrant sharpens our perceptions of the roles that migration law plays in

---

79 See Chapter 7.

liberal nations. It brings into sharper focus the functions of inclusion and exclusion performed by this law, and the values embedded in it which make some migrants highly prized and others illegal. If part of the jurisprudential endeavour is to provide the conscience of law, the inequalities which this analysis reveals should not be ignored or allowed to disappear behind the mask created by naming the other as a transgressor of 'our' laws. The generalizability represented by the increasing prevalence of illegal migration has a nefarious edge.

PART IV:

GLOBALIZATION, CULTURES AND COMPARISONS

Chapter 9

Globalization, Legal Transplants and Unhappiness: Post-Communist Experiences

Adam Czarnota

Introduction

In this short contribution I will sketch the impact of globalization processes on societies in post-communist central-eastern Europe. It seems necessary to start with a simple question: is there any relationship between globalization processes and the collapse of communism?

The geographical area I am covering is the post-communist world and, more closely, post-communist central-eastern Europe. Let me begin with the thesis that the extraordinary changes in that part of the world where we can find more 'history than geography' can be attributed to processes of globalization, but that ten years after the collapse of communist regimes in the region there are no signs of universalization of legal norms despite heavy borrowing from the arsenal of the western legal tradition. In this paper I will try to describe and explain the processes which block universalization of legal norms in that part of the world and create a structure in which legal transplants work in a different way than expected.

I do not think that it is possible at the moment to write a comprehensive, logical piece on the topic. One could ask why not? That is a legitimate question. My answer is first, that we do not yet have any theory of globalization and second, we do not have any theory of post-communist societies.

So I am exploring a dark area with my eyes as open as possible. What I intend to do in this contribution is to show paradoxes and a few examples in order to make the paradoxes more visible. My conclusions are rather provisional, except one for legal scholars: it is impossible to build any theory of law that includes globalization as a variable without taking into account other social phenomena. That means that the only feasible theory of globalized law is a social theory.

Globalization and Unhappiness

Globalization in recent years has become a fashionable keyword. In numerous conferences and journals there are plenty of articles and papers using it. Even in the legal sciences, which are usually far behind the other social sciences, it has become a legitimate term. The question is: how do we understand globalization?; and what is the best methodological approach to investigate the impact of globalization processes within national legal systems?

Before I propose some definition let me relate a story. Leo Tolstoy in *Anna Karenina* wrote that 'all happy families look alike but each unhappy family is unhappy in its own way'. It appears that globalization triggers social processes which stimulate unhappiness in different parts of the world. This unhappiness, however, may take different forms in different parts of the world, and even within the same society. Despite my aim to write about central-eastern Europe, I will start with France.

In his book *The Lexus and the Olive Tree*, which considers a hypothetical situation in which countries are on offer on the stock exchange, Thomas Friedman suggested to potential investors that they buy shares in Taiwan, keep shares in Italy and sell France.[1] His advice was guided by the criterion of how each particular country is able to adjust to globalization. Why buy shares in Taiwan? Because it is a country which has opened itself up to global economic forces. Taiwan treats economic globalization as a big opportunity. Italy treats it with hesitation but is able to read the *Zeitgeist* and find its place in the post-cold war global world. But why sell shares in France? Because, according to Friedman, instead of accepting the trend the French try to swim against the current and attempt to change it which is just a waste of time.

About a year ago the media informed us about the French symbol of swimming against the current – the leader of the French peasants or farmers, Jose Bove. Mr Bove succeeded in the sense that his act of violence against a McDonalds restaurant, which should have been mentioned only as a short note in the tabloids, became a symbol of national struggle against evil global forces with headline news covering it around the world. Another contemporary version of David versus Goliath. In that version Jose Bove is David – representing everything that is local and French against Goliath – representing global forces. More precisely – David represents French traditional culinary art with Roquefort cheese at its heart and Goliath – a fast-food chain offering the same type of food – especially hamburgers – around the world.

---

1 Friedman T, *The Lexus and the Olive Tree* (rev ed), Harper Collins, London, 2000.

The media called Mr Bove a contemporary Robin Hood from Roquefort. The reality, however, is different. Jose Bove does not represent the poor and powerless against the rich and powerful. French farmers receive huge subsidies from the European Union and are protected by a powerful political lobby. Roquefort cheese is a luxurious commodity. Hamburgers are not able to steal customers of Roquefort simply because customers of McDonalds cannot afford it.

The two stories illustrate that the dominant approach to globalization is to treat it as solely an economic force. It is true that the most visible dimension of globalization is the economic one. Nevertheless, there are other dimensions that are not so visible, which accompany economic globalization and have enormous impact on existing social structures.

In the post-communist countries of eastern Europe there are plenty of such local Boves, not as well known to public opinion. There is Lepper – another leader of peasants – in Poland, a leader of miners in Romania (at present in prison), leaders of the smallholders party in Hungary, and there was and still is the boxer turned politician Meciar in Slovakia – just to give some examples. In each country in post-communist central-eastern Europe it is possible to find such leaders who quite often use violence in their protest against evil global forces. All of them play with some local sentiments and emotions. Is this just a game of interests or is something more at stake? It seems that not only economic interests are at stake. Globalization is a cultural revolution *sensu stricto* and is most visible in the post-communist countries of central-eastern Europe where at least since 1945 deep layers of traditions and identities had been frozen by the communist political and ideological superstructure.

The situation is paradoxical because globalization is not about the homogenization of social, cultural and legal identities. Globalization does not question separate national and regional differences but is changing the world into an open space in which, as in the new type of office space without walls, it is possible to see who works and who does not, who is having a nap and who sits at their desk. For people who used to love their own small, uncomfortable space where it was possible to shut the door and escape from control and surveillance, this new situation creates challenge and cultural shock. Change could mean that effort will be noticed and rewarded or that weaknesses will be noticed and accounted for. In the eyes of those local heros like Bove, globalization is the worst evil and possesses all the evil features ascribed to nineteenth century capitalism. It does not have mercy for the weak and rewards only the strong. There is also fear that globalization will change the world into a big global marketplace where it will be possible to buy and sell everything. Where only commodities will be important and there will be no place for values, norms, local and national traditions and cultures. In other words, even central-eastern Europeans fear that globalization, at the end of the day, will just equal the Americanization of their societies and countries.

Globalization – Character of the Process(es)

Globalization as a category is very confusing. Usually it is reduced to economic processes but as I tried to show using some illustrations and metaphors about cheese, globalization could be treated as a process of opening of social space and a process which stimulates global transparency.

Contemporary social theory is not a great help since serious work on conceptualization of globalization has just begun. At the moment the focus is rather on packaging some observable phenomena but not providing us as yet with the comprehensive tools with which to grasp globalization in its entirety. Ulrich Beck[2] – one of the leading social theorists of the contemporary moment – is in my opinion right in claiming that globalization is the challenge for existing paradigms within social theory.

The beginning of social theory was a focus on analyzing societies within the nation state framework. Such an approach provided the nexus between social and legal theory since both accepted the box of the nation state as the starting point for analysis. Globalization requires a radical change in cognitive approach – a jump outside the nation state as the limit for analysis. At the moment we do not have sufficient tools to do this. Within legal theory in particular, the focus is still on nation state legal systems. From this it is possible to draw two important methodological suggestions:

- it is impossible to build a legal theory which includes globalization, without adequate social theory; and
- what is possible to do at present is to describe the impact of globalization processes on national legal systems. In other words, to describe the process of adaptation and resistance to new global social processes within the national legal system. This means that legal scholars with an adequate grasp of social theory could grasp the process of globalization.

These two methodological suggestions do not mean that an intellectual effort to build legal theory that includes globalization should not be attempted. It means only that without adequate social theory such an effort cannot be fruitful.

---

2 Beck U, *What is Globalization*, Polity Press, Malden, Massachusetts, 2000 at 1-20.

In an analysis of local responses to globalization some working definition has to be accepted. Globalization was defined by one of the leading contemporary social theorists, Anthony Giddens, as the 'intensification of worldwide social relations which links distant localities in such a way that local happenings are shaped by events occurring many miles away and vice versa. This is a dialectical process because such local happening may move in an obverse direction from the very distanciated relations that shape them. Local transformation is as much a part of globalization as the lateral extension of social connections across time and space'.[3]

For Giddens, globalization is one of the consequences of modernity. In his conceptualization of globalization two categories play the most important role: time and space. In my opinion he is right that attention paid in social theory to 'society' should be replaced by the problem of how social life is ordered across time and space, what he called 'time-space distanciation'. That is Giddens' proposal to escape from the nation state box approach in social theory. Local involvements and interaction across distance are crucial for understanding globalization. For Anthony Giddens, 'the relations between local and distant social forms and events became correspondingly 'stretched''. Globalization refers essentially to that stretching process, in so far as the modes of connection between different social contexts or regions became networked across the earth's surface as a whole'.[4]

Following a four-dimensional classification of modernity, Giddens also conceptualized globalization as a four-dimensional phenomenon. In my opinion it is a useful tool for presentation of the experiences and the reaction to globalization in societies of post-communist transformations. The four dimensions of globalization are: nation state system, world capitalist economy, international division of labor, and world military order.

The communist system was based on control over these four elements through politics. The nation state system within the so-called communist camp was replaced by an imperial structure with Moscow at the centre. The economy within the system was also controlled by the political system within the Comecon countries. That was supplemented by a peculiar division of labour or what was called specialization of particular countries in some types of industries. And the military element took the form of the Warsaw Pact. The collapse of communism abolished these structures and

---

3 Giddens A, *The Consequences of Modernity*, Stanford University Press, Stanford, California, 1990 at 64.

4 Ibid.

opened the former system to new processes of globalization developed in the world outside the communist camp.

Globalization, Communism, and Post-Communism

From the point of view of post-communist transformation the most important changes are those that have occurred in the nation state system and the world capitalist economy. Communism was a system that aimed to suppress the operation of the world capitalist economy and also change the operation of the nation state system. Following the Bolshevik Revolution in Russia in 1917 and the collapse of the hope for world communist revolution, the policy adopted by the ruling party was to create a system in which the laws of economy would be totally annihilated and replaced by a political decision-making system within central planning. That was the suppression of world economic forces. After the war, in 1944-45, the communists started to build a communist empire with the aim of changing the operation of the world-state system. The satellite states in central-eastern Europe became part of the Soviet Empire. Within this empire those states had different levels of limited sovereignty. Up until 1956 there was an attempt to totally universalize the communist system within the empire. Examples of this attempt include: nationalization of property, collectivization of agriculture, implementation of similar institutions, and also radical policies in the symbolic sphere of culture within particular nation states (for example, socialist realism as the dominant doctrine in aesthetics). From the legal point of view there was the implementation of similar legal institutions within the empire. Some comparative law scholars started to distinguish a separate 'socialist family of law' within the typology of world legal systems.

After Khrushchev's famous secret speech in 1956 the process of de-Stalinization started. Generally it allowed the creation of 'communist regimes with local faces' in the region of central-eastern Europe under communist rule. That meant that some local traditions were taken into account and allowed to flourish with the blessing of the local communist party. The states within the empire differed in the level of sovereignty exercised by the ruling communist elites.

As an example of limitations on sovereignty it is possible to mention the military suppression by Soviet forces of the Hungarian uprising in 1956, and of the Prague Spring by Warsaw Pact military forces in 1968. That practice was later known as the so-called Brezhnev Doctrine of international relations.

The entire communist bloc was based on the principle of cushioning the impact of the world capitalist economy on particular economies through an imperial political system of command economy. It meant that the operation of market forces was suppressed by a political centre. According to communism's original intentions, central planning and suppression of the 'irrational' operation of the market was supposed to bring rationality to economic relations, a more effective use of resources and a more rational and just distribution of goods. The effect was rather disastrous and created what Janos Kornai, the distinguished Hungarian economist, called an 'economy of shortage'.[5] From the environmental point of view, we now know that one outcome was the destruction of the natural environment.

After use of internal resources, the communist economic system started to show difficulties, and was forced to open to the world economy. The pace of the process was different in particular cases, but it is not an exaggeration to say that since the beginning of the 1970s each of the central-eastern European countries was strongly dependent on world economic forces. Each of the countries adopted different strategies to cope with this dependency; this had an effect on their path of escaping from communism later on. This reconnection to the world economy played an important role in the destruction of communism. I do not want to say that the collapse of communism as a peculiar economic and political regime was due to world economic forces. What I do want to say is that it stimulated the acceleration of the change that in the end destroyed the system. The connections with the world economy generated more contradictions within the system. In addition, due to the more active role on the world market of some parts of the communist regimes, some sections of the communist elites became less ideological and more pragmatically oriented. This also had an impact on changes in the system of property rights, most visible in Hungary during Kadar's 'goulash communism' from the early 1970s, and in Poland in the 1980s with the process of enlargement of the second economy and creation of actual private property by the *nomenklatura*. In practice there was a huge difference between the official symbolic lip service to Marxist-Leninist ideology, on the one hand, and economic and political reality, on the other.

The second variable that generated implosion of the communist regimes as a system was changes in the world state system. Since the beginning of the cold war relations between the western world and the communist world were based on a delicate military balance. The two superpowers were engaged in substitute conventional wars; the Korean War, then Vietnam, Afghanistan, not to mention plenty of wars in Africa where both superpowers were indirectly involved. Since the 1970s the

---

5 Kornai J, *Political Economy of a Socialist System*, Harvard University Press, Cambridge, Massachusetts, 1993.

balance slowly changed to the advantage of the western powers. Drawing with a big brush it is possible to say that the collapse of the system was possible when the Moscow elites discovered that it was possible to change the concept of national security. That means resignation from control of what they called the external empire that includes the satellite eastern European states, while at the same time receiving security guarantees for Russia. Then the green light for political change was given and the political breakthrough began.

What I want to stress is that global forces played a very important role in the process of the collapse of communism. They created the necessary but in some cases not sufficient precondition for the political breakthrough. In adopting such a perspective it is necessary to say that the process of implosion of the communist system started much earlier than 1989. It is probable that it began in the early 1970s. What happened in 1989 was a political breakthrough. This clearly was very important but it is impossible to understand what happened in 1989 without taking into account at least the preceding two decades.

Law during the communist time played an increasingly important role in the life of societies under communist rule. From total disregard of law and legal institutions from 1944 to 1956, to a period of law as an instrument of social engineering still subordinated to the ideology, to a kind of semi-independent role due to an attempt by political elites to establish their legitimacy through law. All these elements played a role in approaches to law and the position of law after the political change in 1989.

Legal Transplants and Transitional Justice Problems in Post-Communist Societies

There are at least two possible approaches to law and legal institutions in post-communist countries. One is based on a description of basic legal changes and legal institutions. The second is more ambitious: a description of the operation of those legal institutions. The second approach involves a more theoretical dimension, where the investigators at least try to look below the surface at the 'hidden structure' of law and society. The hidden structure determines the meaning given to new legal institutions and the operation of those institutions within society. In the sketch below I will try to apply both approaches together.

A characteristic feature of the situation after the political breakthrough has been 'revival of the idea of law'. Such a metaphor includes the semi-autonomous role of law. Not law as subordinated to political aims, an instrumental role of law as tool of social engineering, but law as institution – using Habermas' expression – playing a role in the everyday life world itself.[6] What struck observers was basically the lack of any innovations within the legal landscape in the countries of central-eastern Europe. That lack of innovation however appears only on the surface, not in the operation of legal institutions.

Central-eastern Europeans and their elites who articulate interests perceive the change as a 'return to history' or 'joining Europe'– understood as a return to the mainstream of European history. It is a return to normality – understood as removing the barriers and obstacles, among them legal obstacles, created by communism. For a long time, so this understanding went, their history was on the wrong path, and now after the political breakthrough it is possible for particular nations to return to the normal historical road of development, perceived as the same path as that of other western European nations.

A lack of normal political life for almost 40 years creates a background for a very naïve perception of political reality, not only within populations but within new political elites. On the one hand they do not want any experiments with new institutions, yet on the other they believe that by removing the communist institutions through law, social forces will automatically create what they call a 'normal society'. The outcome of this perception was, first, the heavy borrowing of institutions, economic and also legal, from the developed West. This was, let us say, the ideological background for economic and legal changes. The second background was the peculiar type of exit from communism (breakthrough), namely the so-called 'round table talks' in nearly all these countries. The change of the regime was not through revolution that might clear the political scene and open a vacuum for creation of the new political and social institutions but through negotiations between former foes: the so-called opposition and old-communist political elites.

That mode of change of the regimes created needs for copying of legal institutions from the liberal democracies. The character of change became framed by law and both sides stuck to a narrowly perceived, naïve concept of legality.

The paradox was that copying institutions at least in the first phase was totally incompatible with the revival of national tradition. The latter has been reduced to some symbols and emblems around most important national myths. Only one country, Czechoslovakia, had a democratic tradition before communism. The 'recreation' of the market and democracy required legal transplants mainly from western Europe, and especially from the Federal Republic of Germany. The most visible example was the wave

---

6 Habermas J, 'Law as Medium and Law as Institution' in Teubner G (ed), *Dilemmas of the Welfare State*, de Gruyter, Berlin, 1986 at 212.

of first amendments to communist constitutions declaring a 'democratic law governed state' as the new type of regime.

As usual with legal transplants, they do not work in the same way as in the country of origin. In the case of the post-communist countries, the situation is more complicated since they are countries in transition, or to use the metaphor of Elster, Offe and Preuss, involved in 'rebuilding the ship at sea'.[7] In such a situation of conscious transformation, not only of legal institutions but also social institutions, mentalities and attitudes of people, special approaches are required which are not routine but extraordinary.

The beginning of political breakthrough in 1989, in the form of 'round table-talks' which marked negotiated revolutions in the communist part of central-eastern Europe, manifested a return of the idea of law. Paraphrasing Ronald Dworkin's expression 'taking rights seriously' elites of central-eastern European states 'took law seriously'. Very quickly amendments to the constitutions included statements about 'law governed states' – the equivalent of the rule of law. Well, it is very easy to decree but much more difficult to implement rule of law in social life. The hidden principle that underlay that approach is that the model for comparison is a liberal democratic state. It is justifiable from the political point of view since the aspiration of almost all these states is to build liberal democracy. After 12 years of transformation, however, I am not so sure that the outcome will be simple repetition of such a model.

Lack of originality is no bad thing. Certainly there is no shortage of originality in the social operation of new legal institutions during the process of 'transitional justice'. I want at least to mention a few elements regarding these problems.

- The 'original sin' of negotiated revolution – by that I mean legal continuity. From the very beginning there has been coexistence of the old and new law. Quite often the new old law was impossible to replace by new legislation or activism of judges, especially constitutional judges. That structural coexistence created more problems for implementation of the change.
- Short supply of alternative legal personnel – in all post-communist countries (except the former German Democratic Republic) there is a structural problem with new legal personnel. A new type of polity implementing democratic institutions and the rule of law, and also a market economy, requires a specific type of legal professional.

7 Elster J, Offe C Preuss UK, *Institutional Design in Post-Communist Societies: Rebuilding the Ship at Sea*, Cambridge University Press, Cambridge and New York, 1998.

Oppositional movements where they existed had not devoted enough attention to that problem. On the contrary, their ideologies were based on naïve economic and legal thinking. In effect old practices, at least in part, probably quite a substantial part, were reproduced after the transmission of power. Practices, ways of thinking, habits of the profession constitute law and play an important role in the functioning of the legal system. That part of the legacy of the communist regimes is quite often overlooked in thinking about the situation of law and legal institutions in new post-communist countries.

- Legal education – such a situation can be at least partly addressed by putting enough effort into legal education. It looks as though this is not taking place. There were not enough changes in models of legal education and basically the old guard is still controlling the legal academy. In all of the central-European countries there is a push for quantity rather than quality in legal education, not for the benefit of students but for short-term economic gain of the universities and their staff.
- Hidden structures of law – by that I mean conscious activity to subvert proper functioning of law in order to receive some gain. For everybody who knows the operation of the communist regime, it is not a secret that some covert agencies played a very important role in the daily life of that regime. That phenomenon is not reducible only to secret political police but includes also operation of secret police on the level of economic enterprises. Those agencies were dismantled but the personnel is now active in the economy and plays an important role in subverting functioning of the legal systems. This takes place on the level of legislation as well as that of the application of law. With the exception of a few scholars this phenomenon is totally overlooked. It plays an important role in undermining legitimacy of law, its prestige and '*Geltung*'. It puts in danger fragile elements of rule of law and should be seriously investigated. The hypothesis that central-eastern European countries too quickly adopted rule of law principles should not be dismissed but taken seriously. What the citizens of those countries need is not more rights but implementations of policies that will provide the infrastructures to fulfill those rights. Intuition suggests that to a high degree the merely declaratory character of rights is due to the activity of hidden structures.
- Impact of globalization – it is impossible to analyze the transformation in central-eastern European countries without taking into account the contemporary global situation especially globalization forces not only in their economic, but also political, military and cultural dimensions.

Those forces influence the legal dimension of transformation. Manifestations of that are the limited power of the state visible on the level of legislative process, and also soft law – especially as far as regulation of economy is concern. It is true especially in relation to post-communist central-eastern European states that the transformation started in a situation of 'post-sovereign' states. It means that national legal systems are not any more in the form of a pyramid with a Kelsenian *Grundnorm* expressed by the will of the sovereign but are part of a new legal space with legal order composed of different legal systems.

- Postmodern mind – the transformation in post-communist central-eastern European countries has been taking place in a peculiar cultural situation. Before the change there was universal support for democracy, political rights and rule of law. After the change a struggle began about the meaning of those ideas. Societies in contemporary nation states do not share the same values. Even in ethnically homogeneous countries there is pluralism of values with significant influence on law. Law is not supported by one shared meta-narrative as it used to be in the period between the two world wars. Such a situation creates good as well as bad consequences. It is much more difficult for legal institutions to achieve a high level of legitimacy. It is much more difficult even to implement 'law and order'. At the same time scepticism about values stimulates scepticism about political power and makes it much more difficult to abuse law by political power.

It is banal that post-communist transformation did not create any new political and legal ideology but if we look at legal change in the countries in question from the socio-legal point of view we can find not only a laboratory for research but plenty of innovations connected with implementation of new-old blueprints and adaptation of societies to new situations.

Post-Communist Rule of Law

The rule of law in post-communist countries is a 'limping' rule of law, as in practice it functions only in a limited area of social life. Ruti Teitel in her last book elaborated the situation of 'transitional justice' with plenty of internal paradoxes.[8] What is important is that, as she correctly observed, 'rule of law is constitutive and is being constituted' at the same time. That is possible to observe in the operation of constitutional courts and tribunals in the countries in question. They are rather quasi-judicial institutions than purely judicial ones. Rule of law imposes legal limits on any and especially

8 Teitel R, *Transitional Justice*, Oxford University Press, Oxford, 2000.

political power, but the main agent of transformation is the state and its organs. Government through law creates the change of social structure. That requires a high concentration of power in the hands of the executive branch and change in the balance of powers. Eastern European scholars including legal scholars can easily observe this situation of growing concentration. Andras Sajo, a distinguished constitutionalist from the Central European University, presented that unbalanced constitutionalism in his book and warns of the growing authoritarian tendencies from Khazackstan to Hungary.[9]

The situation with the judiciary is also peculiar – in some countries it became very powerful – especially constitutional courts as in Hungary under Judge Solyom.[10] One of his court's famous rulings was based on the concept of the 'invisible Hungarian constitution' – a good base for constitutional review. The same Hungarian scholar, Sajo, wrote that the Constitutional Court + social rights = socialism redivivus. In other countries constitutional courts are not that powerful but play an important role in decisions usually reserved for parliaments about social policies and conflicting values.

In all former communist countries after 1989, constitutional review by constitutional courts or constitutional tribunals was established. In some countries they achieved a very high level of independence, power, and prestige. The main aim was to have a body that would guarantee observance of constitutional rights. Their design was not something newly developed in the post-communist situation (unlike the round table), but a replica of the institutions in the established liberal democracies in the West, in particular western Europe. That is, constitutional review exercised by a specially established constitutional body that exclusively possesses the competence to declare the unconstitutionality of laws. The decisions are made *in abstracto* and are final. There are, however, exceptions to this picture. Only in Estonia is the constitutional review entrusted to the department of the highest court. In all countries except Ukraine the constitutional courts exercise both an abstract and a concrete review – concrete in the sense that they are answering questions on constitutionality coming from the ordinary courts dealing in particular cases with constitutionality issues. In some countries the constitutional review bodies have the power to decide on constitutionality before the law enters into force, but only when asked by the President (Estonia, Hungary, Poland).

---

9 Sajo A, *Limiting Government: An Introduction to Constitutionalism*, Central European University Press, Budapest, 1999.

10 Solyom L and Brunner G, *Constitutional Judiciary in a New Democracy*, University of Michigan Press, Ann Arbor, Michigan, 2000 at 1-65.

The Romanian Constitutional Court is specific in two areas: the abstract review can be exercised only before promulgation of law, and invalidation of such law is not final and can be overridden by a qualified majority in the Parliament.

Such a summary picture shows us that these are bodies with huge power and which hold plenty of repercussions for the concept of democracy and the constitutional concept of separation of powers – if one constitutional body invalidates the decision of another constitutional body the balance does not exist.

Constitutionalism and Quasi-Judicial Institutions: the Example of the Hungarian Constitutional Court

The Court was established as an outcome of political compromise in the round table talks between the democratic opposition forces and representatives of the then communist regime. At that time it was perceived as an institution which would guarantee the constitutionality of the emerging polity. The oppositional forces pushed for the allocation of as many competences as possible to that new institution. The Court was modelled on the Constitutional Court of Germany and represents the flagship institution of the third wave of constitutional courts in Europe. It began work in 1990. Constitutional review exercised by the Court is abstract, in that it does not require a concrete case to be presented before the court. The law establishing the Constitutional Court made provision for a very broad category of standing before the Court which includes not only petitions from some state institutions such as the Parliament, the President, and groups of politicians, but also *actio populare* – any person can petition for constitutional review. This provision established the background for a huge amount of work for the Constitutional Court. Under the presidency of Justice Solyom the Court played an activist role and within a few years made decisions that in effect adjusted the former law adopted under the communist regime to new law based on a totally different axiology. In effect the Court created the new Hungarian constitution and developed a comprehensive catalogue of constitutional rights through its activist role, playing, it is possible to claim, the function of a quasi-legislative body.

Solyom argues that the activism of the Court took place and was necessary in order to minimalize and neutralize the anti-democratic forces that existed in Hungarian society as well as in Hungarian political institutions. So, the critique of the activist judges who play the role reserved for Parliament should be contextualized; the specific Hungarian context was such that this activism was necessary.

In the first few years after 1990 the Constitutional Court was consciously involved, with success, in creation of a hierarchy of constitutional rights in Hungary. The bases of this were the right to life and human dignity. Rights such as freedom of speech, religion, information, and freedom of thought were derived from these basic rights to life and dignity.

Solyom not only defends the activities and jurisprudence of the Court under his presidency, and not only defends the achievements of the Court's rulings, but in general defends the activist approach of the Court. He believes the new judges on the court should follow the path of their predecessors. Further, he wants to see an expansion of the jurisdiction of the Constitutional Court to include individual human rights complaints. An interesting part is his battle to establish the Court's authority in the face of the ordinary judiciary, in particular in controversies relating to justifiability and enforceability of the Constitutional Court's rulings.

Generally in legal literature one finds praise for the activism of constitutional courts in post-communist central-eastern Europe. This is most visible in relation to the Hungarian Constitutional Court. There are plenty of arguments in support of such a thesis. Let me focus on the opposite argument. I am not convinced of the validity of that thesis. It is possible to find plenty of arguments against judicial activism including arguments regarding the lack of democratic legitimacy of judges appointed, not elected, by universal suffrage or by the Parliament. The problem is serious and worthy of serious consideration. There are some arguments that support Justice Solyom as far as 'transitional justice' is concerned. Namely, that what is important is building democratic and rule-of-law-oriented institutions. In the specific time of transformation when the rules of the game are in the process of creation it is better and more effective to place it in the hands of impartial judges than leave it to politicians. On the other hand it is too early to make a judgment as to what has been lost due to the Court's activism. One such thing that comes to mind is the passivity of citizens, not a new argument in the theory of constitutional review. The petrification of the legal institutional structure without the activities of citizens could create a pretty shaky structure that in times of difficulty could fall down quite easily. Such a 'wobbly' institutional structure established from above by wise impartial judges has the potential to alienate citizens and to operate without 'spirit'. But law requires spirit – a spirit that is provided by the normative social structure.

Chou En-Lai, when asked about the impact of the French Revolution, answered that it is too early to say. This represents the long-term point of view. As Maynard Keynes reminds us, from the long-term point of view we will all be dead. I mention this because it is really difficult to make an assessment and we will never know what has been lost. What is needed is serious public debate about this problem.

There is no doubt that so far the constitutional courts in the majority of the post-communist countries have played a generally positive role in the process of institutionalization of constitutionalism. Nevertheless, after 12 years of transformation and consolidation of the constitutional structure a more critical approach is needed. What I mean by critical is serious debate on the location of courts as quasi-judicial bodies in the constitutional structure; discussion of their role in constitutional politics as separate from normal everyday politics; their role as a second or third chamber – depending upon which country we are taking into account – in the legislative process.

A Note on Dealing with the Past and Property Rights

The important problem faced by all these countries is that of dealing with the past – on the one hand this is a question of which legal strategies and institutions should be adopted in order to legally clean the communist past.[11] The Czech solution was the adoption in 1991 of a law on decommunization and lustration, heavily criticized by human rights organizations as being against human rights and also based on the retroactivity of law. Despite this criticism the Czech Constitutional Court confirmed the constitutionality of that statute. Interestingly in a similar case the Hungarian Constitutional Court declared the unconstitutionality of such a law due to retroactivity.

Another area is property rights. I am not going to discuss here the fascinating problem of restitution of property – also one of the dimensions of legal dealing with the past. As everywhere in the market economy post-communist countries resurrected the legal concept of private property. In the legal text it appears the same as in other OECD countries. In practice the situation is different. What is noticed, by scholars such as Staniszkis[12] or Stark, is a new type of property, what they termed 'hybrid property' or 'recombined property'.[13] Shortly speaking, this is based on the legal connection between private and public (state) property.

11 For a brilliant socio-legal analysis of the consequences of not cleansing the past see Los M and Zybertowicz A, *Privatizing the Police-State: The Case of Poland*, St.Martin's Press, New York, 2000.

12 Staniszkis J, *Post-communism: The Emerging Enigma*, Institute of Political Studies Polish Academy of Sciences, Warsaw, 1999.

13 Stark D and Bruszt L, *Postsocialist Pathways: Transforming Politics and Property in East Central Europe*, Cambridge University Press, Cambridge and New York, 1998.

Globalization and the Enigma of Post-Communism

The rule of law in post-communist countries was imposed from above and was not accompanied by profound changes in the value system of the society and its elites. In such a situation the imposition of rule of law and a legal institutional framework connected with it, as a model taken from abroad, was based on skipping the historical stages of its development. That situation creates a peculiar 'limping' operation of rule of law. On its façade it looks like any other liberal democratic country with similar substantive law and similar legal institutions but the system works differently. This is most visible in a situation of crisis. Using a parallel expression, the difference is like that between cars with manual and automatic transmission. Political elites in post-communist countries pretend that they are driving a smooth automatic car but they only pretend. What is actually at work is a vehicle with manual transmission. It is running but not that smoothly and always requires corrections. In the case of post-communist countries a political driver makes corrections. At the same time the skills of people in the driver's seat are different. The drivers change after each election and try to adjust the driving strategy. The passengers are not happy with each driver and they try to find the good one. They also believe that they are in a vehicle with automatic transmission. So the entire situation is paradoxical.

Using more theoretical language I can say that after 1989 new political elites introduced prematurely an institutional system of rule of law as known from the West, that means a self-referential system. That was possible due to the global spread of institutional knowledge. The problem is that the conditions for self-referentiality, not only of the legal system, do not exist. From the point of view of legal sociology there is discrepancy between the potentially self-referential legal system and values accepted by the society. The effect is the malfunctions of the legal system and growing anomie or dissatisfaction with the legal system itself.

Globalization processes play a very important and double role in all of this. On the one hand, due to globalization legal transplants are easily available. Even more there is an expectation that legal institutions will be similar to those in other neighbouring countries. On the other hand, globalization reinforces the preservation of specificity. I am not thinking only about conscious preservation of traditional institutions but rather the unconscious preservation and use of institutions from the communist past in order to be efficient in the new global environment. Those institutions are mainly outside legal worlds, such as organized markets and the hybrid character of the institutional settings. All of this creates the growing social unhappiness with which I started this piece.

Chapter 10

Crime, Terror and Transitional Cultures in a Contracting Globe

Mark Findlay

Introduction

This chapter speculates on the place of crime within global themes of change. It proposes an examination of dichotomous development themes such as globalization through the representation of difference, and its employment in setting social control agendas. Criminalization is an important mechanism for such representations.

In examining the relationship between globalization, crime and transitional cultures, the uneven nature of globalization is revealed, particularly as a motivation for selective socio-economic development. This then is exposed as a natural, if all too often ignored, environment for world crime. As a process of modernization promoted by strong to weak nation states the consumerist ethic of globalization generates new contexts for crime. The secularism of globalization and its attendant distortions of democracy have led to a world where terrorism is the great threat, and world war is now another method of crime control. This highlights the paradox of cultures under challenge and at the same time resilient against globalization, crime and control.

Globalization or Misleading Duality

As with many emergent and contested themes in the analysis of crime and culture, globalization is simple and complex. Put simply in its contemporary manifestation, globalization is the collapsing of time and space; the process whereby through mass communication, multinational commerce, internationalized politics, and transnational regulation we seem to be moving inexorably towards a single culture. The more complex interpretation of globalization is as paradox – wherein there are as many pressures driving us in the direction of the common culture as those keeping us apart.

Today globalization is largely an economic paradigm, meaning modernization and the marketing of predominant consumerist values. In its most recent political incarnation as the 'global alliance against terrorism'. Western economic and military dominion is implicating states with mutual interests in modernization, in the advancement of a common paradigm of justice against fanatic fundamentalism. While terrorism is now a crime against democracy, control is in global war terms and not (as in the past with say Northern Ireland) reliant on criminal justice resolutions alone.[1]

The force of modernization is marked in transitional cultures. So too, crime as a consequence of modernization in transitional cultures is evident, troubling and little recognized. In weak or non-conventional 'democratic' state structures (such as those organized around fundamentalist religious ideology) resistance through crimes of terror is criminalized by the 'global alliance' which can itself be criticized for selectively endorsing state terrorism as a legitimate control response in a climate of global war.

The influence of modernization over developing cultures in transition can be initially destabilising of custom and tradition. Crime such as corruption and fraud, domestic violence and drug abuse (characteristic in modernized societies) is now essential within this process of destabilization, and crime control is expected to restore order. Fundamentalist or anarchistic resistance (such as the recent riots against globalization at meetings of world trade and economic interests) to consumerist and sectarian globalization may galvanize endangered cultures.[2] The colonial and orientalist institutions and processes of criminal sanction and penalty tend to undermine custom along with producing new forms of crime. Transitional cultures governed by weak states are particularly susceptible to the modernization/crime/cultural strain equation.

The more complex interpretation of any relationship between globalization, crime and transitional cultures recognizes the paradoxical manner in which the essence of these cultures transforms crime and control, or is strengthened and endorsed through reaction to their influence.[3] Common themes of religious integrity and economic oppression may foster alliances amongst cultures traditionally excluded from, or exploited through modernization. Globalization, modernization, development, crime and its control are now interrelated in such a predictable and consistent fashion so as to significantly influence global culture and responses to crime.

In its harmonious state, globalization tends to universalize crime problems and generalize control responses. For instance, the war on terrorism is selective but at the same time universalized as an inevitable,

---

1 Despite the fact that the discourse of bringing the criminals to justice is resplendent throughout the discourse and symbolism of political responses to terrorism.

2 See Ignatieff M, 'What Will Victory Look Like?' *The Guardian*, 19 October 2001.

3 See, Findlay M, 'Crime, Community Penalty and Integration within Legal Formalism in the South Pacific' (1997) 21 *Journal of Pacific Studies* 145-66.

unavoidable and unquestionable response to a challenge to 'civilization' and 'democracy'.[4] The unity of globalization is as yet more convincing at a symbolic level. Crime represents unequivocal symbols around which global ethics are confirmed. Crime control claims an irrefutable mandate for global order and a symbolic terrain across which order rules.

An appreciation of crime within globalization is only partial unless control is considered. Control is more than a response to crime. It is the political and economic prize. The globalized strategies of crime control tend also to reveal the impetus for globalization (that is, the conflation of control interests around shared determinants of crime significance and control agendas). Crime and its control, as global political concerns, are now essential features of global culture. The example of drug law enforcement, discussed later, manifests this as does the war on terror.

The commodification of the globe and the pre-eminence of the marketplace have made profit the global ethic. Crime is choices and relationships for profit, except where it is seen to arise from (and support) resistance to sectarian values and free-market (free-trade) economic imperialism. These choices and relationships cross over the boundaries criminalization pretends to maintain. In the context of transitional cultures, the outcomes for both change and consolidation of such culture are important in imaging globalization.

What follows is a brief insight into the connections between crime and globalization within transitional cultures. This rests on considerations of the way crime promotes globalization, the way in which crime is a characteristic of globalization, and how globalization has tended to influence crime and control and its inclusive agendas. In order to contextualize this within transitional cultures it is necessary to also briefly engage with comparativism and to test the significance of contextualizing grounded generalizations.

The Crime/Globalization Nexus

Globalization creates new and favourable contexts for crime. This is the consequence of what Harvey refers to as the 'compression of time and the annihilation of space'.[5] Commercial crime relationships in particular, are set free to benefit from opportunities not dissimilar to those enjoyed by multinational enterprise beyond the jurisdiction of the individual state, and the limitations of single markets.

---

4 Both these notions rely upon a modernization sectarian paradigm of the world and world order.

5 Harvey D, *The Conditions of Postmodernity*, Blackwell, Oxford, 1989 at 293-5.

The process of time-space compression that is globalization has enhanced material crime relationships to an extent where they require analysis in a similar fashion to that of any other crucial market force. The claim of globalization is that: 'spatial barriers have collapsed so that the world is now a single field within which capitalism can operate, and capital flows become more and more sensitive to the relative advantages of particular spatial locations'.[6] The context of crime is such a location.

The globalization of capital from money to the electronic transfer of credit, of transactions of wealth from the exchange of property to info-technology, and the seemingly limitless expanse of immediate and instantaneous global markets have enabled the transformation of crime beyond people, places, and even identifiable victims. Crime now is as much a feature of the emergent globalized culture as every other aspect of its consumerism.

Common themes for crime and globalization are commodification and profit. The marketplace is an essential context for modernization and the version of culture it promotes. Crime's place within the market appears to be crucial for an understanding of the nexus between crime and globalization. Even where crime relationships are those of power and domination, the materialist consequences of crime are rarely denied. These consequences sit well with the motivations behind modern materialist cultures, and with cultural resistance to them.

The collapsing of time and space, while at the same time profound cultural difference is celebrated through global realities like world debt, forces hard up against each other the intolerant and the implacable features of cultures. World political and economic domination through modernization has tended to reignite the most ancient of antipathies.

Conventional resolutions of global conflict such as war state-against-state have been replaced in this phase of globalization by crime as warfare, and warfare as crime control.

Crime and the Global Culture

Globalization is changing our understanding of culture and its significance as a context within which crime is constructed and played out. Until recently, and in recognition of the diversity of world cultures, it was safe to say that crime was culturally specific, and to confine contextual analysis thereby. The recognition of criminalization and resultant punishment as differentiating the individual, whereas global crime and control agendas rely on more generalized paradigms invites an appreciation of crime which is culturally specific as well as universal. Differing levels of analysis allow

6 Waters M, *Globalization*, London, Routledge, 1995 at 57-8.

for these apparent competing visions. Contextual grounding enables the reconciliation of crime as a feature of the universal and the particular culture, an influential feature of both and each.

In the likelihood that '... in a globalized world there will be a single society and culture occupying the planet',[7] a more integrative and dynamic contextual analysis for crime is required, particularly as it sits within any universal culture. This is all the more immediate in the transitional phase of globalization that defies cultural integration. Our world is still far from the universalized culture in all quarters. Globalization is a transitional state. It is illusory and potentially distracting at this stage of the globalization process only to concentrate on 'the collapsing' of time and space without recognising the diversity of human consciousness which remains.[8] 'Globalization as a concept refers both to the compression of and the intensification of consciousness of the world as a whole ... both concrete global interdependence and consciousness of the global whole in the twentieth century'.[9]

The intensification consciousness may also apply to nationalism and state/cultural revival. This may work against the unification of culture through global consciousness at the same time as it is being broadly claimed (by global political, economic and regulatory organizations and 'communities'). The crime and control consequences of this tension are apparent through the formulation and confrontation of international terror.

Globalization is paradoxical in the way it unifies and delineates, internationalizes and localizes.[10] Crime demonstrates a similar duality. While crime on the streets might be viewed as a local issue and crime in the multinational boardroom more as global, there remain important contextual themes common to both, inextricably essential to an understanding of either. This is where an interactive appreciation of crime in context is important to an understanding and analysis of crime as a force for globalization and vice versa, rather than being restricted to representations of crime as criminals, offences or victims: aliens in the 'global village'.

---

7 Ibid at 3.

8 Giddens A, 'Anthony Giddens on Globalization: Excerpts from a Keynote Address at the UNRISD Conference on Globalization and Citizenship' (1996/97) 15 *UNRISD News, (United Nations Institute for Social Development Bulletin)* at 4-5.

9 Robertson R, *Globalization*, London, Sage, 1992 at 8.

10 A criticism of the contemporary application of terms like globalization to studies of crime and culture is the tendency for it to be envisaged as a simple paradox between the local and the global. While presenting a useful analytical tool, such a dichotomy is further away from today's world than considerations of the transnational, regional and cosmopolitan.

Elaborating on the paradox and harmony themes of globalization, international terror has been described as a response to globalization, and the political domination and sectarianism which has fuelled the process of modernization ever since the mercantile phase of globalization during the middle of the eighteenth century. However, while terrorism may be an extreme (and extremist) response to globalization, so globalization is a response to internationalized terror. War is no longer state-to-state, nor is crime control state-to-individual. Extraordinary political and economic alliances are forged for legitimacy in a climate where world superpowers avoid international institutions in order to reconstruct and manipulate world order for clear national interests.

The state as the focus of government within global politics is and is no longer true. Multilateral state alliances are forged to combat individuals and collectives representative of transitional cultures and dominated worldviews. The state as the definer of crime and the monopolist of punishment gives way to global declarations of collective (cultural) deviance, represented in things like the current debate about what is terrorism. The ruling state seems central to these definitions where resistance to any state and in any form is terror. Such definitions commend the international state and its action as beyond terrorism, provided it is not deemed 'rogue' and beyond global ideologies of democracy. Those who are outside this imagery are also excluded from the reordering of world security, and are seen in terms of terror or their support for it.[11]

The focus in globalization literature on the role of the bureaucratized state tends to disguise the importance of corporations and multinational markets as an equally significant force in the transition of cultures. The global agenda for modernization and market economies complements the aspirations of corporate as much as state-centred politics. This is a powerful recognition when addressing the relationship between development and crime in transitional cultures. Where development means commodification and modernization it will be selective, dependant and discriminatory. It will produce in transitional cultures either resisting or on their way to modernization, apparent inequities that may generate crime and require control if development is to proceed and claim legitimacy.

One significant cultural theme in globalization is development. More than modernization, development is a paradigm affecting all world cultures, and an international financial dogma intruding on all societies in transition. Equally relevant to globalization and crime however, are the selective and discriminatory nature and outcomes of development. These may be

---

[11] Milne S, 'Terror & Tyranny' *The Guardian*, 25 October 2001.

criminogenic and productive of new and globalized control agendas consistent with the promotion of modernization.

Along with development, free market economics and the reconstruction of centralized economies motivate change, particularly in Eastern Europe. The discourse generated around these themes of change reflects a tendency to marginalize crime as a 'foreign import' or a 'black market aberration'. This, in turn, diminishes the significance of a crime market within these emergent economies, and ignores the opportunity of using crime as a critical measure of free market economics to achieve reconstruction.

Global priorities such as economic reconstruction largely define the direction of modernization, within contemporary cultural and social development in whatever paradigm. So too are they integral to current representations of crime and crime control, particularly when crime is targeted as a challenge to the realization of such priorities, or as with the search for motives behind the recent extremities of global terror, are seen as an attack on the icons of modernization. However, the place of crime within themes of change is not so straightforward. It is not an irrational response to the universal benefits of modernization. Nor is it an immoral challenge to the 'democratic' hegemony of Western political and cultural supremacy.

As Giddens suggests,[12] whereas globalization was initially the province of Westernized cultures it is now outside and beyond the exclusive control of any particular cultural influence, certainly in terms of globalization as action and reaction. It is the international influence of consumerist and sectarian market economics, rather than the particular impact of culture, which presently fuels globalization (in a somewhat similar fashion to the way in which it shapes transnational criminal enterprise).

For instance, corruption if it is essential to the maintenance of a local black market will exist as the giving and receiving of material advantage. Where corruption is a feature of government, it transforms beyond local exchanges of advantage into processes of influence which become political networks. For corruption to replace the work ethic of the community and the sense of duty of the public official, challenges the rights and responsibilities themes which are identified characteristics of democratic, globalized culture.

Cultures in transition, particularly those assailed by pressures to modernize are living with a transformation of crime and control so often impossible to disentangle from world economic and political priorities. How this transformation simultaneously works towards the paradox of universal culture and resilient individual cultural difference is worthy of

---

12 Above n 8.

comparative analysis. Unfortunately, as regards the interpretation of international terrorism demonstrates, such comparison can only effectively progress from a detailed understanding of the transitional cultures influenced by globalization and presenting a focus for its resistance.

Comparativism

To achieve its fullest potential within globalization, comparative research (and the search for universals around which the comparative project may be mounted) must work at several levels:

- within cultural contexts;
- across two or more contexts within the same culture;
- across time or space within a culture in transition;
- culture to culture; and (not or)
- simultaneously at the local and global levels.

Comparative Research within Cultures

The inference here is that within a particular context we compare selected social or legal variables in order to appreciate their cultural significance. Obviously, this cannot be done in a contextual or cultural vacuum, and to some extent it challenges the discreet application of any of these proposed comparative research distinctions. Having said this, there are some issues of particular relevance to cultures and which need to be addressed within that context. An example of this is the prevailing debate about good governance and its relevance in developing cultures and weak states.

Against good governance, political corruption is a very pertinent example of the need for internally comparative research. One might hold that comparing the behaviour of politicians against the aspirations of a designated leadership code (or statement of ethics) should produce a potent analysis of political corruption, and good governance. This cannot be done without an appreciation of corruption sensitive to its cultural contest, and the impact on it which corruption exerts. The call to cultural relativity here is not designed to weaken aspirations to control the destructive impact of corruption in any culture. Rather it suggests the need to soften the over-simplistic international politics of difference surrounding the issue.

In any political culture, the more powerful bonds of obligation might challenge otherwise non-problematic definitions of corrupt behaviour and might neutralize attempts to label as corrupt behaviours that violate a higher code. The instance of corruption in small Pacific states evidenced through the collapse of the National Bank of Fiji and the bank guarantees scandal in Vanuatu, is revealing.[13] Against international measures, features of these events would seem clearly corrupt and corrupting. Then how is it that many of the public figures associated with such events have survived in political life and even prospered? Through a comparison of certain economic relationships which might be deemed corrupt (or abuses of power) and structures of customary obligation one can appreciate the compromises which exist within the political life of these cultures.

Comparative Research Across Two or More Contexts within Cultures

Important in understanding control and regulation in society is an examination of the relationship between custom (in all its forms) and legality. This suggests the dangers in attempting to appreciate certain legal control 'traditions' without the benefit of comparative research into prevailing 'cultures'.

Along with this realization is the challenge: do we simply approach comparative research within the language and ideas of the dominant legal control tradition or attempt to construct a method for analysis which recognizes the essential difference of the things we are trying to compare?

For example, it would be impossible to understand why insider trading is against the law in certain commercial settings and not others, without possessing a commensurate understanding of prevailing commercial and corporate cultures, with their own imperatives and moralities.

Therefore, it is not enough to engage in a comparative analysis of legal controls and custom as if they exist within the same legal context or discourse. The reasons for their operation within differing contexts is an important focus for analysis as are the often artificial attempts to discuss their reconciliation or recognition.

Comparative Research Across Time or Space within a Culture in Transition

Work that attempts to understand the significance of legal forms and institutions lends itself to this type of analysis. For example, the emergent role of constitutions and constitutional legality in postcolonial Pacific states is much empowered through temporal and spatial comparison.

The constitutional review process in Fiji that led to the 1997 Constitution and the settling of new constitutional arrangements is impossible to appreciate without also tracing the political and social relations of indigenous and Indo-Fijian societies. The extent of this comparative analysis must also reflect the relevant history of the object under review. For instance, understanding the constitutional review

---

13 See, Findlay M, *The Globalisation of Crime: Understanding Transitional Relationships in Context*, Cambridge University Press, New York and Cambridge, 1999 at 77-93.

process, were it only to work from the last post coup constitution would produce a distorted result. The coups and the constitution did not occur within a social or legal vacuum. Nor was the progress to the constitutional review and the new constitutional review arrangements only dependent on issues in the history of Fiji in the 1990s. Researchers seeking to analyze the constitutional review process of 1995-1997 are bound to consider issues such as land ownership, the spread of capital, the development of trade unionism, the influence of chiefly authority, and the emancipation of women in Fiji amongst many trends that emerged in and shaped the country of Fiji from the arrival of the first Indian labourers to the transition to independence.

Another example might be the appreciation of the struggle between fundamentalist Islamic agitation in Indonesia, and the recent attempts to move from military to sectarian forms of government. In particular, the manner in which fundamentalist groups have merged with nationalist independence movements within separatist provinces in Indonesia can only be understood across the time and space of the nation's post independence imperialism. The reaction of international development agencies in attempting specifically to influence the political future of Indonesia is another transitional component of this understanding.

Trend analysis also emphasises the fact that legal research which is comparative must also be multidisciplinary if it is to have the power to influence policy, particularly where social control institutions are multi-levelled and diverse across communities.

Culture to Culture

Research into the existence of judicial independence in different judicial cultures is of this nature. For instance an appreciation of the status of judicial independence within the People's Republic of China following on from the enactment of the Judges Law in 1995 requires a consideration of ideology outside the Chinese justice context.[14] This law purported to limit political interference with the judiciary in China. It promoted the independent tenure of judges, and expanded the functions of the judiciary over judicial interpretation and review of laws and administration.

Despite these initiatives, and the Chinese constitutional endorsement of judicial independence, a comparison between judges' practice in common law traditions with the practice in China would suggest that the Chinese judge is far from independent. But is that a fair comparison? The judiciary

---

14 See, Findlay M, 'Independence and the Judiciary in the PRC: Expectations for Constitutional Legality in China' in Jayasuriya K (ed), *Law, Capitalism and Power in Asia*, Routledge, London, 1999 at 281-99.

in China distinguish independence at the level of the courts, the judiciary, and individual judges. They say the courts are responsible to the people and as such not independent. The judge is subject to the judicial hierarchy (and the National Peoples' Congress (NPC)) and therefore also not independent. But the judiciary as an organ of government is independent. They call it 'independence within the organic whole'.

Is it enough to look at issues like judicial independence only relative to their cultures? Also it is important to search out common characteristics of independence such as professionalism, accountability, and probity to test whether independence can be claimed within its cultural context. In this way mindless relativism is avoided.

Any comparative analysis of globalization and crime in the context of transitional cultures boils down to a consideration of dynamic relationships within and around cultures of change. If we are alleging that crime is an outcome of globalization (through the selective dimensions of modernization and development) then this needs to be established through the relationships of globalization to crime. Also if crime control is now a feature of a globalized world order it might be assumed to play a part in the structuring and duration of globalization as crime. Finally, with crime as a force for further differentiation consistent with modernization how does crime as a force for globalization operate?

Relationships of Crime

Relationships that are criminal essentially depend on choice. Arising from considerations of crime as choice is the need to reveal the stages through which crime relationships are moulded, opportunities responded to, and consequent choice is transacted. In the same way that choice is essential to crime relationships, it is crucial for considerations of control. Strategies for crime control, local and global, and the institutions created to support these, reveal the way in which choices about crime and choices about control are interdependent. Attached to this is the discriminatory representation of what forms of common action and behaviour will be designated deviant or legitimate, and the international political context for this.

Crime is interactive and as such depends on personal relationships and institutional reactions. Unless crime is discussed in terms of interaction, its dynamic influence within global social change may be overlooked. In both local and global language crime and criminality are talked about as if one party to a relationship, or one institution in an administrative process is responsible or responsive. As a result perpetrators are stereotyped, victims are marginalized, control agencies are distorted, and justice policy is misdirected.

For contexts wherein laws regulate behaviour, crime is a trigger for the inception of control relationships. Sometimes the reverse is also true. Usually crime is characterized as a breach of legal prohibitions that are graduated in terms of their seriousness, or the severity of the harm resulting from their violation. While the measure of crime seriousness is a culturally relative exercise, violence against individuals is more often than not an aggravating feature of crime in most community settings.

The significance of regulation and control (through criminalization) represents a utility for globalization. Crime control in the context of globalization is about reshaping opportunities and consequent choices that endorse globalized authorities and interests, endorsing global priorities. In this respect the regulation of crime reveals crucial connections between global politics, criminalization and wider aspirations for control, through which crime and cultures may be restructured in terms of the predominant view of world order.

Therefore, the social positioning of crime is not simply a matter of determining the seriousness of crime or its consequences in a particular cultural setting. The status of the offender or the victim, the priorities of criminal justice agencies, and the perceptions of governments and communities influence the representation of crime, and reactions to it. For example, in both developed and developing societies significant investments of control resources are directed against minor property crimes, public order offences, as well as certain crimes of serious violence, individual against individual. At the same time theft by corporations, environmental destruction, or violence by state agencies against individuals may not receive a similar intensity of control effort or state response. The harm caused, the seriousness of the behaviour, or the extent of victimization does not explain such differential treatment. Nor will the laws against criminal activity necessarily clarify the position. It is the social context of crime that holds the key to its significance. Whether it be a local or global context, the story remains the same.

Globalized Situations of Crime

The unification of global culture is politically motivated through Westernized priorities. One such is the eradication of recreational drug abuse. Whether in a medical or social-order context this common view is enforced even in cultures where traditions differ from the modernized West when it comes to drug production and consumption. In addition, the commercial realities that influence developing agrarian economies may generate an alternative commercial expedient in drug production and export. In these settings international crime control priorities may not make good economic sense.

Drug crime operates in a highly selective and discretionary political and social context. This context is essential to the perpetuation of drug economies, as it is to the maintenance of international political priorities. Without criminalization the profit motive behind drug trafficking would not be ensured. Without criminalization the creation of international law enforcement policies under the authority of uniform legal prohibitions would not be possible. Governments would therefore have to expose their drug control politics to a more sensitive form of analysis, not diverted or distracted by neutral and universal concepts of crime and punishment.

Criminalization is an essential element within discretionary and selective drug control. Without it, the meaning of the supply and demand stages of drug economies would be ambiguous. In fact, the whole monopolistic structure of drug markets, and the distortions of price and purity of supply that arise as a result of market regulation would not be prevalent without the globalized and selective criminalization of drug sale and use patterns. This has led to an internationalized trade (supply and demand) structure, where global prohibitions create global market conditions to exploit regional supply and national demand, through transnational enterprise.

The criminalization of drugs and the drug trade on an international level provides one of the clearest indications of crime's importance for global politics. For example, the recent history of the criminalization of opiate abuse and trade is all about international influence (political and medical).[15] Even today the agenda for the 'war on drugs' is as colonial and imperialist as any recent military excursion.[16]

The hypocrisy of the global drugs/crime problem does not stop at the slippage between medical mission and political intervention. Global economic priorities almost force-feed agrarian-based developing economies to cash crop. The markets for legitimate cash cropping (such as coffee, sugar and cotton) are reliant on the fickle tastes of the developed world. One such market that is uniquely stable and growing is the drugs market. The principal producers of the fashionable drugs of choice are the developing world and the vast market for these lucrative cash crops are in the developed world. And yet where in other economic contexts such

---

15 Ward P and Dobinson I, 'Heroin: A Considered Response' in Findlay M and Hoggs R (eds), *Understanding Crime and Criminal Justice*, Law Book Company, Sydney, 1988.

16 The recent employment by the US government of the Central Intelligence Agency, along with military aircraft and personnel to collaborate with Colombian authorities in raids against the cocaine cartels is an example of the politicization and militarization of drug law enforcement.

supply and demand relationships would be fuelled by legitimate (rather than illegitimate) capital, and barriers to free trade would be attacked, with criminalized drugs the opposite is the case. Global development and economic theory is ignored, or reversed, for the sake of political and health control agendas.

In the context of both local and globalized crime control, consistency is sacrificed. Multinational economic priorities determine that alcohol and tobacco are legitimate while cannabis and opiates are not. Interestingly, it is in the developing world where the crime and health consequences of tobacco and alcohol are most acutely felt that the argument behind their aggressive marketing rests in unbridled free marketeering. The same approach and motivation is criminalized when dealing in proscribed drugs.

Further, the recognition of market structures as the context for controlling drug trade requires a recognition of the impetus for the trade and its control in a globalized context. The outcomes are for oligopoly markets, multinational trading, relationships of commercial interest, and the weakness of state regulation.

Local or Global Crime – or Crime in Transition?

When crime is analyzed within a global context, the world becomes more harmonious and at the same time, more diverse. Globalization and its impact on crime are compared with localized frames of reference. This enables consideration of transitional images and representations of crime such as: homicide and genocide, individual and organized crime, corruption of officials or governments. The latter is uniquely dangerous for the developing world.

One of the most obvious features of social development through modernization has been the establishment and growth of the city, replacing rural life. Urban environments provide one of the clearest contexts within which the connections between crime and youth, crime and gender, and crime and economic disparity might be explored. The city is the image and the context of the modern within which crime is a feature and an impetus for urban change.

As both crime and urbanization are dynamic social phenomena, their relationship has been widely discussed in terms of 'drift'.[17] Fluid commitments to crime often are demonstrated in similar ways as are the choices made by young unemployed males to move to the city.

The urban drift in developing societies largely features young males. As crime is similarly the province of young males, then the link here is not surprising. However it is not so much the process of drift, but its

[17] Matza D, *Delinquency and Drift*, John Wiley, New York, 1964.

subsequent social dislocation which is the important contextual consequence of drift for crime.

For newly independent states in particular, the gradual dismantling of colonial laws restricting movement and access to towns, or the lifting of residency and occupation rules (for example those restrictions enforced in closed, centralized economies in eastern Europe), have stimulated population mobility in developing countries. Add to this the shift in rural populations, due to famine, war, and 'ethnic cleansing', and urban drift has rapidly developed as one of the great migratory characteristics of modern social development. By contrast, a flight from the city has become a migratory pattern of developed countries. Decentralization policies and inner city decay leave the city as little more than a business precinct, denuded of residents. The depopulation of the cities has now become a daily migration, where nightfall sees the routine shift of workers out into the suburbs.

The fear of crime, now one essence of modern city life, is an important stimulus for the exodus. Further, the exodus alters the image of the city in terms of crime danger and vulnerability.

Urbanization trends in developing countries tend to reflect the popular perceptions of the relatively limited developmental opportunities in rural areas. City populations explode as a result and the limited services within these centres in turn rapidly negate those opportunities that may have once existed. In addition, the newly arrived resident is disconnected from familiar rural life supports and is unfamiliar with the formal, institutional welfare alternatives which the city affords, limited as these might be.

To the difficult sociocultural adaptations required of young rural migrants is added the economic reality of restricted employment opportunities, shortages of accommodation and the relatively high cost of urban living. Further, the immigrant worker often does not bring with him those skills and training essential for wage labour in an emerging city. Is it surprising in such a context that crime becomes 'work'?

Urban drift might best be seen in certain developing contexts as a progress of frustration and eventual violent dislocation, from one context of blocked opportunity, to another of diminished or distorted opportunity. These are clearly criminogenic conditions; conditions wherein crime and society are in rapid states of change. However, the concerns for localized crime control such as theft and domestic violence are exacerbated by the globalized conditions leading to marginalization and crime.

The tendency for cultural unification and the implication of common global values essential to globalization stands challenged by the marginalization and cultural vilification as a bi-product of modern economic development, and the protection of supportive climates of world order. How are we to then understand globalization as paradox and the role of crime within it?

Globalization is Paradox

In his consideration of what he calls *global law, local orders* Bauman observes:

> In *Postmodernity and its Discontents* I argued that whether Sigmund Freud was right or wrong in suggesting that the trading-off of a considerable part of personal liberty for some measure of collectively guaranteed security was the main cause of psychical afflictions and sufferings in the 'classic' period of modern civilization – today in the late or postmodern stage of modernity, it is the opposite tendency, the inclination to trade off security in exchange for removing more and more constraints cramping the exercise of free choice, which generates the sentiments of fear and anxiety. It is these sentiments which seek their outlet (or are being channeled) in the concerns with law and order.[18]

Bauman proceeds to disentangle the law and order imperatives of safety, security and certainty that he suggests have been made vulnerable by the late modern career of individual freedom. The response he suggests is the withdrawal into the safe haven of territoriality. What does this say for the emergence of internationalism in criminal justice? Are the safety, security and certainty of procedural integrity in domestic jurisdictions challenged by this trend, or could regionalism and internationalism be seen in fact as an indirect quest for unity underlying allegedly distinct crime control responses within individual jurisdictions?

Herein lies a paradox that is a feature of the relationship between globalization, crime and control:

> In its harmonious state globalization tends to universalize crime problems and generalize crime responses...Crime control claims an irrefutable mandate for global order and a symbolic terrain across which order rules ... Crime and control also offer the potential to conceal the edges and detail of difference through the establishment of symbolic borders of behaviour, status and relationships easily manipulated by global politics.[19]

Within this atmosphere of paradox we are presently witnessing a recasting of globalization away from international organizations and bureaucracies and into political and economic alliances at war with threats to safety and security, be these drug trade, terrorism, corruption or urban

---

18 Bauman Z, *Globalization: The Human Consequences*, Columbia University Press, New York, 1989, 116.

19 Findlay M, *The Globalization of Crime: Understanding Transitional Relationships In Context*, Cambridge University Press, Cambridge, 1999 at 224-5.

decay. There is a consequent trend away from the individuality (and rights and freedoms) of modernization and a retreat into territorial safety with a focus on world order, spatial control and cultural regularization. 'The construction of globalized control strategies, and the global inclination for processes and institutions profoundly out of touch with their local contextual origins, endorses the suggestion that connections between crime and globalization are, in large measure, symbolic'.[20] In this light it could be said that bringing war criminals to justice for crimes against humanity is more about reinforcing world order than it is compensating victims and punishing offenders. 'The real paradox of globalization (and the same might be said for the international criminal justice), however, is the manner in which it makes harmony a mask for diversity, and difference a concealment of fusion'.[21]

Paradox is an important device in the reconciliation of the intangibles that are globalization and crime. This is especially apparent when relating crime to cultural marginalization and resistance. Social and economic development promotes certain interests and marginalizes others. If the analysis of globalization and culture recognizes the functional potential of crime as a response to marginalization, and control as a reassertion of cultural dominance, then it becomes more than an exploration of strain, opportunity and conflict.

---

[20] Ibid.

[21] Ibid at 225.

Index

Aborigines, 162
Achebe, Chinua, 36
Amsterdam School of Argumentation, 21
Anderson, Benedict, 196
Anghie, Antony, 86
Asia Pacific Economic Cooperation, 147, 194
Asia Pacific Economic Cooperation (APEC), 166, 194
Asian Debt Crisis, 80
Association of South East Asian Nations, 194
Austin, John, 21
  Austinian Jurisprudence, 19, 21, 31
Australian Commonwealth, 62
Australian Securities and Investments Commission, 98

Bank for International Settlements, 100, 108
Bauman, Zygmunt, 246
Beck, Ulrich, 216
Bentham, Jeremy, 26, 29, 38, 40, 54
Berman, Harold J, 43, 48, 49, 63
Blackstone, William, 58
Braithwaite, John, 94, 99, 100, 117, 146
British Protective Model, 155
Brubaker, William Rogers, 201
Buchanan, Ruth, 76, 77, 89, 90

canon law, 48, 55, 58, 59, 62, 63
Carens, Joseph, 199
case law, 54, 55, 115, 165, 185
Castles, Stephen, 173
chaos theory, 52
Chinkin, Christine, 100, 119
Chou En-Lai, 227
citizenship, 7, 159, 160, 161, 162, 163, 164, 165, 168, 169, 171, 172, 173, 174, 175, 179, 180, 182, 183, 184, 185, 195, 197, 201, 208
codification, 54, 58, 177
colonialism, 5, 36, 66, 80, 81, 86, 87, 88, 193, 232, 243, 245
communism, 213, 217, 218, 219, 220, 221
  post-communism, 213, 215, 217, 218, 220, 221, 222, 224, 225, 227, 228
Communism, 65
communitarian theory, 35, 110, 111, 145
comparative jurisprudence, 9
comparative research, 238, 239
consumer law, 61
contracts, 58, 59, 60, 61, 94, 109, 115, 120, 122
corruption, 2, 7, 9, 32, 34, 35, 36, 37, 38, 39, 40, 41, 48, 66, 232, 237, 238, 244, 246
Cotterrell, Robert, 110, 111
crime, 8, 9, 106, 180, 200, 231, 232, 233, 234, 235, 236, 237, 241, 242, 243, 244, 245, 246, 247
  control, 231, 232, 233, 234, 236, 237, 241, 242, 243, 244, 245, 246
  criminalization, 233, 234, 242, 243
  drug trade, 243, 244, 246
  urban drift, 244, 245
critical theory, 29
cross-border transactions, 58, 94, 95, 96, 98, 105, 108, 109, 112, 125

Declaration of the Rights of Man and Citizen, 1789, 60
developing countries, 79, 140, 148, 151, 245

domestic law, 56, 60, 129, 151
Drahos, Peter, 94, 99, 100, 117, 146
Dworkin, Ronald, 29, 32, 45, 197, 222

Ehrlich, Eugen, 103
English Law Commission, 37
environmental law, 61
European Coal and Steel Community Treaty (1951), 50
European Community, 53, 108, 134, 146, 147, 197
  Common Code of Conduct for Lawyers, 108
European Convention on Human Rights, 38, 180
European Convention on Nationality, 1997, 165, 184
European Court of Human Rights, 174, 180
European Court of Justice, 166
European Union, 9, 25, 45, 50, 53, 55, 62, 166, 171, 194, 197, 200, 203, 204, 205, 206, 215
  Treaty on European Union (1992), 50
Evatt, Elizabeth, 183
Export Processing Zones, 74
extraterritoriality, 98, 101

feminist theory, 82, 85
Fine, Ben, 84
Fletcher, George, 32
Foucault, Michel, 81
free trade, 47, 50, 61, 74, 191, 208, 244
Friedman, Jonathan, 168
Friedman, Thomas, 214
Fung, Archon, 133, 139

General Agreement on Trade and Tariffs (GATT), 166
generalizability, 1, 2, 3, 4, 5, 6, 7, 8, 9, 22, 28, 30, 41, 73, 78, 81, 209
Giddens, Anthony, 74, 96, 103, 189, 217, 237
global business regulation, 94
global economy, 73, 75, 76, 77, 83, 91, 168, 191, 194
global governance, 75, 76, 83, 85, 90, 91
global society, 47
globalization theory, 7, 8, 188, 190, 191, 192, 193, 207
Goldblatt, David, 190
governance theory, 110, 111, 124

Hague Convention on Certain Questions Relating to the Conflict of Nationality Laws, 1930, 165, 177
Hart, Herbert, 16, 31, 32, 45
Harvey, David, 26, 97, 233
Held, David, 26, 166, 189, 190, 191, 192, 193
Hirst, Paul, 191, 194, 197, 202
historical location, 1
human rights law, 25, 45, 176, 179, 185
Hurrell Andrew, 192, 208

International Accounting Standards Commission, 101
International Association of Insurance Supervisors, 100, 108
International Bar Association, 108
  Code of Ethics, 108
International Bond Dealers Association, 108
international case law, 175, 184
international commercial law, 54, 60
International Criminal Court, 21
  Rome Statute, 21
international economic law, 5, 54, 77, 83
International Labour Conference, 129, 130, 135, 148, 151
International Labour Organization, 6, 129, 130, 131, 133, 134, 135, 136, 137, 138, 143, 144, 146, 147, 148, 149, 151, 153, 154, 155, 156, 157, 173
  Somavia, Juan, Director-General, 139

Thomas, Albert, Director-General, 130
international law, 5, 7, 25, 47, 64, 86, 89, 90, 94, 98, 99, 100, 101, 102, 103, 117, 124, 161, 163, 164, 165, 167, 174, 175, 176, 178, 179, 181, 182, 183, 184, 185, 195, 197, 198, 201, 203, 243
private, 45, 46, 47
public, 25, 26, 32, 46, 47, 76, 99, 100, 101, 102, 130, 176, 177
international legal norms, 2, 173
International Monetary Fund, 5, 22, 76, 77, 78, 79, 80, 81, 88
International Organization for Standardization, 61
International Organization of Securities Commissions, 5, 94, 96, 98, 100, 101, 102, 103, 104, 105, 106, 108, 111, 114, 115, 116, 117, 118, 119, 120, 121, 122, 123, 124, 126
Emerging Markets Committee, 116, 118
Technical Committee, 116, 117
international refugee law, 198
International Swaps and Derivatives Association, 108
international trade, 57, 83, 85
international trade law, 83, 84, 86
international war crimes, 45
Iran–US Claims Tribunal, 174
Islamic law, 25, 60

Jayasuriya, Kanishka, 102, 110, 124, 203, 204, 205
jurisprudence
analytical, 21, 29, 31, 32, 34, 41
feminist, 30, 82
functional, 30
general, 1, 5, 19, 22, 23, 24, 26, 27, 28, 32, 123
sociological, 16, 19, 30

Kahn-Freund, Otto, 131
Kennedy, Paul, 166, 168
Keynes, Maynard, 227
Kornai, Janos, 219

labour law, 6, 61, 109, 129, 131, 132, 141, 144, 155, 156, 157
legal education, 22, 26, 34, 43, 55, 56, 57, 223
legal ordering, 3, 4, 5, 6, 24, 26, 27, 30, 32, 41, 76, 90, 129
legal philosophy, 18, 23, 31
legal pluralism, 3, 9, 23, 28, 76, 94, 95, 105, 110, 111, 112, 125
legal science, 4, 43, 52, 53, 55, 57, 67, 68, 214
legal theory, 1, 3, 15, 16, 18, 20, 21, 23, 24, 26, 30, 72, 76, 81, 82, 96, 129, 189, 205, 216
critical, 82
Legomsky, Stephen, 199
liberal theory, 8, 196
Llewellyn, Karl, 17

MacCormick, Neil, 33, 46, 205, 206
Mansfield, Lord, 58
maritime law, 58, 179
Martens, Judge, 181
Marx, Karl, 46
McGrew, Anthony, 189, 190, 191
mercantile law, 43, 57, 62
migration
illegal, 7, 187, 188, 194, 195, 199, 200, 201, 202, 203, 204, 206, 207, 208, 209
migration law, 7, 169, 187, 188, 190, 193, 195, 196, 197, 199, 206, 207, 208
migration
illegal, 8, 207
Mill, John Stewart, 51
multinational corporations, 135, 138, 140, 147, 150, 151, 152, 153, 157, 172
municipal state law, 26, 76

Napoleonic Code, 60
nation state, 4, 5, 6, 7, 8, 23, 24, 25, 26, 27, 30, 41, 45, 47, 65, 75, 89, 94, 96,

104, 105, 109, 111, 112, 114, 120, 121, 122, 124, 125, 126, 134, 138, 149, 150, 157, 159, 163, 165, 166, 167, 168, 170, 171, 172, 173, 174, 181, 183, 184, 185, 187, 188, 190, 193, 195, 196, 198, 201, 202, 203, 204, 207, 216, 217, 218, 224, 231
nationality, 7, 159, 161, 164, 165, 168, 174, 175, 176, 177, 178, 179, 180, 181, 182, 183, 184, 185, 188, 208
natural justice, 4, 53, 125
Nelken, David, 93, 119
non-governmental organizations, 100, 101, 102, 141, 143, 146, 168, 170, 171, 172
  Amnesty International, 100, 170
  Greenpeace, 100, 170
Noonan, John, 36, 39
normative pluralism, 4, 23, 76, 105, 111
North American Free Trade Agreement (NAFTA), 90, 146, 147, 166, 194
Nottebohm case, 175, 176, 177, 178, 179, 180, 185, 197
Nussbaum, Martha, 26

O'Rourke, Dara, 133, 139
Ohmae, Kenichi, 190
Organisation for Economic Co-operation and Development (OECD), 109, 138, 139, 146, 147, 148, 151, 152, 228
Ouroga, Cecilia Medina, 183

Parsons, Talcott, 16
Picciotto, Sol, 102
Pound, Roscoe, 16, 17, 20

Ratcheting Labour Standards, 6, 133, 139, 140, 141, 142, 143, 144, 145, 146, 147, 148, 149, 150, 151, 152, 153, 154, 155, 156
Rawls, John, 29, 197
refugees, 198, 200
  Refugee Convention, 198
Reich, Robert, 191
Robertson, Roland, 74
Roman law, 52, 57, 60
Rose-Ackerman, Susan, 38
Rosenstock-Huessy, Eugen, 51, 58
Ruggie, John, 191, 203
rule of law, 4, 16, 53, 125, 197, 222, 223, 224, 228, 229

Sabel, Charles, 133, 139, 145
Sajo, Andras, 225
Santos, Boaventura de Sousa, 23, 74, 76, 91, 95, 102, 112, 113, 114, 116, 118, 120, 122
Schlesinger, Rudolph, 33
Schofield, Philip, 40
Sen, Amartya, 36
Smith, Adam, 51
Smith, Anthony, 196
social theory, 8, 30, 96, 213, 216, 217
soft law, 100, 102, 119, 120, 123, 223
Solyom, Judge, 225, 226, 227
sovereignty, 5, 7, 32, 43, 45, 50, 62, 63, 64, 66, 67, 75, 85, 86, 87, 88, 102, 105, 110, 129, 134, 135, 160, 165, 166, 167, 169, 175, 176, 179, 181, 185, 187, 188, 191, 195, 199, 201, 202, 203, 204, 205, 206, 207, 218
  maritime, 64
Soysal, Yasemin, 173
Standard Minimum Rules
  for the Treatment of Prisoners, 2, 14
Stone, Julius, 1, 3, 15, 16, 17, 18, 27, 29, 31, 41, 131, 190
  legal reasoning, 3, 28, 31
subsidiarity, 4, 53, 134
Summers, Robert, 33

Teitel, Ruti, 224
terrorism, 9, 231, 232, 236, 238, 246
  endorsing state terrorism, 232
Teubner, Gunther, 103, 104, 111, 125, 152, 157
The World Bank, 22, 35, 36, 38, 76
  Shihata, Dr Ibrahim, 35
Third World, 52, 77, 78, 80, 81, 84, 88

Thompson, Grahame, 191, 194, 197, 202
Torpey, John, 195
trade law, 61, 83, 84, 85
trade theory, 85
transnational securities transaction, 95, 109, 112, 114
Transparency International, 36, 37, 38, 41
  Corruption Perception Index, 38
treaties, 50, 55, 98, 99, 100, 102, 165, 173
Treaty Establishing the European Economic Community (1957), 50
Twining, William, 1, 2, 3, 4, 5, 7, 8, 9, 44, 45, 55, 57, 67, 72, 74, 76, 78, 81, 82, 89, 90, 91, 93, 95, 105, 123, 129, 131, 153, 157, 159, 165, 186, 188
Two Swords theory, 63

UNIDROIT Principles, 58
United Kingdom
  Nolan Committee, 40
United Nations, 45, 61, 62, 143, 166, 170, 172, 173, 178, 197
  Committee for the Elimination of Racial Discrimination, 62
  Compensation Commission, 174, 178
  Congress on the Prevention of Crime and the Treatment of Offenders
    Standard Minimum Rules for the Treatment of Prisoners, 14
  General Assembly, 166
  International Court of Justice, 61, 166, 174, 176
  International Covenant on Civil and Political Rights, 1966, 164, 175, 181, 182
  International Criminal Tribunal, 61
  Security Council, 166
  Universal Declaration of Human Rights, 10 December 1948, 50, 53
United Nations Convention Against Organized Crime 2000, 204
  Protocol to Prevent, Suppress and Punish Trafficking in Persons, Especially Women and Children, 204
United States of America, 17, 25, 47, 62, 64, 82, 88, 163, 199, 200, 201
University of London, 55

Walzer, Michael, 196
Wapner, Paul, 168
Weber, Max, 56
Weiss, Linda, 191
Witte, John Jr, 50, 62
Woods Ngaire, 192, 208
World Bank, 143, 146
world economy, 8, 24, 44, 138, 165, 191, 194, 219
World Trade Organization, 5, 22, 45, 51, 61, 76, 83, 85, 88, 90, 138, 166, 191
  Dispute Settlement Body, 86, 88

Young, Iris Marion, 172

£70.00